H Bell

Law of Landlord and Tenant as Administered in Bengal

Act VIII of 1869, B.C. Second Edition

H Bell

Law of Landlord and Tenant as Administered in Bengal
Act VIII of 1869, B.C. Second Edition

ISBN/EAN: 9783337312497

Printed in Europe, USA, Canada, Australia, Japan

Cover: Foto ©Suzi / pixelio.de

More available books at **www.hansebooks.com**

THE
LAW OF LANDLORD AND TENANT

AS ADMINISTERED IN BENGAL.

(ACT VIII OF 1869, B.C.)

BY

H. BELL, M.A., C.S.,
OF THE MIDDLE TEMPLE, BARRISTER-AT-LAW.

Second Edition — Revised.

BY

H. MILLETT,
OF LINCOLN'S INN, BARRISTER-AT-LAW,

AND

C. HORACE REILY,
OF THE MIDDLE TEMPLE, BARRISTER-AT-LAW.

CALCUTTA:
THACKER, SPINK & CO.,
Law Publishers and Booksellers.

1874.

CALCUTTA: PRINTED BY THACKER, SPINK & CO.

PREFACE TO THE SECOND EDITION.

IN publishing the second edition of Mr. Bell's work, we have abstained from all comment, and have only added those cases which have been decided since the first edition was published. We have also revised the marginal notes according as recent decisions have necessitated such change.

H. M.
C. H. R.

April 8th, 1874.

PREFACE TO THE FIRST EDITION.

The passing of Act VIII of 1869 of the Bengal Council appeared to me a favourable opportunity for bringing out a new edition of the Law of Landlord and Tenant, as current in Bengal. The present work is an attempt to illustrate each section of the Law by a well-arranged Digest of the various decisions of the learned Judges of the High Court, and copious extracts are given from the reports, in order to illustrate the principles upon which the decisions are based.

It will be observed that Act VIII of 1869 has made no change in the substantive Law, it is merely a re-enactment of Act X of 1859, with the procedure sections omitted. To make, therefore, the book useful to officers who have still to administer Act X of 1859, I have noted the corresponding sections of that Act in the margin.

In conclusion, I take this opportunity of acknowledging the obligations I am under to Mr. Chapman, whose work upon the Rent Law contains the most complete abstract of all the earlier rulings upon Act X of 1859.

H. BELL.

CONTENTS.

	Page
PREAMBLE	1
Application of the Act only to landlord and tenant	ib.
Where relationship of landlord and tenant exists	ib.
Where relationship of landlord and tenant does not exist	2
Object of Act X of 1859	ib.
I—INTERPRETATION OF "COLLECTOR"	ib.
II—RYOTS ENTITLED TO A POTTAH	3
Right of tenant to possession and quiet enjoyment	ib.
Limit to landlord's implied guarantee against eviction	ib.
What suits for rent are cognizable under the Act	4
The right to a pottah	ib.
Rights of parties under lease	ib.
Leases granted by lessors with limited interest	ib.
Payment of rent in kind	5
Tenant is estopped from denying landlord's title	ib.
Registration of lease	ib.
Stamp-duty chargeable on lease	ib.
III—RYOTS HOLDING LANDS AT FIXED RATES	6
Fixed rates of rent explained	ib.
Not affected by consolidation of jumma	7
Nor by subdivision of jumma	ib.
Date of Permanent Settlement	8
Holding from Permanent Settlement secure against auction-purchaser	ib.
But not if the rent has changed	ib.
If land has been held at a fixed rent, the nature of the holding need not be considered	ib.
IV—PRESUMPTION IF RENT HAS NOT CHANGED FOR 20 YEARS	9
Whether presumption applies to talookdars	ib.
When benefit of presumption can be claimed	ib.
When benefit cannot be claimed	10
Presumption only applies to cases of landlord and tenant	ib.
The pleadings must be consistent with holding from Permanent Settlement	ib.
Proof necessary to establish presumption	12
Evidence required to prove receipts	13
A break in the holding rebuts the presumption	ib.
But not if tenant has been unlawfully evicted	ib.
Value of jumma-wasil-bakee papers as evidence	14
Value of canoongoe papers	ib.
The presumption applies only to ryots	ib.
V—RYOTS HAVING RIGHT OF OCCUPANCY TO WHAT POTTAHS ENTITLED	15
VI—RIGHT OF OCCUPANCY AFTER 12 YEARS' HOLDING	ib.
The section retrospective in its operation	ib.
Distinction between occupancy-ryot and middleman	ib.

CONTENTS.

	Page
Occupancy only acquired in agricultural lands	16
Who are not entitled to a right of occupancy	ib.
Who are entitled to a right of occupancy	17
Loss or determination of right	18
Right to sublet	ib.
Right of occupancy hereditary, not necessarily transferable	19
Right of occupancy may be transferred with consent of zemindar	ib.
Under what circumstances right of occupancy can be acquired in neej-jote land	20
Neej-jote land passes to purchaser on sale of zemindaree	ib.
Ryot failing to prove pottah can plead right of occupancy	ib.
Court to determine rates of rent	ib.
Question discussed as to whether right of occupancy is transferable or not	ib.
VII—RIGHT OF OCCUPANCY WHEN BARRED BY TERMS OF WRITTEN CONTRACT	22
General effect of the section	23
VIII—RYOTS NOT HAVING OCCUPANCY RIGHTS	24
Non-occupancy ryot cannot sue for a pottah	ib.
Landlord can only demand fair and equitable rent	ib.
And can only enhance after notice	ib.
General conclusions	ib.
IX—COURT TO FIX PERIOD OF POTTAH IN CERTAIN CASES	25
Section only applies to suits for pottahs	ib.
Ryot suing for pottah must stand or fall by pleadings	ib.
Equitable rates cannot be decreed to a ryot who claims fixed rates	ib.
X—GRANTOR OF POTTAH ENTITLED TO KABULIAT	26
Landlord cannot sue trespasser for kabuliat	ib.
Nor the holder of lakhiraj land	ib.
Tender of pottah	27
Landlord failing to prove rent claimed, suit to be dismissed	ib.
No suit for kabuliat for portion of holding	28
Shareholder cannot sue joint tenant for kabuliat	ib.
Unless by special agreement rent has been separately paid	29
Miscellaneous	ib.
Registration of kabuliat	ib.
Stamps on kabuliats	ib.
XI—DAMAGES FOR EXACTION OF RENT	30
Cesses cannot be recovered over and above rent	ib.
Contract to collect an illegal cess invalid	ib.
What are illegal cesses	ib.
Illegal exactions	31
Receipts	ib.
Damages must be awarded if receipts withheld	ib.
Stamps on receipts	32
Appropriation of payments	ib.
XII—LANDHOLDER NOT TO COMPEL ATTENDANCE OF RYOT	32
XIII—DAMAGES FOR EXTORTING PAYMENT BY DURESS	33
XIV—NOTICE OF ENHANCEMENT	ib.

CONTENTS.

	Page
Notice must be served before suit for enhancement	34
In what cases notice necessary	ib.
Notice must specify grounds of enhancement	ib.
In case of non-occupancy ryots, grounds must be those stated in section 8	ib.
Requisites of notice	35
Good notices	ib.
Bad notices	ib.
Section applies to intermediate tenures	36
Effect of notice	37
Judgment operates as notice	ib.
Failure to prove notice	ib.
By whom to be issued	ib.
On whom to be served	38
Separate notice to be served for each holding	ib.
Unless the holdings have been consolidated	ib.
Objection taken in special appeal	39
Ryots in Government and resumed estates	ib.
Declaratory decree	ib.
XV—MODE OF CONTESTING ENHANCEMENT OF RENT	ib.
Complaint by ryot of excessive demand of rent	ib.
Right of taking initiative not to apply to non-occupancy	40
In suits under section, Court cannot fix rates of rent	ib.
When sufficiency of notice can be contested by suit	ib.
XVI—DEPENDENT TALOOKS	ib.
Application of section	ib.
Enhancement of rent of dependent talookdars	41
Section 51 of Regulation VIII of 1793	ib.
To what section 51 applies	ib.
Special custom	ib.
Rule to be followed when no customary rate exists	42
Abatement	ib.
What tenures are permanent and transferable	ib.
Construction of leases	44
Grounds of enhancement of permanent transferable tenures	45
Accretions to under-tenures	ib.
Leases with defined boundaries	46
Include all land within those boundaries	ib.
But where boundaries not specified, ryot must pay for excess land	ib.
Unless the land has been held at an uniform rent from the Permanent Settlement	ib.
Jungle-boorie leases	47
Where a maximum customary mentioned rent cannot be raised beyond that amount	ib.
Ghatwalee tenures	ib.
Held upon conditions of service	ib.
If service dispensed with, ghatwal holds free of service	ib.
Effect of Government sales on under-tenures	48
Scope of the Sale Regulation	ib.
Under-tenures not void, but voidable	ib.

	Page
And the rights of annulling under-tenures must be exercised within a reasonable time	49
Shikmee lakhirajdar cannot be disturbed	ib.
XVII—Presumption from holding at Unchanged Rent for 20 years	ib.
XVIII—Grounds of Enhancement of Rent of Occupancy-Ryot	50
This section applicable only to ryots and agricultural lands	ib.
Under no circumstances can an occupancy-ryot's rent be enhanced beyond what is fair and equitable	51
Prevailing rates	ib.
Ryots of the same class	ib.
Places adjacent	52
Increase in the value of the produce or productive powers of the land	ib.
The principle of proportion to be followed in adjusting obsolete rates	ib.
When rule of proportion applies	53
The increase in the value of the produce must be an increase in the natural and ordinary course	ib.
The increase must have been brought about otherwise than by the agency or expense of the ryot	ib.
A ryot who converts arable land into orchard land, only liable for arable land rates	54
Where plaintiff fails to prove his case, suit must be dismissed	56
XIX—Abatement of Rent	57
Ryot not restricted to the grounds of abatement mentioned in this section	ib.
When area is diminished by diluvion, ryot can either sue for abatement, or for a refund of the excess taken from him	ib.
Or may set up the fact of a diminution in answer to a claim for arrears of rent	58
Other causes which entitle a ryot to abatement	ib.
Dispossession through defect of lessor's title	ib.
Principle upon which abatement is to be made	ib.
Any ryot or under-tenant can sue for abatement though not under this section	59
When land has been resumed through defect of lessor's title	ib.
Or damage caused by act of God	ib.
Fraud	60
Zemindar cannot sue Government for abatement	ib.
XX—Relinquishment does not apply to Ryots with Lease	61
Notice unless followed by relinquishment invalid. Verbal notice in what cases sufficient	ib.
Absconding of ryot tantamount to relinquishment	ib.
Service of notice by Collector	ib.
Relinquishment of part of a holding not permitted	ib.
Stamp on notice	ib.
XXI—Definition of "Arrear of Rent"	62
Discretionary power vested in Courts to award interest on arrears of rent	ib.

	Page
Tenant bound to tender payment	62
Waiver of interest	ib.
Interest not awardable in addition to damages	ib.
Meaning of "established usage"	ib.
XXII—EJECTMENT OF RYOT FOR ARREARS	63
Ryot not liable to ejectment for arrears due in the middle of the year	ib.
The receipt of rent of a subsequent year bars ejectment for arrears of previous year	ib.
Holder of mokurruree ijara not under this section	ib.
Remedy in case of unlawful ejectment	ib.
XXIII—CANCELMENT OF LEASE FOR ARREARS	ib.
Application of section	64
No suit after arrears received	ib.
Equitable relief in cases of forfeiture	ib.
Courts will not adjudge forfeiture if subtantial relief can otherwise be granted	ib.
A tenant holding over is bound by the conditions of forfeiture contained in the lease	65
Unless they have been waived by the landlord	ib.
Appointment of sezawul does not determine lease	ib.
XXIV—SUITS AGAINST SURBURAKARS	ib.
XXV—PROPRIETOR'S RIGHT TO SURVEY AND MEASURE HIS ESTATES	66
Can a proprietor not in receipt of rents measure?	ib.
A proprietor not in possession cannot measure	ib.
The right to measure not affected by the land having been let out on fixed leases	67
Zemindar cannot measure lakhiraj lands	ib.
XXVI—REGISTRY OR TRANSFER OF UNDER-TENURES	ib.
Transferable ryottee tenure need not be registered	ib.
No express penalty provided for non-registration	68
Zemindar need not recognize transfer	ib.
Effect of improper transfer	69
No division of tenure without consent of zemindar	ib.
Recognition by landlord supplies the place of registration	ib.
When lease has been taken benamee, the landlord may sue real tenant	ib.
Rights of unregistered transferree	70
Suit lies to compel registration	ib.
XXVII—TO WHAT SUITS LIMITATION OF ONE YEAR APPLIES	ib.
Saving of limitation provided by this Act	71
"One year" to be calculated by British calendar	ib.
Illegal ejectment	ib.
XXVIII—LIMITATION IN SUITS FOR POTTAHS	71
XXIX—LIMITATION IN SUITS FOR ARREARS OF RENT	72
Section not affected by Limitation Act	ib.
No deduction of time allowed for minority, &c.	ib.
Where tenure is sold for arrears of rent and the sale is reversed, the arrears are held to accrue from reversal of sale	ib.
Rent must be certain before suit for arrears will lie	73
Declaratory decree not a cause of action	ib.

CONTENTS.

	Page
Dismissal of initiative suit by ryot voids proviso	74
Miscellaneous	ib.
XXX—LIMITATION IN SUITS AGAINST AGENTS	75
Meaning of "agent"	ib.
Cannot grant leases unless specially authorized	76
Limitation in suits against agents	ib.
Fraud	ib.
Principal must use due diligence in discovering fraud	ib.
XXXI—SUITS FOR BALANCE AFTER DEPOSIT	77
Deposit to be made after rent has become due	ib.
Notice must be in form of Schedule B	ib.
Effect of reversal of sale after deposit	ib.
XXXII—NAIBS TO BE DEEMED AUTHORIZED AGENTS	ib.
General power of attorney	78
Suit to be brought in name of principal	ib.
XXXIII—COGNIZANCE OF SUITS	ib.
XXXIV—PROCEEDINGS TO BE REGULATED UNDER CODE OF CIVIL PROCEDURE	ib.
Section 119 of Civil Procedure made applicable to rent suits	79
XXXV—JURISDICTION IN CERTAIN SUITS	79
XXXVI—PROVISION WHEN LAND IS SITUATED IN DIFFEERENT JURISDICTIONS	ib.
XXXVII—PROCEDURE WHEN MEASUREMENT IS OPPOSED	ib.
Separate application for each ryot not necessary	80
A shareholder of joint estate cannot sue alone	ib.
Jurisdiction	ib.
XXXVIII—MEASUREMENT BY COLLECTOR WHEN TO BE MADE	ib.
Who may apply for measurement	81
Grounds on which application may be granted	82
One application may include many ryots	ib.
Intervenor	ib.
Power of the Collector	ib.
Proceedings must be in strict accordance with terms of section	ib.
Objection to be taken at the time of proceedings	ib.
No proceedings valid under this section to enhance rents	ib.
XXXIX—PROCEEDINGS ON COMPLETION OF MEASUREMENT	83
XL—COLLECTORS' POWERS	ib.
XLI—MEASUREMENT TO BE MADE BY PERGUNNAH POLE	ib.
Weight to be given to canoongo papers in fixing the standard	84
XLII—REGISTER OF SUITS	ib.
XLIII—FORM OF PLAINT	ib.
XLIV—AWARD OF DAMAGES IN ARREARS	ib.
Under what circumstances damages are to be awarded	85
Are in lieu of interest	ib.
XLV—AWARD OF COMPENSATION TO DEFENDANT	ib.
XLVI—PAYMENT INTO COURT AFTER TENDER	86
When defendant entitled to set-off	ib.
Tender must be made and refused before deposit	ib.
Zemindar entitled to know interest of depositor	ib.
XLVII—PROCEDURE TO BE FOLLOWED	ib.
Stamp on deposits	87

CONTENTS.

	Page
XLVIII, XLIX.—Payment into Court after Action brought	87, 88
L—Suits in which Arrests before Judgment cannot issue	ib.
LI—Mesne Profits may be claimed in Suits for recovery of Land	ib.
Separate suits for mesne profits	89
When cause of action accrues	ib.
Wrongful possessor liable to execution-creditor for mesne profits	ib.
LII—Suits for Ejectment or Cancelment of Lease	ib.
Equitable relief afforded by this section extends to lease-holders	ib.
Time how computed	90
Discretionary with Court to extend time	ib.
Section does not apply to middlemen	ib.
LIII—Immediate Execution in certain Cases	ib.
Effect of holding over after expiry of lease	91
Where landlord consents	ib.
Where landlord dissents	ib.
LIV—Execution not stayed pending Appeal	ib.
Ejectment of non-occupancy ryots and under-tenants holding over after the lease has expired.	ib.
LV, LVI—Refusal to grant Pottah or execute Kabuliat	92
LVII—Simultaneous Execution against Person and Property prohibited	ib.
LVIII—Execution in Suits under Rs. 500 not to issue after 3 years	ib.
Costs of execution to be reckoned as part of judgment	93
Application for execution if presented before the lapse of 3 years can be carried out after the expiration of 3 years	ib.
The 3 years must be reckoned from date of final judgment	ib.
LIX—Procedure on Sale of Under-tenure	94
Transferable under-tenures hypothecated to landlord for rent	ib.
Tenure cannot be resold a second time	95
Defaulting tenant cannot himself purchase	ib.
Only the property of the judgment-debtor can be sold	ib.
Is a sale under an *ex-parte* decree which is afterwards set aside valid?	ib.
Effect of reversal of decree on sale	96
Effect on sale when decree is barred by limitation	ib.
LX—Contents of Notice of Sale of Under-tenure	ib.
LXI—Under-tenures not to be sold whilst other Execution in force	ib.
Immoveable property other than the under-tenure in arrear not to be sold till moveable property is exhausted	97
Execution must issue against moveable property first	ib.
LXII—Payment of Decree by person interested in the Tenure	98
Effect of deposit by under-tenant of rent due	ib.
LXIII—Procedure where Under-tenure is claimed by third Party	ib.
An unregistered under-tenant cannot sue for a reversal of a sale except in cases of fraud	ib.

CONTENTS.

	Page
This section applies only when relation of landlord and tenant exists	99
LXIV—Execution of Decrees in favor of Sharers	ib.
A co-sharer cannot cause sale of tenure or his share of rent	ib.
LXV —Execution against Immoveable Property	100
LXVI—Auction-Purchaser of superior Tenure	ib.
Incumbrances not void—only voidable	ib.
Notice condition precedent to cancellation of tenure	101
What rights preserved	ib.
Fraud	ib.
Collusive sale	ib.
House no incumbrance	ib.
When cause of action arises to auction-purchaser	ib.
LXVII—Suit to compel Registration	ib.
LXVIII to LXXI—The Law of Distraint	102, 103
Gomasta cannot distrain unless specially authorized	ib.
Ratification of illegal distress by landlord	ib.
LXXII to XCV—Procedure to be followed	104—110
XCVI—Suits by Third Parties claiming the Property distrained	111
XCVII to XCIX—Suits for Damages for Illegal Distraint	112
Penalty for illegal distraint	113
C—Time within which such Suits are to be brought	ib.
CI—Resistance of Distraint	114
CII—Appeals under the Act	ib.
Meaning of "District Judge"	ib.
Meaning of suit	115
Where no appeal lies	ib.
CIII—Review of Judgment	ib.
CIV—Small Cause Court not to have Jurisdiction	ib.
CV—Power to issue Process free of charge	ib.
CVI—Application of Act	116
CVII—Enactments repealed	ib.
CVIII—Pending Suits	ib.
CIX—Chota Nagpore Tenures Act not affected	117
CX—Nor Act VII of 1868 (B. C.)	ib.
CXI—Title of Act	ib.
Schedule A	ib.
Schedules B and C	118
Schedule D	119

LIST OF CASES.

A.

Abdool Ali *v.* Yah Ali Khan, 28.
Addoyto Churn Dey *v.* Peter Doss, 17.
Afsurooddeen *v.* Mussamut Shorooshee Bala Dabea, 57, 58.
Ahmed Ali *v.* Golam Gafar, 50.
Ahmuty *v.* Brodie, 32.
Ajoodhya Pershad *v.* Mussamut Emam Bundi Begum, 19.
Akhoy Sunkur Chuckerbutty *v.* Rajah Indroboushun Deb Roy, 26, 34.
Allender *v.* Dwarkanath Roy, 69.
Alum Chunder Shah *v.* Moran and Co., 65.
Amanutulla, in the matter of, 114.
Ambika Debi *v.* Pranhari Dass, 98.
Amirto Lall Bose *v.* Arbach Kazee, 51.
Anand Lall Mookerjee *v.* Kalika Persaud Nissa, 70.
Anundolall Chowdry *v.* Hills, 12.
Anund Moyee Chowdhrain *v.* Chunder Monee Dossia, 37.
Anunt Manjhee *v.* Joy Chunder Choudhry, 82.
Attimollah *v.* Shaik Saheboollah, 46.
Augur Singh *v.* Mohini Dutt Singh, 64.

B.

Baboo Dhunput Singh *v.* Gooman Singh, 36, 43.
Baboo Dwarka Doss *v.* Gopal Doss, 61.
Baboo Gauri Baijnath Persad *v.* Budhoo Singh, 89.
Baboo Gokhlanund *v.* Lalljee Sahoo, 90.
Baboo Gopal Lall Thakoor *v.* Kumur Ali, 46.
Baboo Gopal Lall Thakoor *v.* Teluck Chunder Roy, 44.
Baboo Nundo Loll *v.* Smith, 82.
Baboo Purmessuree Persaud Narain Singh *v.* Aghur Singh, 88.
Bacharam Paul *v.* Asgur Fakeer, 87.
Bakranath Mundle *v.* Binodram Sen, 24, 34.
Bala Thakoor *v.* Meghburn Singh, 82.
Bamasoondery Dassyah *v.* Radhika Chowdhrain, 41.
Banee Madhub Banerjee *v.* Bhagbut Pal, 14.
Banee Madhub Chowdry *v.* Tara Prosunno Bose, 35.

Barry *v.* Abdool Ali, 58.
Beckwith *v.* Kisto Jeebun Buxshee, 62.
Bejoy Gobind Bural *v.* Bheeko Roy, 14.
Bejoy Gobindo Bural *v.* Junnobee Bromonya, 38.
Bejoy Gobind Singh *v.* Karoo Singh, 77.
Bengal Government *v.* Nawab Jafur Hossein Khan, 43.
Bepin Behary Choudhry *v.* Ram Chandra Roy, 69.
Bhagabat Prosad Singh *v.* Durg Bijai Sing, 46.
Bhagruth Dass *v.* Mohasoop Roy, 53.
Bharut Chunder Sein *v.* Oseemooddeen, 1, 4.
Bharut Roy *v.* Gunga Narain Mohapattur, 69.
Bhiro Chandra Mazumdar *v.* Bamundas Mookerjee, 89.
Bhogeeruth Shikdar *v.* Ram Narain Mundur, 30.
Bhogobutty Churn Bhuttacharjea *v.* Tameerooddeen Moonshi, 84.
Bholanath Ghosal *v.* Kedarnath Banerjee, 101.
Bholanath Mookerjee *v.* Brijo Mohun Ghose, 31.
Bhooputtee Roy *v.* Umbika Churn Banerjee, 70.
Bhowanee Prosad Chuckerbutty *v.* Mussamut Coroona Mye, 60.
Bhurut Chundra Aitch *v.* Gourmonee Dossee, 47.
Bibee Reazoonissa *v.* Shaikh Dad Ali, 56.
Bibee Suhodwa *v.* Smith, 19.
Biddell *v.* Chuttardharee Lall, 76.
Binode Behary Roy *v.* Masseyk, 55.
Binode Ram Sein *v.* Deputy Commissioner, Sonthal Pergunnahs, 48.
Binodee Lall Ghose *v.* Mackenzie, 37.
Bipro Dass Dey *v.* Mussamut Sakermonee Dassee, 46.
Bissen Lall Dass *v.* Ranee Khyrunnissa Begum, 16.
Bissessur Chuckerbutty *v.* Woomachurn Roy, 53.
Bonmallee Churn Mytee *v.* Shooroop Hootai, 56.
Boydonath *v.* Ramjoy Dey, 36.
Brindabun Dey *v.* Bisona Bibee, 51.
Brae *v.* Kumal Shaha, 72.

Brohommoyee Bewah, in the matter of, 89.
Brojonath Choudhry v. Stewart, 51.
Brojonath Dey v. Shumboo Chunder Chatterjee, 31.
Brojonath Kundu Chowdry v. Lakhi Narayan Addi, 45.
Brojonath Kundu Chowdry v. Lowther, 50.
Brojonath Kundu Chowdry v. Stewart, 54.
Brojonath Paul Chowdry v. Heera Lall Paul, 58.
Brojo Soondur Mitter v. Kalee Kishore Choudhry, 41.
Buduroonissa Choudhrain v. Chunder Coomar Dutt, 50.
Bullen v. Lalit Jha, 3.
Bunchanund v. Hurgopal Bhadery, 42.
Burmah Chowdry v. Sreenund Singh, 30.
Burodakant Roy Bahadur v. Radha Charan Roy, 36, 56.
Butabee Begum v. Kooshai, 16.
Bydnath Shaha v. Jadub Chunder Shaha, 20.
Byjnath Dutt Jha v. Mussamut Patsohee Dobain, 6.
Byjnath Koonwar v. Saheb Koonwar, 37.
Bykunt Ram Roy v. Mussamut Shoorfoonissa Begum, 74.

C.

Campbell v. Abdul Huc, 93.
Campbell v. Kishen Dhun Audhikaree, 2, 4.
Cazee Syud Mahomed Agmul v. Chunder Lall Panday, 61.
Choudhry Khan v. Gour Jana, 47, 54.
Chunder Coomar Banerjee v. Azeemooddeen, 50.
Chunder Kanto Surma v. Bissessur Surmah Chuckerbutty, 95.
Chunder Monee Chowdrain v. Debender Nath Roy Chowdry, 31.
Chunder Monee Dassee v. Dhuroneedhur Lahory, 38.
Chunder Mun Chowdhry v. Sriman Chowdhry, 37.
Chunder Nauth Nag Chowdhry v. Assanoolla Mundul, 26.
Chundra Kanth Mookerjee v. Dhun Sing Roy, 46.
Chytunno Chunder Roy v. Kedernath Roy, 62.
Collector of Bograh v. Dwarkanath Biswas, 2.

D.

Damudar Roy v. Nimanand Chuckerbutty, 101.

Dariao v. Dowluta, 18.
David v. Ramdhun Chatterjee, 55.
Deen Doyal Lall v. Mussamut Thakroo Koonwar, 74.
Deen Dyal Paramanick v. Juggeshur Roy, 64.
Degumber Mitter v. Gobindo Chunder Haldar, 38.
Desaratulla v. Nawab Nazim Nazar Ali Khan, 97.
Dhalee Paramanick v. Anund Chunder Tolaputtur, 30.
Dhomree Sheikh v. Bisessur Lall, 19.
Dhukhina Mohun Roy v. Kureemullah Mookhtear, 9.
Dhunput Singh Doogar v. Rahmon Mundul, 76.
Dhunput Singh Roy Bahadur v. Vellayat Ali, 69.
Dhun Sing v. Chunderkant Mookerjee, 12.
Digumber Mitter v. Gobindo Chunder Haldar, 76.
Din Doyal Lal v. Mussamut Thukroo Konwar, 58.
Din Doyal Paramanick v. Prankissen Paul Chowdhry, 62.
Dindoyal Paramanick v. Radha Kishore Debi, 73.
Dinobundhoo Bhadooree v. Prankishen Sircar, 38.
Dinobundhoo Chowdhry v. Dinonath Mookerjee, 82.
Dinobundoo Dey v. Ram Dhone Roy, 8.
Dinonauth Doss v. Gogon Chandra Sen, 36, 37.
Dinonath Panday v. Roghoonath Panday, 72.
Dirganj Singh v. Foorsut, 18.
Dookee Ram Sircar v. Gowhar Mundul, 29.
Doonee Mahtoe v. Sheo Narain Singh, 106.
Doorgachurn Mullick v. Bhoormon Manjee, 18.
Doorga Churn Surmah v. Jampa Dassee, 29.
Doorga Mohtoon v. Kannye Lall Ajha, 25.
Doorga Pershad Pal Chowdry v. Jogesh Prokash Gungopadhy, 96.
Doma Roy v. Melon, 56.
Domunulla Sirkar v. Mahomondie Nushyo, 21.
Dowlut Ghazee Choudhry v. Moonshee Munoor, 95.
Doyal Chund Sahoy v. Nobin Chandra Adhikari, 115.
Doyamoyee Chowdrainee v. Bholanauth Ghose, 74.

LIST OF CASES.

D'Silva v. Raj Coomar Dutt, 39.
Dukhin Mohun Rai v. D'Abreau, 52.
Dumaine v. Attam Singh, 39.
Durga Charan Mazumdar v. Mahomed Abbas Bhuya, 66.
Dwarkanath Chuckerbutty v. Bhowanee Kishore Chuckerbutty, 66, 80, 82.
Dwarkanath Haldar v. Huree Mohan Roy, 38.
Dyaram v. Bhobindun Naraen, 45.

E.

Elahee Bux Chowdry v. Roopun Telee, 7, 12.
Elahi Bux Chowdry v. Roopchund Telee, 7.
Erskine v. Ram Coomar Roy, 61.
Eshan Chunder Ghose v. Hurrish Chunder Banerjee, 17.
Eshan Chunder Roy v. Khajah Asanoollah, 73.

F.

Fakiruddin Mahomed Ahason v. Phillipps, 65.
Farquharson v. Dwarkanath Singh, 47.
Fitzpatrick v. Wallace, 16.
Foschola v. Hurrochunder Bose, 12, 50.

G.

Gaur Lal Sirkar v. Rameswar Bhumik, 20.
Geetum Singh v. Buldeo Kahar, 102.
Gholam Khejur v. Erskine, 67.
Ghoora Singh v. Otar Singh, 11.
Gobin Chunder Bose v. Alimooddeen, 101.
Gobind Chunder Chunder v. Kristokanto Dutt, 4.
Gobindchunder Dutt v. Baboo Hurronath Roy, 41.
Gobind Kumar Chowdhry v. Huro Chandra Nag, 36.
Gobind Monee Debia v. Deno Bundhoo Shaha, 46.
Golam Ali v. Baboo Gopal Lal Thakoor, 44, 47, 56.
Golam Asgar v. Lakhimani Debi, 96.
Golam Chunder Dey v. Nuddiar Chand Adheekaree, 94, 99.
Golam Mahomed v. Asmut Alee Khan Chowdhry, 25, 27, 29.
Goluck Kishore Acharjee v. Kesta Majhee, 82.
Goluckmonee Deben v. Asssimoodeen, 76.
Goor Dial v. Ramdut, 16.
Goorooprosad Sirkar v. Philippe, 64.
Gooroo Prosunno Banerjee v. Sree Gopal Chowdry, 2.
Gopaul Chunder Bose v. Muthoora Mohun Bonnerjee, 12.
Gopaul Mundul v. Soobhudra Boistobee, 94.
Gopeekisto Gosamee v. Ram Comul Misry, 69.
Gopee Mohun Roy v. Sibchunder Sein, 15, 17.
Gopeenath Jannah v. Jetao Mollah, 28.
Gopenunda Jha v. Lalla Gobind Pershad, 3.
Gora Chund v. Godadhur Chatterjee, 40.
Goreeb Mundul v. Bhoobun Mohun Sein, 17.
Goroodass Mundul v. Shaikh Durbaree, 11.
Gouree Nath Rai v. Ramgutty Chunder, 52.
Gour Huree Sing v. Beharry Raut, 20, 22.
Grant v. Bunkshee Deo, 47.
Greeschunder Ghose v. Kallykristo Holdar, 10.
Grish Chandra Ghose v. Iswar Chandra Mookerjee, 36.
Grish Chunder Ghose v. Ram Tono Biswas, 36.
Grish Chunder Sein v. Eastern Bengal Jute Company, 86.
Gubdoo Mull v. Hoolasee, 37.
Gunga Gobind Sen v. Gobind Chunder Doss, 74.
Gunga Gobind Roy v. Kala Chund Surma, 71.
Gunga Narain Chowdry v. Kofa Tali, 40.
Gunga Narain Dass v. Sharoda Mohun Roy, 13, 29.
Gunga Pershad Singh v. Ramloll Singh, 40.
Gunga Ram Bearer v. Ujoodhyaram Mytee, 56.
Gureebollah Puramanick v. Fukeer Mahomed Kholoo, 31.
Gyan Chunder Roy v. Kalee Churn Roy Chowdry, 94.
Gyaram Dutt v. Gooroochurn Chatterjee, 12.

H.

Hameed Ali v. Afnoddeen, 28.
Haran Chundra Pal v. Mukhta Soondari Chowdhrain, 17.
Harasoondari Dasi v. Kistumani Chowdhrain, 101.
Haree Persad Malee v. Koonjo Behary Shaha, 1.
Hari Prosonno Roy v. Bhugwan Chunder Panda, 65.

LIST OF CASES.

Haro Doss v. Gobind Bhuttacharjee 18, 61.
Heeramonee v. Gunganarain Roy, 61.
Heeroo v. Dhobee, 18.
Hem Chunder Chatterjee v. Poornu Chunder Roy, 11, 37.
Hera Lall Seal v. Poran Matteah, 93.
Herrick v. Sixby, 46.
Hill v. Khowaj Sheikh Mundle, 26.
Hills v. Besharuth Meer, 7.
Hills v. Hurololl Sein, 7, 13.
Hills v. Ishur Ghose, 25.
Hills v. Pauch Cowrie Sheikh, 39.
Hora Mohun v. Umesh Chunder Dutt, 85.
Horokishen Banerjee v. Joykishen Mookerjee, 59.
Hubebool Hossein v. Allender, 4.
Huree Churn Bose v. Meharoonissa Bibee, 69.
Hureehur Mookerjee v. Biressur Banerjee, 18.
Hureehur Mookerjee v. Jodoonath Ghose, 68.
Hureekishore Ghose v. Komodineekant Banerjee, 74.
Huree Mohun Mookerjee v. Gora Chand Mitter, 70.
Huree Pershad Malee v. Koonjo Behari Shaha, 26.
Hurish Chunder Chuckerbutty v. Sreemutty Huree Bewah, 115.
Huro Chunder Goho v. Dunn, 19.
Huronauth Roy v. Gobin Chunder Dutt, 56.
Huronath Roy v. Jogender Chunder Roy, 75.
Huro Pershad Chuckerbutty v. Sreedam Chunder Chowdry, 107, 115.
Huro Soonduree Chowdhrain v. Anund Mohun Ghose Chowdry, 41.
Hurrish Chunder Koondoo v. Alexander, 16.
Hurrish Chunder Koondoo v. Mohinee Mohun Mitter, 3.
Hurrish Chunder Mookerjee v. Annund Chunder Chatterjee, 70.
Hurro Chunder Mookerjee v. Mohesh Chunder Dhopa, 13.
Hurro Mohun Mookerjee v. Ranee Lalun Monee Dossee, 43.
Hurronath Roy v. Bindo Bashinee Debia, 41, 50.
Hurronath Roy Chowdry v. Goluck Nath Chowdhry, 73.
Hurro Prosad Chowdry v. Shama Persaud Roy Chowdry, 39.
Huruck Lall Shaha v. Sreenibash Kurmokar, 71.
Hurruck Sing v. Toolsee Ram Sahoo, 11.
Hurryhur Mookerjee v. Paddolochun Dey, 8.
Hurry Mohun Mozumdar v. Dwarkanauth Sen, 115.
Hyder Buksh v. Bhudendro Deb Coomar, 17, 20.

I.

Imdad Hossein v. Stack, 27.
Indromonee Burmonee v. Sooroop Chunder Paul, 28.
Indur Chunder Dugar v. Brindabun Bihara, 28.
Ishur Chunder Doss v. Nittyanund Doss, 10.
Isshur Ghose v. Hills, 15.
Iswar Chandra Chuckerbutty v. Bistu Chandra Chuckerbutty, 101.
Iswar Chandra Sen v. Bepin Behari Roy, 115.

J.

Jadub Chunder Haldar v. Etburry Lashkur, 53.
Jadub Chunder Haldar v. Etwaree Lushkur, 39, 54, 80.
Jadunath Kundu Choudhry v. Braja Nath Kundu, 96.
Jallalooddeen v. Burn, 84.
Jan Ali v. Gooroo Dass Roy, 74.
Jan Ali v. Jan Ali Choudhry, 95.
Jan Ali Choudry v. Ishan Chunder Sein, 77.
Jan Ali Chowdry v. Nittyanand Bose, 90.
Janokee Bullab Chuckerbutty v. Nobin Chunder Roy Chowdry, 46.
Jaun Alio. Jan Ali, 56.
Joba Sing v. Meer Najeeb Oollah, 44.
Jokee Lall v. Nursing Narain Sing, 97.
Jonarhdn Acharjee v. Haradhun Acharjee, 63.
Joy Dhut Jha v. Bayeeram Singh, 20.
Joy Kissen Mookerjee v. Raj Kissen Mookerjee, 42.
Joylall Sheikh v. Brojonath Paul Chowdry, 113.
Joy Monee Dassee v. Huronath Roy, 73.
Juggessur Patty v. Ishanchunder Ghose, 56.
Juggut Chunder Dutt v. Panioty, 46.
Jumant Ali Shah v. Chowdhry Chutturdhari Shahi, 91.

K.

Kabeel Shaha v. Radhakissen Mullick, 17.
Kadir Gazee v. Mahadebee Dossia, 64.

LIST OF CASES.

Kalam Sheik v. Panchu Mandal, 2.
Kalee Churn Singh v. Ameerooddeen, 16.
Kalee Doss Ghose v. Lall Mohun Ghose, 115.
Kalee Doss Nundee v. Ramguttee Dutt Sein, 66.
Kalee Kishen Biswas v. Sreemutty Jankee, 16.
Kalee Kishore Chatterjee v. Ramchurn Shah, 15, 18.
Kalee Pershad v. Shah Lutafut, 14.
Kallee Chunder Choudhry v. Rutton Gopal Bhadooree, 51.
Kallee Churn Dutt v. Shooshee Dossee, 7.
Kalee Nath Chowdry v. Humee Bibee, 36.
Kali Coomar Das v. Sheik Anees, 76.
Kali Kamal Mozumdar v. Shib Sukul, 71.
Kamikhaprasad Roy v. Srimati Jagadambi Dasi, 5.
Kanchun Mollah Dossea v. Rajendro Chunder Roy Choudry, 77.
Karoo Lall Thakoor v. Luchmeeput Doogar, 16, 22, 68.
Karoo Loll Thakoor v. Forbes, 89.
Karunakar Mahati v. Niladhro Chowdhry, 43.
Kashee Nath Deb v. Moharanee Shibessuree Debea, 39.
Kasheenath Lushkar v. Bamasoonduree Debea, 8.
Kasheenath Punee v. Lukhmonee Pershad Patnaik, 69.
Kasheenath Roy Chowdry v Mynuddeen Chowdry, 62.
Kashee Singh v. Onraet, 61.
Kasimuddi Khandkar v. Nadar Ali Tarafdar, 44, 47.
Katyanee Dabee v. Soonduree Dabee, 12.
Kazee Khuda Nawaz v. Nubo Kishore Raj, 7, 13.
Kebul Kishen Dass v. Jaminee, 66.
Kenaram Mullick v. Ramcoomar Mookerjee, 8.
Kenny v. Mookta Soonderee Debea, 76.
Ketul Gain v. Nodur Mistree, 17.
Khaski Roy v. Farzand Ali Khan, 37.
Khasroo Manddar v. Prem Lall, 71.
Kheeromonee Doss v. Bejoy Gobin Burral, 14.
Khetter Paul Singh v. Lukhee Narain Mitter, 70.
Khoda Buksh v. Akoot Gazee, 29.
Khola Mundel v. Piroo Sirkar, 56.
Khoobaree Rai v. Roghoobur Rai, 94.

Khoondkar Abdur Ruhman v. Wooma Chunder Roy, 35, 53.
Kolodeep Narain Singh v. Government of India, 44.
Koolodeep Narain Singh v. Mahadeo Singh, 47.
Komla Kant Doss v. Pogose, 59.
Komul Lochun Roy v. Moran and Co., 73.
Komul Lochun Roy v. Zumerooddeen Sircar, 12.
Koontee Debee v. Hirdoynath Duncepa, 101.
Koylash Chunder Dey v. Joy Narayan Jalooah, 29.
Kriteebash Mytee v. Ramdhan Kharah, 13.
Kristo Chunder Goopto v. Elahee Buksh, 41.
Kristo Motee Debia v. Fukeer Chunder Khan, 37.
Kristo Protibar v. Alladinee Dossee, 86.
Kumala Kant Ghose v. Kalu Mahomed Mandal, 30.
Kumar Paresh Narayan Roy v. Gour Sundar Bhumick, 35.
Kunda Missa v. Gunesh Singh, 10.

L.

Lakhikant Das Choudhry v. Ram Doyal Das, 89.
Lalla Ram Sahoy v. Dodraj Mahtoo 93.
Limond v. Gour Soonder Chowdry, 46.
Luchmun Pershad v. Holas Mahtoon, 5.
Lullo Singh v. Thakoor Pershad, 90.
Lutchmee Persaud v. Ram Golam Singh, 10.
Luttefun-nissa Bebee v. Baboo Poolin Beharee, 14.

M.

Mackintosh v. Gopee Mohun Mozumdar, 91.
Mackintosh v. Womesh Chunder Bose, 77.
Madan Mohun Biswas v. Stalkart, 50.
Madhub Chunder Ghose v. Radhika Chowdhrain, 73.
Madhusudan Kundu v. Ramdhan Ganguli, 100.
Maharaja Dheraj Mahtab Chand Bahadoor v. Chittro Coomaree Bebee, 58.
Maharajah Dheraj Mahtab Chand v. Srimati Debkumaree Debi, 62.
Maharajah Ranmath Sing v. Huro Lall Pandey, 26.
Maharajah Tejchund Bahadoor v. Srikant Ghose, 4.
Mahomed Gazee v. Shunkur Lall, 61.

c

LIST OF CASES.

Mahomed Myanoboo Hek v. Mahomed Syud Khan, 26.
Mahomed Yacoob Hossein v. Sheikh Chowdry Waheed Ali, 7.
Malodee Nashyo v. Bullubee Kant Dhur, 61.
McGiveram v. Dariaw Chowdhry, 38.
McGiveran v. Hurhkoo Singh, 35.
Meah Jan Munshi v. Kurrumamayi Debi, 69, 95.
Meetoonjoy Chowdhry v. Khetter Nauth Roy, 99.
Meheroonissa Bibee v. Hur Churn Bose, 95.
Mirtunjoy Sirkar v. Gopaul Chunder Sirkar, 69.
Mirza Nadir Beg v. Muddurram, 17.
Miterjeet Singh v. Tundun Singh, 11.
Modee Hudden Jorwardar v. Sanders, 46.
Modhoosoodun Koondoo v. Gopeekishen Gossain, 37.
Modhoosoodun Moozumdar v. Brojonath Koond Chowdry, 72.
Mohamed Aynuddeen v. Baboo Rajendra Chandra Neogi, 42.
Mohamed Bahadur Mozoomdar v. Raja Rajkishen Singh, 82.
Mohamed Singh v. Mussamut Mughy Chowdhrain, 29.
Moharanee Inderjeet Koer v. Khwaja Abul Hossein, 62.
Mohesh Chunder Chakladar v. Gunga Monee Dossee, 73.
Mohima Chunder Dey v. Gooroo Doss Sein, 41.
Mohun Gobind Sein v. Nittaye Holdar, 29.
Mohunt Buloram Doss v. Jogendra Nath Mullick, 63.
Mohunt Jalhu v. Koylash Chunder Dey, 1, 26.
Modhoo Shoodun Singh v. Moran & Co., 78.
Mooktakeshee Dossia v. Pearee Choudrain, 69.
Mookhtakeshee Dossee v. Koylash Chunder Mitter, 17.
Moolook Chand Mundul v. Modhoosoodun Bachuspatty, 82.
Moonshee Mahomed Munoor Meah v. Sreemutty Jybunee, 115.
Moran and Co. v. Anund Chunder Mozumdar, 12.
Mothooranath Chatterjee v. Khetternauth Biswas, 39.
Mothooranath Gungopahdya v. Sheeta Monee, 50.
Moulvie Abdool Jubba v. Kalee Churn Dutt, 17.

Mrityun Joya Sirkar v. Gopal Chandra Sirkar, 69, 86.
Mitterjeet Singh v. Toondun Singh, 7.
Mudhoo Manjee v. Rajah Nilmoney Singh, 34.
Muhesh Dutt Pandey v. Seetul Sonar, 72.
Mukandi Lal Dubei v. Crowdy, 18.
Muneekurnicka Chowdhrain v. Anundmoye Chowdhrain, 11.
Munee Kurnika Chowdry v. Anund Moyee Chowdry, 41.
Muneeram Acharjee v. Sreemutty Tarungo, 89.
Munerooddeen v. Mahomed Ali, 18.
Mun Mohun Ghose v. Husrut Sirdar, 11.
Muneeruddeen v. Mahomed Ali, 61.
Munsoor Ali v. Bunoo Singh, 12.
Munsoor Ali v. Harvey, 60.
Mussamut Balool Bebee v. Juggut Narain, 90.
Mussamut Drabamayi Guptia v. Tarachurn Sein, 79, 115.
Mussamut Gobind Monee v. Rajendra Kishore Chowdhry, 71.
Mussamut Hukeem-oon-nissa v. Bhoorin, 20.
Mussamut Hoymobutty Dossee v. Sreekishen Nundee, 4.
Mussamut Kishenbutty Misrain v. Roberts, 4.
Mussamut Lakhee Kowar v. Roy Hari Krishna Singh, 43.
Mussamut Luteefun v. Shaik Meah Jan, 95.
Mussamut Mohun Koowar v. Baboo Zoraman Singh, 5.
Mussamut Reazoonissa v. Tookun Jha, 13.
Mussamut Safuroonissa v. Saree Dhoobee, 94.

N.

Naim Chand Borooah v. Mooraree Mundul, 19.
Naimudda Jowardar v. Scott Moncrieff, 51.
Nand Lall Ghose v. Sidi Nazir Ali Khan, 90.
Nanku Roy v. Mahabir Prasad, 19.
Nara Kant Mozumdar v. Rajah Barodakant Roy Bahadur, 37.
Nawab Nazim, The, v. Ram Lal Ghose, 39.
Nidhi Krishna Bose v. Ram Dass Sen, 16.
Nilkomul Sein v. Danesh Shaikh, 17.
Nil Madhab Karmokar v. Shibu Pal, 17.

LIST OF CASES. xix

Nityanund Ghose v. Kissen Kishore, 2, 56.
Nizamat Ali v. Romesh Chunder Roy, 27, 28.
Nobin Chunder Chowdry v. Gooroo Gobind Surmah Mojoomdar, 30.
Nobin Chunder Rai v. Luckee Prea Dabee, 61.
Nobin Kishen Mookerjee v. Shib Pershad Pattuck, 68.
Nobo Coomar Bose v. Kishen Chunder Bonnerjee, 69.
Nobokanto Dey v. Raja Baroda Kanth Roy Bahadur, 62, 85.
Nobokishore Bose v. Pandul Sircar, 41.
Nobokisto Koondoo v. Nazir Mahomed Sheikh, 115.
Nobokisto Mookerjee v. Ramessur Goopto, 90.
Nobokristo Mojoomdar v. Tara Monee, 42.
Noor Mohamed Mundle v. Hurriprosonno Roy, 51.
Nubo Kishen Mookerjee v. Sreeram Roy, 69.
Nubo Kishore Biswas v. Jadub Chunder Sircar, 101.
Nubo Kishore Bose v. Pandul Sircar, 50.
Nubo Kishore Mundul v. Fukeer Paramanick, 56.
Nuddea Chand Poddar v. Modhoo Soodhun Day Poddar, 61.
Nudhee Dass v. Shah Baboo Bunwaree Lall, 1.
Nuffer Chunder Paul Chowdry v. Poulson, 39, 50.
Nuffer Chander Shaha v. Gossain Jysingh Bharuttee, 44.
Nund Dhunpat v. Tara Chand Pritheeharee, 84.
Nund Kishore Lall v. Kureem Buksh Khan, 26.
Nund Kishore Singh v. Ranee Ismed Kooer, 69.
Nundo Lall Roy v. Gooroo Churn Bose, 99.
Nyamutulla Ustagur v. Gobind Churn Dutt, 21.

O.

Oojan Dewan v. Prannath Mundul, 112.
Ooma Churn Biswas v. Shibnath Bagchee, 67.
Ooma Tara Debi v. Peena Bibee, 74.
Orjoon Sahoo v. Anund Singh, 30.

P.

Pandit Sheo Prokash Misser v. Ram Sahoy Singh, 18, 23.
Pandy Bishonath Roy v. Bhagrut Singh, 10.

Panioty v. Juggut Chunder Dutt, 50.
Pearce Mohun Mookerjee v. Rajkristo Mookerjee, 80.
Pelaram Kotal v. Nundcoomar Chuttoram, 56.
Poolin Beharee Sen v. Watson, 54.
Poolin Beharee Sein v. Neemaye Chund, 11.
Poorno Chunder Roy v. Stalkart, 29.
Poulson v. Modoosoodun Paul Chowdhry, 72.
Pran Bandhu Sirkar v. Sarbasundari Debi, 94.
Prankissen Bagchee v. Monmohinee Dassee, 55.
Prankisto Dey v. Bissumbher Sein, 4.
Pratab Chandra Binwa v. Rani Swarnamayi, 89.
Prem Chand Laha v. Addoito Doss, 114.
Pring Lall v. Brockman, 51.
Prosonno Coomar Paul Chowdhry v. Koylash Chunder Paul Chowdhry, 70.
Prosunno Coomar Paul Choudhry v. Radhanath Dey Choudhry, 54.
Prosunno Moyee Debia v. Chunder Nath Chowdry, 67.
Puddo Lochun Bhadooric v. Chunder Nath Roy, 74.
Puddo Monee Dossia v. Puromanund Sein, 47.
Punchanun Bose v. Peary Mohun Deb 44.
Pureejan Khatoon v. Bykant Chunder Chuckerbutty, 66.
Puring Bhuggut v. Donzelle, 80.
Purmanund Sein v. Puddo Monee Dossia, 52.

R.

Radha Bullub Ghose v. Beharee Lall Mookerjee, 35.
Radha Kishore Roy v. Ameer Chunder Mookerjee, 76.
Radha Madhub Pal v. Kalee Churn Pal, 61.
Radha Mohun Mundul v. Buksha Begum, 90.
Radha Mohan Naskar v. Jadu Nath Das, 113.
Radha Monee Dossia v. Moharanee Shibessuree Debia, 37.
Radhika Pershad Sadhoo v. Gooroo Prosunno Roy, 70.
Raja Kristo Chunder Mundraj v. Poorosuttum Doss, 29.
Raja Nilmani Singh v. Annada Prosad Mookerjee, 58.

Raja Nilmani Singh v. Madhab Singh, 47.
Rajah Satyasaran Ghosal v. Mohesh Chunder Mitter, 44.
Raja Suttyanand Ghosal v. Zahir Sikdar, 62.
Rajah Burodakant Roy v. Seebsunkeree Dossee, 34.
Rajah Leelanund Singh v. Nirput Mahtoon, 2.
Rajah Suttyanund Ghosal v. Huro Kishore Dutt, 41.
Raj Chunder Rai v. Kishen Chunder, 66.
Raj Kishore Mookerjee v. Hureehur Mookerjee, 7, 13.
Rajkishore Mozoomdar v. Heeralall Bukshee, 70.
Raj Mahomed v. Banoo Roshmah, 13.
Rajmohun Mitter v. Gooroo Churn Aytch, 55.
Rajnarain Roy Chowdry v. Olivia Atkins, 12.
Raj Narain Roy v. Muddoo Soodun Mookerjee, 71.
Rakal Dass v. Kinooram Holdar, 11.
Rau Chandra Choudhry v. Subal Patro, 113.
Ram Chunder Choudhry v. Hurrish Chunder Choudhry, 37.
Ram Chunder Dutt v. Juggeshchunder Dutt, 10, 41.
Ram Coomar Bhuttacharjea v. Ram Coomar Sein, 64.
Ram Coomar Dhara v. Bhoyrub Chunder Mookerjee, 52.
Rhadhika Prosunno Chunder v. Urjoon Manjhee, 62.
Ram Bhurossee Singh v. Syud Mahomed Asguree Khan, 40.
Ram Dyal Sing v. Baboo Latchmi Narayan, 7.
Ramessur Audhikaree v. Watson & Co., 26.
Ram Ghose v. Radhachurn Gangooly, 17.
Ram Gobind Roy v. Syud Kushuffudooza, 49.
Ram Jeebun Bose v. Tripoora Dossee, 37.
Ramjeebun Choudhry v. Pearyloll Mundle, 94.
Ramjoy Mundle v. Kallymohun Roy Chowdry, 103.
Ramjoy Singh v. Nagar Gazee, 28.
Ramkant Chowdry v. Brojomohun Mozumdar, 76.
Ramkant Chuckerbutty v. Raja Mohesh Chunder Singh, 56.
Ramkant Dutt v. Gholam Nubby Choudhree, 42.

Ram Khelawan Singh v. Mussamut Soondra, 91.
Ram Lal Chuckerbutty v. Tara Soondari Baramonya, 14.
Ram Lall Ghose v. Lalla Pecum Lall Doss, 10.
Ram Lochun Goopto v. Bamasoonduree Dabee, 14.
Ram Mohon Ghose v. Modhoo Soodun Choudhry, 24.
Rammonee Chuckerbutty v. Alla Buksh, 29.
Ram Mungul Ghose v. Lukhee Narain Shaha, 16.
Ramnarain Mitter v. Nobin Chunder Moordaferash, 89.
Ramnarain Nundee v. Toyluck Chunder Biswas, 46.
Ramnath Lal Bhakt v. Watson and Co., 9.
Rampershad Vogut v. Ramtohul Singh, 4, 31.
Ramrutton Sircar v. Chunder Mookee Dabea, 7.
Ranee Asmad Koer v. Maharanee Indurjeet Koer, 89.
Ranee Durga Sundari v. Brindaban Chandra Sirkar, 18.
Ranee Durga Sundari Dassee v. Bibee Umdatannissa, 50.
Ranee Krishto Monee Debia v. Ram Nidhee Sirkar, 66.
Ranee Shooruth Soondaree Dabee v. Brodie, 32.
Ranee Shornomoyce v. Blumhardt, 16, 50.
Ranee Shornomoyee v. Gouri Prosad Doss, 45.
Ranee Shornomoyee v. Maharajah Suttes Chunder Roy, 49.
Ranee Shornomoyee v. Shooshee Mokhee Burmonia, 73.
Ranee Shurut Soondaree Dabya v. The Collector of Mymensingh, 62.
Rani Sarat Soondari Debi v. Watson, 28.
Rao Baneeram v. Ramnath Saha, 90.
Rasmonce Dabya v. Ramjoy Saha, 31.
Rashum Bebee v. Bissonauth Sircar, 55.
Raye Kumul Dassee v. Jhoroo Mollah, 113.
Reed v. Sreekishen Sing, 20.
Remanund Ghose v. Shorendronath Roy, 18.
Rhidoykrishna Ghose v. Koylash Chandra Bose, 93.
Romanauth Dutt v. Joykishen Mookerjee, 37.

LIST OF CASES.   xxi

Romanath Ruckit v. Chand Huree Bhooya, 27, 29.
Rughooban Tewaric v. Bishendutt Doobey, 14.
Run Bahadoor Singh v. Muloorun Tewaree, 67.
Runglal Sahu v. Piali Dhar, 67.
Rushton v. Girdharee Tewaree, 37.
Rutton Monee Dabee v. Kumolakant Talookdar, 18.
Ryesunnissa Begum v. Bydonath Shaha, 35.

S.

Saddanundo Maiti v. Nowrattam Maiti, 42.
Sadhoo Jha v. Bhugwan Chunder Opadhya, 91.
Sadhoo Singh v. Ramanoograha Lall, 51, 52.
Sadhun Churn Bose v. Gooroo Churn Bose, 69.
Saduck Sirkar v. Mohamoya Debia, 8.
Saduk Sircar v. Sreemutty Mohamoya Dabea, 14.
Saleeboonissa Khatoon v. Mohesh Chunder Roy, 34.
Sameena Beebee v. Koylas Chunder Roy, 32.
Samiraddi Khalifa v. Huris Chandra, 94.
Santiram Panja v. Bycunt Panja, 80.
Sarbanand Panday v. Ruchia Panday, 84.
Sarkies v. Kali Coomar Roy, 68.
Saroda Soondaree Dabya v. Hazee Mahomed Mundul, 61.
Savi v. Chand Sirkar, 63.
Savi v. Issur Chunder Mundul, 4, 74.
Savi v. Jeetoo Meah, 51.
Savi v. Obhoy Nath Bose, 58.
Shah Ali Hossein v. Nanda Khan, 90.
Shaikh Danoollah v. Shaikh Amanutollah, 4.
Shaikh Dilbur v. Issur Chunder Roy, 115.
Shaikh Husmut Ali v. Onree Thakoor, 39.
Shaikh Misser v. Kazee Syud Naser Ali, 92.
Sham Chaud Koondoo v. Brojonath Paul, 95.
Sham Churn Koondoo v. Dwarkanath Kuberaj, 12.
Sham Jha v. Durga Roy, 55.
Sharoda Persaud Gangooly v. Raj Mohun Roy, 83.
Sharoda Soondari Debia v. Goonee Sheik, 4.
Sheikh Afzul v. Lalla Gurnarain, 99.

Sheikh Bhoolloo v. Ram Narain Mookerjee, 96.
Sheik Enayutulla v. Sheikh Elaheebuksh, 60.
Sheikh Gholamee v. Iman Buskh, 40.
Sheikh Jainooddeen v. Poornochunder Roy, 13.
Sheikh Mahomed Chaman v. Rampersad Bhagat, 17.
Sheikh Mahomed Kaloo Chowdry v. Fedaye Shikdar, 28.
Sheikh Mohamed Shuhurroollah v. Mussamut Romya Bibi, 77.
Sheikh Moheem v. Sheikh Raheemoollah, 24, 40.
Sheik Peer Bux v. Mouzah Ally, 63.
Sheik Peer Bux v. Sheikh Mealijan, 17.
Sheoburn Lal v. Ram Pertab Singh, 8, 40.
Sheodie Mahtoon v. Hurreekishen, 20, 25.
Sheopaul Singh v. Nubbee Ashruf Khan, 90.
Sheopershad Tewary v. Mussamat Moleema Beebee, 103.
Shib Chunder Bose v. Ram Chand Chand, 26.
Shibdas Bandapadhya v. Bamandas Bandapadhya, 101.
Shib Narain Dutt v. Ekra Moonissa Begum, 36.
Shibpershad Doobey v. Promathanath Bose, 14.
Shib Ram Ghose v. Pran Pria, 27.
Shoorendro Mohun Roy v. Bhuggobut Churn Gangopadhya, 82.
Showdaminee Dassee v. Hurrunchunder Surmah, 54.
Showdamonee Dassee v. Shookool Mahomed, 53.
Shushee Bhoosun Banerjee v. Nubo Coomar Chatterjee, 80.
Siboo Jelya v. Gopal Chunder Chowdry, 16.
Sobha Mahtoon v. Pabaroo, 34.
Solano v. Soobum Roy, 82.
Sree Misser v. Crowdy, 82.
Sreemutty Alladinee Dassee v. Sreenath Chunder Bose, 14, 115.
Sree Nubudeep Chunder Sirkar v. Lalla Sheeb Loll, 24.
Sreeram Chatterjee v. Lakhan Magilla, 51, 52, 53.
Sreeram Biswas v. Juggernauth Dass Mohunt, 55.
Sreeram Bose v. Bissonath Ghose, 19.
Sri Gopal Mullick v. Dwarkanauth Sein, 36, 39.
Srimati Jannoba v. Grish Chandra Chuckerbutty, 35, 37.

LIST OF CASES.

Srimati Manmohini Choudhrain v. Prem Chand Roy, 83.
Srimati Saudaminee Debia v. Sarup Chandra Roy, 1.
Srinath Ghose v. Haronath Dutt Chowdry, 95, 101.
Sristeedhur Chuckerbutty v. Koonjo Behary Biswas, 115.
Sooda Mookhea Dassee v. Ram Guttee Kurmokar, 12.
Soorasoondera Debia v. Golam Ali, 56.
Soudaminee Debia v. Mohesh Chunder Mookerjee, 2, 27.
Sudyc Purrira v. Boistum Purrira, 18.
Sukhawatoolah v. Puthoo Goldar, 57.
Sumbhoo Chunder Singh v. Ram Narain Doss, 95.
Summeeruddeen Lushkar v. Hurronath Roy, 8, 13.
Surahutoonissa Khanum v. Gyanee Buktur, 51.
Suroop Chunder Mozumdar v. Jardine, Skinner, and Co., 4.
Syed Ahmed Riza v. Agore, 24.
Syed Jeshon Hoosein v. Bakur, 26.
Syud Ameer Hossein v. Sheo Sahae, 17.
Syud Soojat Ally v. Huree Thakoor, 36.

T.

Tara Chand Dutt v. Mussamut Wakamoonissa Bibee, 49.
Tara Monee Debia v. Joykisto Mookerjee, 74.
Tara Monee Koonwaree v. Jeebun Munder, 77.
Tara Pershad Roy v. Soorjokant Acharjee Chowdry, 19.
Tarinee Churn Bose v. Shumboonath Panday, 114.
Tarinee Kant Lahoree v. Koonj Beharee Awasty, 41.
Tarini Charan Ganguli v. Watson, 42.
Thakooranee Dossee v. Bisheshur Mookerjee, 6, 15, 27, 53.
Thakooranee Mahtab Kooer v. Buldeo Singh, 34.
Thakoor Pershad v. Nowab Syud Mahomed Baker, 5.
Thekmee Beldar v. Ramkishen Lall, 34.
Thukree Rai v. Heeramun Singh, 114.
Tilak Patak v. Mahabir Panday, 61.
Tirbhobun Singh v. Jheno Lall, 90.
Tirth Nund Thakoor v. Mohur Mundul, 35.
Tofaoll Khan v. Woopdan Khan, 91.
Tommy v. Soobba Kurim Lall, 91.
Troylucko Tarenee Dossia v. Mohima Chunder Muttuck, 75.
Tweedie v. Ram Narain Doss, 67.

U.

Umbika Churn Mundle v. Ramdhun Mohurrir, 26.
Umes Chandra Roy v. Shashidhar Mookerjee, 89.
Umurt Lal Bose v. Soorubee Dossee, 95.
Unoda Persaud Banerjee v. Chunder Shekur Deb 76.
Unopoorna Dossee v. Oomachurn Doss, 19.
Unopoorna Dossee v. Radha Mohun Pattro, 17.
Upendra Mohun Tagore v. Thanda Dasi 69.
Urjoon Sahoy v. Rajah Nilmoney Singh Deo, 99.

W.

Watson v. Collector of Rajshaye, 69.
Watson & Co. v. Bhoonya Kunwur Narain Singh, 67.
Watson & Co. v. Choto Joora Mundul, 10.
Watson & Co. v. Juggeshar Atta, 44.
Watson & Co. v. Koer Jogendro Narain Roy, 18.
Watson & Co. v. Ramdhan Ghose, 35.
Watson & Co. v. Ram Soonder Panday, 69, 70.
Watson & Co. v. Ranee Shurat Soonderee Dabee, 19.
Wise v. Bansee Shaha, 82.
Wise v. Lakhoo Khan, 82.
Wise v. Ram Chunder Bysack, 64.
Woma Moye Burmonya v. Bokoo Behara, 17.
Woodoy Churn Dhur v. Kalee Tara Dasi, 28.
Wooma Churn Dutt v. Grish Chunder Bose, 35.
Wooma Churn Sett v. Haree Pershad Misser, 68.
Woomakanto Sirkar v. Gopal Singh, 16.
Woomanauth Roy Chowdhry v. Deb Nath Roy Chowdhry, 39.
Woomanath Roy Chowdhry v. Rogoo Nauth Mitter, 49.
Wooma Nath Tewaree v. Koondun Tewaree, 17.
Woomesh Chunder Chatterjee v. Sheik Kumuroodden Lushkur, 64.
Woomesh Chunder Gooptoo v. Rajnarain Roy, 101.

Y.

Yakoob Ali v. Kaernollah, 26.

Z.

Zubeeroodeen Paiker v. Campbell, 46.
Zumeerudnissa Khanum v. Phillipe, 31.

GLOSSARY OF TERMS.

ABWAB—Miscellaneous cesses, imposts and charges levied by zemindars and public officers.

AMEEN—A confidential agent, or a commissioner employed generally to take charge of an estate, to measure lands on it, &c.

BASTOO—Land used for building purposes.

BENAMEE—Holding in the name of another person; the person so holding is the *benameedar*.

BHAGDAREE—A joint tenancy—See p. 18.

BHAOLEE—A tenure where part or the whole of the rent is payable in kind.

BHIKYA—See section 11, page 31.

BUKOOMAT—A certain illegal cess.

BYE-HOWLADAREE—See *Howala*.

CANOONGOE—Pergunnah accountant.

CHAKERAN—A service tenure, that is, land held either rent-free or at a nominal rent by persons who are liable to perform service, in lieu of wages.

CHOWPAL—A shed in which the village community assemble for public business (generally erected by the headman of the village and used by him as an office).

DAKILAS—Receipts for money or goods payment of revenue or rent.

DOWL—Paper containing statement of the gross rental of an estate.

DUR-IZARADAR—See *Izara*.

DUR-PUTNEEDAR—See *Putnee-Talook*.

GHATWALEE—A service tenure held on payment a certain quit-rent, or by the performance of certain police duties. *Ghatwal* is the holder of such tenure.

GORABUNDEE—A holding of land which is surrounded by *khals*, or tidal streams.

HAT—A market held only on certain days of the week.

HOWALA—A description of tenure in Eastern Bengal. An intermediate holding of a part of an estate or of a farm under a zemindar or talookdar, to whom a stipulated portion of the rents collected from the ryots is paid. *Neem-howala*—a division of the above. *Bye-howala*—a division of *neem-howala*.

ISTIMRARI—Perpetual, generally has reference to a tenure.

IZARA—A farm of the rents of lands at a specific amount; the farmer or lessee is the *izaradar*; and any person to whom the rents are again farmed by the *izaradar* is the *dur-izaradar*.

JAGEER—A tenure common under the Mohammudan Government on which the public revenues of a given tract of land were made over to a servant of the state, together with the powers requisite to enable him to collect and appropriate such revenue, and administer the general government of the district; now considered family property of which the holders cannot be rightfully dispossessed, and to which their legal heirs succeed without fine.

JEEBKA—See section 16, p. 42.

JOTE—A holding.

JULKUR—The right of fishing.

JUMMA—The rental of an estate; the total amount of rent or revenue payable by a cultivator or a zemindar including all cesses as well as land tax.

JUMMA-WASIL-BAKEE—The amount of collections and outstanding balances; an account showing the particulars of the revenue to be paid, the instalments discharged, and the arrears due.

KHAMAR—Land of which the revenue was paid in kind, or of which the produce was divided in determinate shares between the cultivator and the revenue-payer or zemindar; applied also to lands originally waste, but which having been brought into cultivation were retained by zemindars or were let out at a very small rent.

KHAS—A tenure by which the value is assessed according to the crop, but it generally means holding in actual possession.

KHOODKASHT—Sowing, cultivating one's own ground; a *khoodkasht* ryot is a ryot residing in the village which he cultivates.

LAKHIRAJ—Rent or revenue free land.

MAL—Rent-paying.

MAL CUTCHERRY—The chief office or court house of the zemindar where the tenants pay in their rents.

MALIK—A master, an owner, a proprietor.

MIRASI or **MOURUSEE**—Hereditary.

MODAFUT—Properly *Muzafut*, annexed, added, resumed as lands.

MOKURREE—Fixed; generally referring to a fixed rate of rent.

MOUZAH—A village, understanding by that term a cluster or clusters of habitations and all the lands belonging to their proprietary inhabitants. A *mouzah* is defined by authority to be "a parcel or parcels of land having a separate name in the revenue records, and of known limits."

MOUZAH LI or **MOUZAH ASLI**—The chief village in that originally settled.

NAIB—A head agent for collecting rents and managing property.

NAJAI—A certain illegal cess.

NEEJ-JOTE—Lands cultivated by the proprietors or revenue payers by themselves and for their own benefit, also land allowed to be set apart for the private maintenance of a zemindar.

NEEM-HOWALA—See *Howala*.

NIRKH or **NERIKH**—Tariff; the standard rate at which the lands of a village or district are assessed.

OOTBUNDEE, properly **OTBANDI**—Settlement of rent to be paid for cultivating waste land, also a settlement of revenue with reference to the quality of the land—See p. 18.

POTTAH—A deed of lease.

PURGUNNAH—A district or tract of country comprising many villages.

PATIT or **POTEET**—Uncultivated lands; also a term for reduced rent on lands which a ryot is allowed by his lease to retain without cultivating.

PATITABAD—The cultivation of fallow lands: a tenure under which waste lands were held on favorable terms, on condition of bringing them into cultivation.

PURVI-BHIKYA—See section 11, p. 30.

PUTNEE-TALOOK—A talook held at a fixed rent in perpetuity by the lessee and his heirs for ever. This particular tenure is regulated by Regulation VIII of 1819. The lessee is called the *putneedar*, or holder of the *putnee*. He has the power of sub-letting the talook, and the sub-lessee is then called the *dur-putneedar*. The *dur-putneedar* in his turn has the power of sub-letting the talook, and the third lessee is called the *se-putneedar*.

PUTWAREEAN—Fees paid to Putwarees or village accountants.

RASADI or RUSSUDEE—Progressively increasing or decreasing, as the annual amount of revenue.

SEER—Arable land originally excluded from the village assessment either in consequence of neglect of cultivation or forfeiture; it generally, however, in the Upper Provinces corresponds to *neej-jote* in Lower Bengal.

SEZAWUL—A person appointed to collect rents.

SHIKMEE-TALOOK—An under or dependent talook.

SURBARAKAR—A manager, a steward.

TUKSHISHI-TALOOK, properly TASHKIS-TALOOK—A subordinate or dependent talook held of a superior upon payment of revenue according to the current rate of the district.

TULUBANA—Fees paid to a subordinate officer for serving processes, issuing summons, &c.

TUPPAH—A small tract or division of country, smaller than a pergunnah, but comprising one or more villages.

TABULAR STATEMENT

Placing in juxtaposition the Sections of Act VIII of 1869 (B. C.) and the corresponding Sections of former Acts.

Act X, 1859.	Act VIII, 1869 (B. C.)	Act X, 1859.	Act VIII, 1869 (B. C.)	Act X, 1859.	Act VIII, 1869 (B. C.)
1	Omitted.	32	29	120	76
2	2	33	30	121	77
3	3	34—68	Omitted.	122	78
4	4	69	32	123	79
5	5	70—75	Omitted.	124	80
6	6	76	9	125	81
7	7	77	Omitted.	126	82
8	8	78	52	127	83
9	10	79	Omitted.	128	85
10	11	80	55	129	86
11	12	81	56	130	87
12	13	82—91	Omitted.	131	88
13	14	92	58	132	89
14	15	93—104	Omitted.	133	90
15	16	105	59—61	134	91
16	17	106	63	135	92
17	18	107	Omitted.	136	93
18	19	108	64	137	94
19	20	109	65	138	95
20	21	108—111	Omitted.	139	96
21	22	112	68	140	Omitted.
22	23	113	69	141	97
23—26	Omitted.	114	70	142	98
27	26	115	71	143	99
28	Omitted.	116	72	144	100
29	24	117	73	145	101
30	27	118	74	146—168	Omitted.
31	28	119	75		

Act VI. 1862 (B. C.)	Act VIII, 1869 (B. C.)	Act VIII, 1865 (B. C.)	Act VIII, 1869 (B. C.)
2	44	4	59
3	45	5	60
4	46	6	62
5	47	16	66
6	31	17	67
7	48		
8	49		
9	25, 37		
10	38		
11	41		
12	43		
17	58		

ABBREVIATIONS OF REPORTS.

Agra	Reports of cases decided by the High Court of the North-West Provinces at Agra from June 1866 to December 1868.
Agra Rev. App.	Ditto, Revenue Appeals.
* All.	Reports of cases decided by the High Court of the North-West Provinces at Allahabad, from January 1869.
Board's Rep.	Decisions under the Rent Laws, published at the instance of the Board of Revenue at Calcutta.
B. L. R.	Bengal Law Reports.
B. L. R., A. C.	Ditto, cases in the Appellate Civil Jurisdiction.
B. L. R., F. B.	Ditto, Full Bench cases.
B. L. R., P. C.	Ditto, Privy Council cases.
B. L. R., S. N.	} Ditto, Short notes printed in the Appendix.
B. L. R., App.	
B. L. R., Sup. Vol.	Ditto, Supplemental Volume of Full Bench cases.
Ind. Jur , O. S.	Ind. Jur. (Old Series).
Ind. Jur.	Ditto (New Series).
Marsh.	Cases determined by the High Court at Calcutta from 1862 to 1864, by Walker Marshall, Official Reporter to the Court.
Moo. I. A.	Moore's East Indian Appeals.
W. R.	Sutherland's Weekly Reporter.
W. R., 1864	Ditto, cases determined in 1864.
W. R. (Act X)	Ditto, cases under Act X of 1859.
W. R., F. B.	Ditto, Full Bench cases.
W. R., P. C.	Ditto, Privy Council cases.
W. R., Sp.	Ditto, Special number of Full Bench cases.

* When these Reports were first published, the first three numbers began with fresh paging instead of being paged consecutively; it has therefore been found necessary in places to put a, b or c in order to mark more clearly the page at which the report is to be found.

THE
LAW OF LANDLORD AND TENANT.

ACT NO. VIII OF 1869.

PASSED BY THE LIEUTENANT-GOVERNOR OF BENGAL IN COUNCIL.

(*Received the assent of the Lieutenant-Governor on the 21st August 1869, and of the Governor-General on the 15th October 1869.*)

An Act to amend the procedure in Suits between Landlords and Tenants.

WHEREAS it is expedient to amend the procedure in suits between landlords and tenants in the Provinces subject to the Lieutenant-Governor of Bengal; It is enacted as follows :— PREAMBLE.

Preamble.

The Act only applies to suits between landlords and tenants. The Court must therefore in a disputed case determine judicially the fact of the existence or the non-existence of the relations of landlord and tenant before it can decide whether it has jurisdiction under the Act or not—*Haree Persad Malee* v. *Koonjo Behary Shaha*, Marsh., 99. A ryot therefore cannot sue for a pottah when he is out of possession, for then the relationship of landlord and tenant does not exist— *Bharut Chunder Sein* v. *Oseemooddeen*, 6 W. R. (Act X), 56 ; *Nudhee Dass* v. *Shah Baboo Bunwaree Lall*, 2 Board's Rep., 92. Nor will a suit for a kabuliat lie unless the plaintiff shows that the relationship of landlord and tenant subsists between himself and the defendant. He cannot compel a trespasser to execute a kabuliat and become his tenant- *Mohunt Jalha* v. *Koylash Chunder Dey*, 10 W. R., 407.

Application of the Act only to landlord and tenant.

A decree of a Civil Court in a suit (the plaint of which referred to section 30 of Regulation II of 1819, and section 10 of Regulation XIX of 1793) which declared the right of the zemindar to assess rent on land not proved to have been held under a grant prior to 1st December 1790, is sufficient to establish the relationship of landlord and tenant between the zemindar and the party against whom the right of assessment was declared—*Srimati Saudaminee Debia* v. *Sarup Chandra Roy*, 8 B. L. R., App., 82 ; 17 W. R., 363. And where a party occupies land within a zemindary as tenant-at-will on the terms of paying rent, a purchaser from the zemindar has the right to treat him as tenant unless the zemindar has transferred his right, such as by granting a

Where relationship of landlord and tenant exists.

2

2   THE LAW OF LANDLORD AND TENANT.

SECTION 1.

Where relationship of landlord and tenant does not exist.

putnee of the land to a third party—*Gooroo Prosunno Banerjee* v. *Sree Gopal Chowdry*, 20 W. R., 99. An alluvial formation accreted to a ryot's jote and the proprietary right in the accretion was claimed by the Government on one hand and the neighbouring zemindar on the other. The ryot held his jote under Government, but wishing apparently to make sure of the land whichever way matters might turn out, he sued the landlord for a pottah. The Court, however, held that the suit was not maintainable. Section 2 of Act X of 1859, observed Peacock, C.J., enacts that "'every ryot shall be entitled to receive a pottah from the person to whom the rent of land held or cultivated by him is payable.' In this case the rent of the jote is payable to Government; and as the accretion was to the jote, the plaintiff has no right to demand a pottah from the zemindar or his ijaradar. He is not the ryot of his zemindar or ijaradar, nor is rent payable by him to the zemindar or his ijaradar for accretion"—*Campbell* v. *Kishen Dhun Audhikaree*, Marsh., 67. Under the provisions of Regulation V of 1799, section 5, and Regulation V of 1827, section 3, the Collector took charge of a sub-tenure as administrator of a deceased person to whom the sub-tenure belonged; it was held he was in no sense the tenant of the superior landlord, and consequently no suit for rent would lie against him—*Collector of Bograh* v. *Dwarkanath Biswas*, 4 B. L. R., App., 80; 13 W. R., 194. Where the lands in question had been declared in a previous litigation between the parties to be *mál* lands of the plaintiff's zemindary wrongfully held by the defendant under an invalid lakhiraj title, it was held that such fact was not sufficient to convert the defendant into a tenant of the plaintiff—*Sowdaminee Debia* v. *Mohesh Chunder Mookerjee*, 19 W. R., 262. Where defendant was an undertenant in respect of land which his lessor held under a *modafut* from the zemindar, and subsequently the lessor left, and the zemindar gave to the defendant a pottah for part of the lands covered by the *modafut*, and the plaintiff a pottah of the whole land covered by the original *modafut*, but did not asssign any of his rights as zemindar to the plaintiff to recover or enhance the rents reserved in the pottah he had granted to the defendant, it was held in a suit for a kabuliat at an enhanced rate that the plaintiff and defendant were not in the position of landlord and tenant—*Kalam Sheikh* v. *Panchu Mandal*, 3 B. L. R., A. C., 253; 11 W. R., 128. Further, as to the position of landlord and tenant in Bengal, see the remarks in *Nityanund Ghose* v. *Kissen Kishore*, W. R., 1864 (Act X), 82.

Object of Act X of 1859.

It has been said that the object of Act X of 1859 was to re-enact the provisions of existing laws relative to the rights of ryots and not in any way to destroy those rights. If therefore a person had a *gorabundee* tenure before the passing of that enactment, the enactment of that Act in nowise deprived him of his rights—*per* Kemp, J., in *Rajah Leelanund Sing* v. *Nirput Mahtoon*, 17 W. R., 306.

Act X, 1859, section 2.

Interpretation of "Collector."

I. In the construction of this Act the word "Collector" shall include a Deputy Collector in charge of a subdivision or other officer exercising the powers of a Collector of a district or of a Deputy Collector in charge of a subdivision, by whatever designation such officer may be called.

II. Every ryot is entitled to receive from the person to whom the rent of the land held or cultivated by him is payable, a pottah containing the following particulars:—

Ryots entitled to a pottah.   *Section 2.*

The quantity and boundaries of the land; and where fields have been numbered in a Government survey, the number of each field.

The amount of annual rent.

The instalments in which the same is to be paid.

And any special conditions of the lease.

If the rent is payable in kind, the proportion of produce to be delivered and the time and manner of delivery.

When a ryot has received a lease from his landlord he has a right to demand that he shall be put into undisputed possession of the land leased to him; and if he is dispossessed of any portion, he is entitled to an abatement. "According to English law," observed Peacock, C.J., "if the land demised be evicted from the tenant, or recovered by a title paramount, the lessee is discharged from the payment of the rent from the time of such eviction; and if he is evicted from part, the rent is to be diminished in proportion to the land evicted; and it has been held that when a lessee is evicted by title paramount to that of his lessor, an apportionment of rent may take place in an action brought for the rent"—*Gopenunda Jha* v. *Lalla Gobind Pershad,* 12 W. R., 109. The delivery of possession on the part of the landlord is ordinarily a condition necessary for the maintenance of an action for rent; and a landlord cannot sue upon a lease unless possession has been given—*Hurrish Chunder Koondoo* v. *Mohinee Mohun Mitter,* 9 W. R., 582; *Bullen* v. *Lalit Jha,* 3 B. L. R., App., 119. But this obligation on the part of the landlord to place his tenant in possession, and secure him in the quiet enjoyment of the lands leased, extends only to guarantee the tenant against evictions and disturbances caused by himself, or any person claiming under him, or paramount to him; for it is "obvious to sound reason and common sense, that ₁if one man demises property to another, he ought to take care that he has himself a right to that which he demises; and consequently, that no person claiming paramount to him, that is, by a title superior to his, shall interfere with the enjoyment of his tenant. But the case is quite different when somebody who has no title at all—some mere trespasser—thinks proper to interfere with the tenant's enjoyment. In such a case the law of the land vindicates the tenant's rights, and he is bound to resort to that law; and he may sue the wrong-doer without having recourse to his landlord, whom it would be unreasonable to expect to indemnify him against every wanton trespass committed by third persons—*Andrew's case,* Cor. Eliz., 214; Shep. Touch., 166. Upon the whole, the law upon this subject may be summed up by saying, that the landlord, in the absence of express agreement, is under an implied obligation to indemnify the tenant against eviction or disturbance by his own act, or the acts of those who claim under or paramount to him; but not against the tortious acts of third persons, for which the law of the realm affords the tenant a direct

Right of tenant to possession and quiet enjoyment.

Limit to landlord's implied guarantee against eviction.

SECTION 2. remedy against those who commit them"—Smith's Landlord and Tenant, p. 210. So where a landlord grants a lease to a third party it amounts to dispossession, and he is responsible for the loss caused to the tenant—*Hubebool Hossein* v. *Allender*, 14 W. R., 43. And where the zemindar so interferes with the possession of the tenant as to induce the under-tenants to pay rent to him (the zemindar), the interference amounts to dispossession—*Mussamut Hoynobutty Dossee* v. *Sreekishen Nundee*, 14 W. R., 58. But where the tenant is dispossessed by no fault of the landlord, he is bound to pay rent—*Gobindchunder Chunder* v. *Kristokanto Dutt*, 14 W. R., 273.

What suits for rent are cognizable or not under the Act. Where the suit is to make the defendant liable for compensation in the shape of rent, it is not a suit for rent under this Act—*Mussamut Kishenbutty Misrain* v. *Roberts*, 16 W. R., 287. Nor is a suit for rent derivable by a lessor from tolls collected by a lessee from person resorting to a hât—*Savi* v. *Issur Chunder Mundul*, 20 W. R., 146.

The right to pottah. A ryot is not entitled to a pottah from a person to whom he does not pay rent—*Campbell* v. *Kishen Dhun Audhikaree*, Marsh., 167; and the mere fact of there being no pottah but only a kabuliat does not release the zemindar from the conditions of the kabuliat—*Shaikh Danoollah* v. *Shaikh Amanutollah*, 14 W. R., 147; and where the ryot is out of possession he cannot sue for a pottah—*Bharut Chunder Sein* v. *Oseemooddeen*, 6 W. R. (Act X), 56.

Rights of parties under lease. Where a lease is granted in perpetuity at a fixed rent, and the lessor reserves no reversionary interest in the land or in the trees, the ownership of the trees is in the lessee—*Sharoda Soondari Debia* v. *Goonee Sheik*, 10 W. R., 419. Where the lease merely gives a right of julkur, or fishery, the tenant has no right in land covered by the water—*Suroop Chunder Mozumdar* v. *Jardine, Skinner and Co.*, Marsh., 334. Where a zemindar after granting a lease collected the rents from the ryots, it was held that the rents were to be credited to the lessee in payment of the rent, and the lessee could sue the zemindar for excess—*Rampershad Vogut* v. *Ramtohul Singh*, Marsh., 655. A lessee whose lessors have never been in possession of the lands comprised in the lease, has a right to bring an action to establish the title of the lessors, if he makes them co-defendants in the suit along with the parties in possession—*Prankisto Dey* v. *Bissumbher Sein*, 2 B. L. R., A. C., 207; 11 W. R., 80. A lease for seven years was granted by the Rajah of Burdwan of a farmed pergunnah. The lease was not executed in writing, but the terms of the holding were defined by a notice sent by the Rajah to the tenants of the property. The lessee died before the termination of the term, when the lessor evicted the lessee's representatives and granted a fresh lease to another at an increased rent. Held, in a suit by the representatives to recover compensation for loss of profits, that the act of dispossession was wrongful, the remainder of the term by the Hindoo law surviving to the representatives of the deceased lessee, and damages to be paid by the lessor calculated upon the increased rental awarded—*Maharaja Tejchund Bahadoor* v. *Srikanth Ghose*, 3 Moo. I. A., 261.

Leases granted by lessors with limited interest in the land. It sometimes happens that a person, having only a limited interest in an estate, grants a lease beyond his own powers; in such cases the lease holds good to the extent of the lessor's interests. Thus a lease in perpetuity granted by a Hindoo widow, who has only a life-interest in the property, is good for the widow's lifetime, though void

against those who have a reversionary interest in the estate—*Mussamut* SECTION 2.
Mohun Koowar v. *Baboo Zoraman Singh*, Marsh., 166; see also
Kamikhaprasad Roy v. *Srimati Jagadamba Dasi*, 5 B. L. R., 509.

Where a lease provides for the payment of the rent in kind, the Payment of rent proportion of produce to be delivered, and the time and manner of in kind.
delivery, are to be specified. If the tenant neglects to deliver the
stipulated proportion of the produce at the time agreed upon, the
landlord will be entitled to sue for damages estimated at the market
value of the crop at the time when the produce should have been
delivered. If after that time prices fall, the tenant has no right to
inflict on the landlord a loss by giving him anything less than the
equivalent of that, which he would have received, if the tenant had
done his duty and handed over the Bhaolee rent when it became due.
On the other hand the landlord has no right to make the tenant
responsible for the possible profit which he might have made, if the
grain had been delivered at the proper time—*Luchmun Pershad* v.
Holas Mahtoon, 2 B. L. R., App., 27; 11 W. R., 151. A zemindar
may sue to convert rent paid in kind into rent paid in money. The
fact of a ryot having paid rent in kind for a number of years is no
bar to enhancement—*Thakoor Pershad* v. *Nowab Syud Mahomed
Baker*, 8 W. R., 170.

A tenant is estopped from denying his landlord title to the property, Tenant is estopped of which he is tenant, by section 116 of the "Indian Evidence Act, landlord's title.
1872," which is as follows:—" No tenant of immoveable property or
person claiming through such tenant, shall, during the continuance
of the tenancy, be permitted to deny that the landlord of such tenant
had, at the beginning of the tenancy, a title to such immoveable
property, and no person who came upon any immoveable property by
the license of the person in possession thereof, shall be permitted to
deny that such person had a title to such possession at the time when
such license was given."

By clause 4 of section 17 of Act VIII of 1871, the Registration Act, Registration of " Leases of immoveable property from year to year or for any term lease.
exceeding one year, or reserving a yearly rent," must be registered before
they can be admitted as evidence, and they must by section 23 be
presented for that purpose within four months of their execution. The
word "lease" for the purposes of that Act by section 3 "includes a
counterpart, a kabúliyát, an undertaking to cultivate or occupy, and an
agreement to lease." The registration of leases for a term not exceeding
one year is by section 18 optional.

All leases, except leases granted to cultivators, are chargeable under Stamp-duty
Act XVIII, 1869, with the following rates of stamp-duty:—Schedule lease.
1, No. 19.

(a.) Where the lease is expressed to be for a term of less than one year. { The stamp-duty with which a bond (No. 5) for the total amount payable under such lease is chargeable.

(b.) Where the lease is expressed to be for a term of not less than one year, but not more than three years. { The stamp-duty with which a bond for the total amount payable under such lease during the first year of the term is chargeable.

Section 3.	(c.)	Where the lease is expressed to be for a term exceeding three years, or where no term is expressed.	The stamp-duty with which a conveyance for the total amount payable under such lease during the first year of the term is chargeable.
	(d.)	Where the lease is granted in consideration of a fine or premium and where no rent is reserved.	The stamp-duty with which a conveyance for the amount so paid is chargeable.
	(e.)	Where the lease is granted in consideration of a fine or premium, and also of a rent.	The stamp-duty with which a conveyance for the amount of the fine or premium is chargeable, in addition to the stamp-duty with which the lease would be chargeable in case no such fine or premium had been paid.

When a complete lease has been executed, stamped, and registered, if another document is prepared and executed with a view to alter the first, and substitute new terms as far as rent is concerned, it requires under the Stamp Act to be itself stamped with the stamp provided for a lease— *Byjnath Dutt Jha* v. *Mussamut Patsohee Dobain*, 20 W. R., 36.

Under the interpretation given in the Stamp Act, section 3, clause 15, "a lease includes any instrument (not being a counterpart) of which one person lets or agrees to let, or takes or agrees to take, immoveable property to or from another." And section 6 provides that in the absence of an agreement to the contrary, the expense of providing the proper stamp shall be borne in the case of a lease by the lessee. But a "lease granted to a cultivator, unless a fine or premium be paid in consideration of such lease," is exempt from stamp-duty. Act XVIII, 1869, s. 15, cl. 9.

Act X of 1859, section 3.

Ryots holding land at fixed rates to receive pottahs.

III. Ryots who, in any province to which this Act may apply, hold lands at fixed rates of rent, which shall not have been changed from the time of the Permanent Settlement of such province, are entitled to receive pottahs at those rates.

Fixed rates of rent explained.

By the term "fixed rates of rent," to quote the decision of Peacock, C.J., in the great Rent Case, "is meant, not merely fixed and definite sums payable as rent, but also rates regulated by certain fixed principles. Such, for instance, as a certain proportion of the gross of the net produce of every biggah, or such a sum of money as would give to the ryot any fixed rate of profit after payment of all the expenses of cultivation. *Id certum est quod certum reddi potest*, is a maxim of law"—*Thakooranee Dossee* v. *Bisheshur Mookerjee*, B. L. R., 1 Sup. Vol., 202; 3 W. R., (Act X), 108. In a subsequent case, it was held by Trevor and E. Jackson, JJ., that no rate of Bhaolee rent, varying yearly in amount with the varying amount of the gross produce of the land, though fixed as to the proportion which it is to bear to such produce, is a fixed unchangeable rent of the nature alluded to in this section. Bayley, J., dissented, holding that "a contract to pay half in kind did not involve a varying rate, being as much a fixed contract as if it were to pay a half of Rs. 100 or any other sum"—*Mahomed Yacoob Hossein* v. *Sheikh Chowdhry Waheed Ali*, 4 W. R. (Act X), 23; 1 Ind. Jur., 29. The decision of Trevor and Jackson, JJ., is however disapproved of in *Ram Dayal Sing* v. *Baboo Latchmi Narayan*, 6 B. L. R., App., 25; 14 W. R., 385. The weight of authority therefore seems to be in favor of the view adopted by the Chief Justice and Mr. Justice Bayley. Act XI, 1859, section 37, when speaking of ryots who cannot be ejected by an auction-purchaser, places in the same category those who have a right of occupancy at a fixed rent, and those who hold at rates assessable according to fixed rules. And in another case it was held that an arrangement by which a certain rent in cash is to be paid in lieu of rent in kind, does not show a variation in the rate of rent, but is tantamount to saying that the money rate represents and is equivalent to what was before paid in another way—*Miterjeet Sing* v. *Toondun Singh*, 3 B. L. R., App., 88; 12 W. R., 14. Similarly, the change of Sicca Rupees into Company's Rupees does not alter the fixity of the rate—*Kallee Churn Dutt* v. *Shooshee Dossee*, 1 W. R., 248. Nor does a trifling difference in the jumma necessarily affect the fact of an uniform payment—*Elahee Bux Chowdry* v. *Roopun Telee*, 7 W. R., 284. Thus a reduction in the jumma of one anna and three pie was held to be merely a nominal variance, not sufficient to alter the fixed character of the holding—*Ramrutton Sircar* v. *Chunder Mookee Dabea*, 2 W. R. (Act X), 74. And where a number of jummas, which have been held at fixed rates, are consolidated into one holding, the fixity of the rent is not affected by the consolidation—*Kazee Khuda Nawaz* v. *Nubo Kishore Raj*, 5 W. R. (Act X), 53. "This principle applies equally to jummas which have been derived in part or in whole with the consent of the landlord, and which are subsequently consolidated into one jumma. The presumptions of section 4, Act X, 1859, are not restricted to holdings, but refer simply to the fact that land has been held by a ryot at a rent which has not been changed for a period of twenty years before the commencement of the suit"—*Raj Kishore Mookerjee* v. *Hureehur Mookerjee*, 10 W. R., 117. In the same way the subdivision of a holding does not necessarily destroy the continuity of the tenure in respect to the rate of rent. The question in such cases is, whether "the rate of rent paid for each biggah has remained unchanged for the period prescribed by law? If it has, that rate cannot be altered. The zemindar, by consenting to a subdivision of, addition to, or subtraction from, the total holding of the ryot, does not destroy the continuity of the tenure in respect of the rate of rent, and the rent paid for each biggah of land. It is undoubtedly true that the zemindar might refuse to consent to a subdivision of the tenure, or to a contraction of the holding, and might say,—'I will hold the whole tenure responsible for the whole rent'"—*Hills* v. *Huro Lall Sein*, 3 W. R. (Act X), 135. Similarly, the division of a ryot's tenure among his heirs does not destroy the continuity of the holding, and as long as the entire rent is paid by their joint contributions the old holding will be preserved; but the entire holding will be vitiated if one of the joint tenants makes default—*Hills* v. *Besharuth Meer*, 1 W. R., 10. When a tenant holding land which had paid an uniform rent since the Permanent Settlement, relinquished a portion of his holding, and received a fresh pottah from his landlord, in which a deduction was made for the relinquished land, it was held that the fixity of rent for the remaining

SECTION 3. portion was not affected by the arrangement. The pottah was merely the confirmation of the tenancy already existing—*Keneram Mullick* v. *Ramcoomar Mookerjee*, 2 W. R. (Act X), 17. In the same way an increase in the rent on account of additional lands is not an increase in the rates of rent—*Summeeruddeen Lushkar* v. *Hurronath Roy*, 2 W. R. (Act X), 93. So to bring himself within this and the following section a ryot need only show that the particular land which is the subject of the suit, not the whole tenure of which it may once have formed a part, has been held at an unchanged rent since the Permanent Settlement—*Kasheenath Lushkar* v. *Bamasoonduree Debea*, 10 W. R., 429.

Date of Permanent Settlement. The tenant must not only have held at fixed rates, but he must show that the rates have not changed since the time of the Permanent Settlement. By the Permanent Settlement is meant the Permanent Settlement of Bengal, Behar, and Orissa, which was sanctioned in 1793, and not the Permanent Settlement of any particular estate which was afterwards made—*Sheoburn Lall* v. *Ram Purtab Singh*, 3 W. R., (Act X), 20.

Holding from Permanent Settlement secure against auction-purchaser. When a ryot has held at a fixed rent from the time of the Permanent Settlement he is entitled to demand a pottah at the fixed rate at which he has held, and his rent cannot be enhanced even by an auction-purchaser at a sale for arrears of revenue—*Saduck Sirkar* v. *Mohamoya Debia*, 5 W. R. (Act X), 16; 1 Ind. Jur., 77. The ryot is equally protected, whether the sale of the estate was made under the former sale law, Act I of 1845, or the existing law, Act XI, 1859. Under Act I, 1845, section 26, a tenure was only secure from enhancement when it had been held at a "fixed rent more than twelve years before the Permanent Settlement;" but this has been modified by section 1, Act X, 1859, which says, that such parts of section 26, Act I, 1845, as relate to the enhancement of rents and the ejectment of tenants by the purchaser of an estate sold for arrears of Government revenue, are declared subject to certain modifications: one of which is that contained in section 3, *viz.*, that a ryot who has held at a fixed rate of rent, which has not been changed from the time of the Permanent Settlement, is entitled to receive a pottah at that rate—*Hurryhur Mookerjee* v. *Paddolochun Dey*, 7 W. R., 176, Full Bench. But a tenant who has held

But not if the rent has changed. land since the Permanent Settlement, but at a varying rate, acquires no right under this section; his position is in no respect superior to an ordinary ryot, with a right of occupancy; and consequently he is only entitled to a pottah at fair and equitable rates—*Dinobundoo Dey* v. *Ram Dhone Roy*, 9 W. R., 522.

If land has been held at a fixed rent from Permanent Settlement the nature of the holding need not be considered. In deciding cases under this section, it is only necessary to consider whether the ryot has held at a fixed rent, and from the Permanent Settlement. "The right of exemption from enhancement is founded upon the simple fact of the land having been held at a fixed rate of rent from the time of the Permanent Settlement. When it has been proved that the land has been so held, no further question arises as to whether it was so held under an *istimraree* or *mokururee* pottah, or whether the person claiming the right to enhance is an auction-purchaser or not. Sections 3 and 4 of Act X make no mention of the nature of the pottah under which the land has been held, or of the right under which a fixed rent has been paid without alteration, but exempt from assessment lands which have been held at fixed rents from the time of the Permanent Settlement. The presumption required to be made is not that the land has been held by the ryot and his ancestors, or by him and the persons who had power to alienate it to him, but simply that it has been held at a fixed rent"—*Ramnath Lal Bhakt* v. *Watson and Co.*, 1 Board's Rep., 169, *per* Peacock, C.J.

SECTION 4.

IV. Whenever, in any suit under this Act, it shall be proved that the rent at which land is held by a ryot in any such province has not been changed for a period of twenty years before the commencement of the suit, it shall be presumed that the land has been held at that rent from the time of the Permanent Settlement, unless the contrary be shown, or unless it be proved that such rent was fixed at some later period.

Act X, 1859, section 4.

Presumption if rent of land be not changed for twenty years.

Probably the words " in any suit under this Act" were not intended to limit the presumption to cases under that Act—*per* Norman, J., in *Dhukhina Mohun Roy* v. *Kureemallah Mooktear*, 12 W. R., 243. Under this ruling it is doubtful whether the presumption of twenty years could not be urged in a suit by a zemindar against a talookdar for enhancement of rent under Regulation VIII of 1793, section 51.

Whether presumption applies to talookdars.

The grounds on which a ryot can still claim the benefit of the presumption in cases where he sets up a pottah may be said to be summarized in the following Full Bench case, where Peacock, C.J., in delivering judgment, says: " Then comes the question, what would comply with those words 'unless the contrary be shown, or unless it be proved that such rent was fixed at some later period?' If a defendant sets up that he came in under a pottah subsequent in date to the time of the Permanent Settlement, it appears by his own showing that he has not held from the date of the Permanent Settlement. But if he should say 'I hold under a pottah prior to the time of the Permanent Settlement, and I have been paying rent for the last twenty years at a uniform rate' and should prove that he had held at the same rate of rent for a period of twenty years next before the commencement of the suit, the fact of his having stated that he held under a pottah would not deprive him of the benefit of the presumption arising from the uniform payment of rent even if he should fail to prove that his pottah was genuine. So, if he were to say, 'I have held for a period of twenty years at the same rate; I hold a pottah of a date subsequent to the Permanent Settlement, but that pottah was granted to me in confirmation of a prior holding;' that would not rebut the presumption arising from the proof of his having held at a rent what has not been changed for a period of twenty years next before the commencement of the suit. It is only when, by evidence, or by his own showing it appears that his holding commenced, or that his rent was fixed, at a period subsequent to the date of the Permanent Settlement that the presumption created in his favor by section 4, Act X of 1859 is rebutted. A ryot is not precluded from the benefit of his having held at a fixed rate of rent which had not been changed from the date of the Permanent Settlement, or of any presumptive evidence to that effect, merely from the fact of his stating that he held under a pottah not inconsistent with

When benefit of presumption can be claimed.

3

10   THE LAW OF LANDLORD AND TENANT.

SECTION 4. that presumption, though he might fail to prove the pottah"—
Greeschunder Ghose v. *Kally Kristo Holdar*, 6 W. R. (Act X), 58.
As a confirmation of the views above expressed the Privy Council says,
"a pottah may be a confirmatory grant only, there is nothing in accepting such a grant inconsistent with the presumption that a prior title existed"—*Ramchunder Dutt* v. *Juggeshchunder Dutt*, 19 W. R., 353.
But the setting up of a pottah found to be a forgery was held to be no bar to the presumption arising under this section—*Ishur Chunder Doss* v. *Nittyanund Doss*, 6 W. R. (Act X), 70.

When benefit cannot be claimed.
On the other hand if a ryot pleads a holding for more than twenty years at a uniform rent on a pottah subsequent to the Permanent Settlement, the defence voids the presumption, and the case must be decided according to the pottah—*Lutchmee Persaud* v. *Ram Golam Singh*, 2 W. R. (Act X), 130; *Watson and Co.* v. *Choto Joora Mundul*, Marsh., 68; *Ram Lall Ghose* v. *Lalla Pecum Lall Doss*, Marsh., 403; *Kunda Missa* v. *Gunesh Singh*, 6 B. L. R., App., 120; 15 W. R., 193.

But the presumption only applies to cases in which the relation of landlord and tenant exists.
When, however, a ryot sets up an adverse proprietary title to his landlord, which he fails to establish, he is not entitled to the benefit of the presumption. In the case of *Pandy Bishonath Roy*, the defendant pleaded that he was a jageerdar; but being unable to prove his jageer title, he was not allowed to fall back upon any right which he might have acquired from any lengthened occupation of the land. "A party," the Court observed, "may have subordinate rights awarded when they *arise out of the principal right which he pleads.* But when a party pleads distinctly a jageerdar's proprietary right against a malik's proprietary right, a Court cannot award a subordinate right of occupancy, which in no way arises out of a jageerdar's proprietary right, but out of a regular right never pleaded by defendant, and, in fact, incompatible with defendant's case"—*Pandy Bishonath Roy* v. *Bhagrut Singh*, 7 W. R., 145. In other words, where a defendant has held as a trespasser, and not as a ryot, he cannot claim the benefit of the presumption which the law makes in favor of ryots. For further cases as to the relationship of landlord and tenant, see pp. 1 and 2.

The pleadings must be consistent with the fact of holding from Permanent Settlement.
When a defendant wishes to avail himself of the benefit of the presumption of an unchanged rent for twenty years, he must take care that there is nothing in his pleadings which is inconsistent with a holding from the time of the Permanent Settlement. Thus, in *Watson and Co.* v. *Chota Joora Mundle*, the defendant set up a pottah which had been granted in 1212 at a rent of Rs. 12 per annum, and alleged that he had been in possession more than fifty-seven years at that rent, but did not plead possession from the time of the Permanent Settlement; it was held by the Court that the defence itself rebutted the presumption. "Section 4," observed Peacock, C.J., "makes the payment of rent for twenty years, without alteration of the amount, presumptive evidence that the land has been held at that rent from the time of the Permanent Settlement; and unless the presumption is rebutted, the ryot is entitled by section 3 to a pottah at that rate, and his rent, consequently, cannot be enhanced. But in this case the defendant did not rely upon the fact that the land had been held at a rate of rent which had not been changed from the time of the Permanent Settlement, but upon a pottah alleged to have been granted in 1212, long after the Permanent Settlement. His own defence rebutted the presumption; and although he failed upon the ground that the pottah

was not a genuine one, he never alleged, in his answer, that the rent SECTION 4. of Rs. 12 had been paid from the time of the Permanent Settlement, as he ought to have done if he intended to rely upon that defence"— Marsh., 68. At the same time it is not absolutely necessary that occupation from the time of the Permanent Settlement should be actually pleaded, provided there is nothing in the defendant's answer inconsistent with such fact. When "the ryot tenders proof and succeeds in proving that he has paid rent at one uniform rate for twenty years, then the presumption imperatively arises, unless the contrary be shown, that the rent has been unchanged from the time of the Permanent Settlement: and upon that presumption so arising the defendant is entitled to the whole legal consequences of that state of things. If the tenant succeeds in proving that he has held at one uniform rate for twenty years, then the Court is bound to go on, and presume that the land has been held at that rent from the time of the Permanent Settlement"—*Rakal Dass Tewaree* v. *Kinooram Holdar*, 7 W. R., 242; see also *Hurruck Sing* v. *Toolsee Ram Sahoo*, 11 W. R., 84; and *Mun Mohun Ghose* v. *Husrut Sirdar*, 2 W. R. (Act X), 39. To the same effect are *Goroodass Mundle* v. *Shaikh Durbaree*, 5 W. R. (Act X), 16; and *Muneekurnicka Chowdhrain* v. *Anundmoye Chowdhrain*, 8 W. R., 6. The defendant therefore need not plead in words that the tenure is "from the decennial settlement." A plea that the tenure is the grandfather's inherited by the successors and of long standing, is sufficient—*Hem Chunder Chatterjee* v. *Poornu Chunder Roy*, 3 W. R. (Act X), 162. The plea of holding at the same rent for forty or fifty years is not sufficient to raise the presumption—*Ghoora Singh* v. *Otar Singh*, 4 W. R., (Act X), 15. But there is a contrary decision to this where the defendant did not expressly plead that he had held at a fixed rate from the time of the Permanent Settlement, but stated that he had paid an uniform rent since 1829. This answer the Court held in no way rebutted the presumption. "The defendant," observed Norman, J., "stated his title as well as he could, alleging payment of rent at an uniform rate from 1829, nearly forty years ago, as far, no doubt as his recollection can go, and says in effect,—'I claim the presumption that the rate was fixed from an earlier period,' that is to say, from a time prior to the Permanent Settlement"—*Poolin Beharee Sein* v. *Neemaye Chand*, 7 W. R., 472. It must be observed in this case that the defendant did not plead that his tenancy *commenced* in 1829, but merely produced proof to show that he had paid an uniform rent since 1829; and the Court inferred from the particular facts of the case that he meant to plead that his tenancy dated from the time of the Permanent Settlement. Thus, when a ryot pleads that he and his family have held certain lands from generation to generation, and claims the benefit of the twenty years' presumption, he will be supposed to have dated his claim from the time of the Permanent Settlement; but where a tenant fixes some particular date, as the one from which his tenancy commenced, no matter how remote that may be, if subsequent to the Permanent Settlement, he cannot claim the benefit of the presumption arising under this section—*Miterjeet Sing* v. *Toondun Singh*, 3 B. L. R., App., 88; 12 W. R., 14. So where in a suit for enhancement a ryot or talookdar pleads the section and claims the benefit of the presumption of the section, it is

12 THE LAW OF LANDLORD AND TENANT.

SECTION 4.

Proof necessary to establish the presumption.

tantamount to his having named the Permanent Settlement—*Dhun Sing Roy* v. *Chunderkant Mookerjee*, 4 W. R. (Act X), 43.

In establishing the presumption of an unchanged rent for twenty years, it is not absolutely necessary that the defendant should show actual payment for every separate year. " An uniform payment may be proved by evidence very much short of the production of the receipts for each and every year during such period"—*Komul Lochun Roy* v. *Zumerooddeen Sirdar*, 7 W. R., 417. Nor need he prove receipts for twenty consecutive years before the date of suit if he happens to have lost the dakhilas for one or two years—*Katyanee Dabee* v. *Soonduree Dabee*, 2 W. R. (Act X), 60. More especially where the landlord refuses to take rent a few years before suit—*Gyaram Dutt* v. *Goorochurn Chatterjee*, 2 W. R. (Act X), 59. But it has also been held that " uniformity of *rent* during the twenty years *immediately* preceding the commencement of the suit must be proved"—*Rajnarain Roy Chowdhry* v. *Olivia Atkins*, 1 W. R., 45. As to the proof of uniform rent for twenty years the decisions all tend to show that it is not necessary to prove for each separate year of the twenty, provided the receipts extend over the period of twenty years. The most recent explanation on this point is thus given by Phear, J. " We will add that the Judge ought not to presume a uniform rent for the twenty years preceding suit upon evidence which only touches a portion of that period. For instance, suppose the evidence to satisfy him that the rent had been uniform for eighteen years before suit, he would be wrong in presuming from that alone that it must have been uniform for two more also, or in other words for twenty years on the whole. On the other hand, to support a finding of uniformity for any given number of years, it is not necessary that there should be evidence bearing directly upon *every* year of that number. It is sufficient if the whole space of that time is included between limits upon which the evidence bears, provided that that evidence is such as to lead to the belief that the rent was uniform throughout the intervening period"—*Foschola* v. *Hurrochunder Bose*, 8 W. R., 284. Nor is it necessary that the ryot should show that he has paid the exact amount of rent in each year. " The varying amounts of rent paid by the defendant in each year are not inconsistent with the uniformity in the amount of payment required by law to warrant the presumption. It is not uniformity in the amount actually paid that is required to raise the presumption, but only uniformity in the rate agreed upon"—*Moran and Co.* v. *Anunchunder Mozumdar*, 6 W. R., (Act X), 35. " It is quite possible that a ryot may not have paid his rent regularly, in which case there would be a variation in the amount of rent as shown by the receipts. If this kind of variation were to be the test, no ryot would be safe, and the object of the law would be frustrated"— *Sham Churn Koondoo* v. *Dwarkanath Kubeeraj*, 19 W. R., 100. An unexplained and immaterial variation of one anna, or of one rupee in sixty, will not affect the question of uniform payment of rent—*Munsoor Ali* v. *Bunoo Singh*, 7 W. R., 282; *Anundolall Chowdry* v. *Hills*, 4 W. R. (Act X), 33. Nor will any trifling difference in jumma affect it—*Elahi Bux Chowdry* v. *Roopchund Telee*, 7 W. R., 284; see also *Gopaul Chunder Bose* v. *Muthoora Mohun Bonnerjee*, 3 W. R., (Act X), 132. Nor will the sale of a portion of the tenure involving a distribution of the rent over two parts—*Soodha Mookhea Dassee* v. *Ram Guttee Kurmokar*, 20 W. R., 419. An abatement of rent by order of a Civil Court in consequence of diluvion does not prove alteration in SECTION 4. the rate of rent, so as to affect the presumption—*Mussamut Reazoonissa* v. *Tookun Jha*, 1 B. L. R., S. N., 18; 10 W. R., 246. Additional rent for additional lands and an exaction of a small illegal cess are not such variations as would void the presumption—*Sumerooddeen Lushkur* v. *Hurronath Roy*, 2 W. R. (Act X), 93. A zemindar by consenting to a subdivision of, an addition, or subtraction from, the total holding does not destroy the continuity of the tenure in respect of the rate of the rent—*Hills* v. *Hurrololl Sein*, 3 W. R. (Act X), 135. The consolidation of several tenures into one cannot deprive a ryot of the benefit of the presumption—*Kazee Khoda Newaz* v. *Nubo Kishore Raj*, 5 W. R. (Act X), 53. And this principle applies to jummas which have been derived, in part or in whole, with the consent of the landlord, and which are subsequently consolidated into one jumma—*Rajkishore Mookerjee* v. *Hurryhur Mookerjee*, 1 B. L. R., S. N., 8; 10 W. R., 117. In the absence of documentary evidence to show that a pottah of 1239 was merely confirmatory of a previous pottah, the possession of a ryot claiming under that pottah will commence from the date of his pottah—*Sheikh Jainooddeen* v. *Poornochunder Roy*, 8 W. R., 129. It is, of course, impossible to lay down any precise rule as to the amount of evidence that is required to raise the presumption. The circumstances of each case differ, and the defendant must give such evidence as will reasonably satisfy the Court that the land has been held at an unchanged rent. In one case the deposition of the defendant and the evidence of a single witness were held sufficient, but the High Court observed, that in suits for enhancement it would not generally be sufficient for the ryot to swear that he had paid rent at a uniform rate for more than twenty years; but that he should prove such payments by *dakhilas*, or other good independent evidence—*Hurro Chunder Mookerjee* v. *Mohesh Chunder Dhopa*, 5 W. R. (Act X), 89.

In proving receipts it is not, of course, expected that the ryot will Evidence required summon every agent of his landlord who may have given him receipts, to prove receipts. but he must give *primâ facie* evidence to show that they are genuine documents. If a ryot produces *dakhilas*, and swears that he received them from the land-owner or his agent, or gives other *primâ facie* evidence of their genuineness, and the landlord or his agent does not come forward and deny them, or give evidence to show that they are not genuine, that may be taken as *primâ facie* evidence against him, if the evidence of the ryot is believed—*Kriteebash Mytee* v. *Ramdhan Kharah*, 7 W. R., 526; 2 Ind. Jur., 197. So whether the writer of the receipt be or be not alive or producible, it would be *primâ facie* quite sufficient if the ryot deposed that he himself on paying his rent received the receipt from the zemindar's gomastah to whom he paid his rent, and that the gomashta gave it to him saying that it was a receipt for the rent so paid—*Gunga Narain Dass* v. *Sharoda Mohun Roy*, 3 B. L. R., A. C., 230; 12 W. R., 30; see also *Raj Mahomed* v. *Banoo Rashmah*, 12 W. R., 34.

In rebutting the presumption arising from a twenty years' holding, the A break in the landlord must show either that the rent has been changed, or that the holding rebuts rent was fixed subsequent to the Permanent Settlement. A break or presumption. interruption in the holding of the land would be sufficient to rebut the presumption: but if a ryot holding at a particular rent was unlaw- But not if tenant fully evicted, he would not necessarily cease to hold at that rent. has been unlawfully evicted.

SECTION 4.

Value of jumma-wasil-bakee papers as evidence.

"Eviction, though it would put an end to the ryot's possession, would not destroy his holding: and therefore if the ryot is restored to possession, he is restored to his original holding, if that holding would not have ceased to exist but for the eviction"—*Luttefun-nissa Bebee* v. *Baboo Poolin Beharee Sen*, W. R., Sp., 91. Nor is a tenant's protection swept away by a sale for arrears of revenue—*Saduck Sircar* v. *Sreemutty Mohamoye Dabee*, 5 W. R. (Act X), 16; 1 Ind. Jur., 77. In another case, where the ryot proved a uniform payment for twenty years, it was held that the presumption was not rebutted by the omission of all mention of the holding in certain *jumma-wasil-bakee* papers produced from the office of the Canoongoe and dated 1229—*Ram Lochun Goopto* v. *Bamasoonduree Dabee*, 6 W. R. (Act X), 95. The value to be attached to *jumma-wasil-bakees* and Canoongoes papers as proof on the part of the plaintiff in rebutting the presumption of an uniform rent was discussed by Norman, J., as follows:—"A *jumma-wasil-bakee* might be admissible, under section 43, Act II, 1855, as a book regularly kept in the way of business, but as such it would be corroborative and not independent proof of the facts stated therein. Very possibly the paper may be made evidence. The writer of it may be produced. Refreshing his memory from the paper (*see* section 45), he might be able to state what rent the defendant paid in the year in question; and then to corroborate his testimony, the paper may be put in under section 43. If it is proved that the writer is dead and cannot be found, the document may be put in as an entry made in the ordinary course of business under section 39, Act II, 1855. As to the Canoongoes papers, it is not stated that the estate was held khas or under attachment in 1227: and if not, it is probable that the entries in the Canoongoes papers are not evidence against the defendant. If they simply give the rate of rent, they will probably have been made from mere hearsay in the first instance"—*Kheeromonee Dossee* v. *Bejoy Gobin Burral*, 7 W. R., 533; see also *Ram Lal Chuckerbutty* v. *Tara Soondari Baramonya*, 8 W. R., 280; *Beejoy Gobind Bural* v. *Bhekoo Roy*, 10 W. R., 291. But when *jumma-wasil-bakee* papers are produced by the zemindar at the citation of the ryot they are not merely corroborative but good and sufficient evidence—*Shibpershad Doobey* v. *Promothanath Ghose*, 10 W. R.,193.

Value of Canoongoes papers.

The presumption only applies to ryots.

It must be remembered, that it is only ryots who can claim the benefit of the presumption under this section. Thus, where several joint owners by arrangement among themselves permit one of their number to hold a portion of the joint property, paying a sum to the others, this arrangement does not convert the occupier into a ryot holding land at a particular rate of rent. It is a temporary arrangement among the joint owners of a particular time, and cannot, either in conjunction with or without a further holding, such as is here shown, be a basis for the presumption mentioned in this section—*Roghooban Tewarie* v. *Bishendutt Doobey*, 2 W. R. (Act X), 92. It seems, however, that when one co-sharer holds land in excess of his share at an agreed rent, he can be sued for such rent by the others—*Kalee Pershad* v. *Shah Lutafut Hossein*, 12 W. R., 418; and the same opinion is held in *Sreemutty Alladinee Dossee* v. *Sreenath Chunder Bose*, 20 W. R., 258; and this and the previous section will also apply to lands which had been held under an invalid lakhiraj grant, and had been resumed subsequent to the Permanent Settlement—*Banee Madhub Banerjee* v. *Bhagbut Pal*, 20 W. R., 466.

V. Ryots having rights of occupancy, but not holding at fixed rates as described in the two preceding Sections, are entitled to receive pottahs at fair and equitable rates. In case of dispute, the rate previously paid by the ryot shall be deemed to be fair and equitable, unless the contrary be shown in a suit by either party under the provisions of this Act.

Sections 5 & 6.
Ryots having right of occupancy, but not holding at fixed rates, to receive pottah.
Act X, 1859, section 5.

A ryot with a right of occupancy is entitled to hold his land upon paying a fair and equitable rent. The law presumes that the rent at present paid is fair and equitable, and this rent cannot be enhanced except after service of a notice under section 14, and upon one of the grounds stated in section 18—*Isshur Ghose* v. *Hills*, W. R., Sp., 148; and *Thakooranee Dassee* v. *Bisheshur Moorkerjee*, B. L. R., 1 Sup. Vol., 202; 3 W. R. (Act X), 110.

The question of what is a fair and equitable rent for occupancy ryots to pay is further discussed under section 18.

VI. Every ryot who shall have cultivated or held land for a period of twelve years shall have a right of occupancy in the land so cultivated or held by him, whether it be held under pottah or not, so long as he pays the rent payable on account of the same; but this rule does not apply to *Khamar*, *Neej-jote*, or Seer land belonging to the proprietor of the estate or tenure and let by him on lease for a term, or year by year, nor (as respects the actual cultivator) to lands sublet for a term, or year by year, by a ryot having a right of occupancy. The holding of the father or other person from whom a ryot inherits shall be deemed to be the holding of the ryot within the meaning of this Section.

Act X, 1859, section 6.
Right of occupancy of ryot cultivating or holding land for twelve years.

This section is retrospective in its operation; so that ryots who had cultivated or held land for twelve years before the passing of Act X of 1859 became occupancy-ryots as soon as that Act came into force—*Thakooranee Dassee* v. *Bisheshur Mookerjee*, B. L. R., 1 Sup. Vol., 202; 3 W. R. (Act X), 29. It is sometimes difficult to draw a distinction between a ryot with a right of occupancy and a middleman: for occupancy does not necessarily imply cultivation, and middlemen do not come within this section—*Gopee Mohun Roy* v. *Sibchunder Sein*, 1 W. R., 68. In one respect an occupancy-ryot differs little from a middleman; he can sublet the whole of his land without in any way forfeiting his own rights, or conferring any rights of occupancy on the sub-lessee—*Kalee Kishore Chatterjee* v. *Ramchurn Shah*, 9 W. R., 344. In such cases it is always difficult to determine the status of a ryot. In one case it was held that in deciding whether a tenant is an occupancy-ryot or a middleman, the origin of the holding should be looked to; and

The section retrospective in operation.
Distinction between occupancy-ryot and middleman.

SECTION 6. if a tenancy when first created was clearly a ryottee tenancy, that no subsequent arrangement which the original cultivator might make with sub-lessees would deprive him of his occupancy rights—*Karoo Lall Thakoor* v. *Luchmeeput Doogur,* 7 W. R., 15. And Bayley, J., says:—" I further think that the benefits of section 6 are not restricted to those who with their own hands till the soil, but extend to those who are *bonâ fide* actual cultivators in the sense that they derive the profits from the *produce* directly, and are not middlemen who have no connection with the produce except by receiving the rents in cash or kind from those who do directly derive their profits from the produce"—*Kalee Churn Singh* v. *Ameerooddeen,* 9 W. R., 579. Again, in a former case, it was held that the mere fact of a ryot subletting would not of itself make him a middleman. " The real question which the Judge should have tried is whether the defendant was or was not a ryot, or one who held land under cultivation by himself or others who took for him under his supervision as a superior cultivator, or whether he was a middleman, because he really did not cultivate in the sense of section 6, but was a general leaseholder or speculator in land rent"— *Ram Mungul Ghose* v. *Lukhee Narain Shaha,* 1 W. R., 71. In the same way a person who takes an ijara, or farming lease, of a whole village is a middleman and not a ryot—*Hurrish Chunder Koondoo* v. *Alexander,* Marsh., 479. But the section will apply not only to lands cultivated, but also to lands held, and therefore a person who is considered by the zemindar as the holder may acquire the right—*Butabee Begum* v. *Khooshai,* 2 All., 24.

Occupancy only acquired in land used for agriculture.

But the land must be used for agricultural purposes, otherwise no right of occupancy is acquired. Thus, it was held that a tenant who had obtained a plot of ground for building a house, obtained no rights of occupancy in the land. " The occupation," observed Phear, J., "intended to be protected by this section, is occupation of land considered as the subject of agricultural or horticultural cultivation, and used for purposes incidental thereto, such as, for the site of the homestead or the dwelling-house of the mali"—*Kalee Kishen Biswas* v. *Sreemutty Jankee,* 8 W. R., 251. Similarly, no right of occupancy is acquired in land used for the erection of a school or a church—*Ranee Shornomoyee* v. *Blumhardt,* 9 W. R., 552. But where a tenant, who was a breeder of horses, had occupied land for grazing, it was held that he had acquired a right of occupancy in it—*Fitzpatrick* v. *Wallace,* 11 W. R., 231. There can, however, be no right of occupancy in anything but land ; a ryot who has held a julkur for a number of years obtains no right of occupancy in it—*Woomakanto Sirkar* v. *Gopal Singh,* 2 W. R. (Act X), 19. So that when the julkur dries up, the land below does not, as a matter of course, become the right of the holder of the julkur—*Bissen Lal Dass* v. *Ranee Khyrunnissa Begum,* 1 W. R., 78. Nor is there any in a tank used only for the preservation and rearing of fish and not forming a part of any grant of land or an appurtenance to any land—*Siboo Jelya* v. *Gopal Chunder Chowdry,* 19 W. R., 200; *Nidhi Krishna Bose* v. *Ram Doss Sen,* 20 W. R., 341. Nor can any right be acquired of cutting grass or other spontaneous produce—*Goor Dial* v. *Ramdut,* 1 Agra, F. B., 15. As to further cases on these points, see the notes to section 18, p. 50.

Who are not entitled to a right of occupancy.

This section applies merely to ryots who pay rent for the land they hold and cultivate ; and where a person by his own confession does not

THE LAW OF LANDLORD AND TENANT. 17

fall within the category of a ryot he cannot claim a right of occupancy. SECTION 6.
Thus " occupation by a trespasser or cultivation by a trespasser could
not confer a right under this Act, and could not be taken into account
in considering whether a person had occupied as a ryot for twelve years"—
Sheik Peer Bux v. *Sheikh Meahjan*, W. R., Sp., 146. To the same effect
are *Gooreeb Mundul* v. *Bhoobun Mohun Sein*, 2 W. R. (Act X), 85;
and *Eshan Chunder Ghose* v. *Hurrish Chunder Banerjee*, 10 B. L. R.,
App., 5.; 18 W. R., 19. And when a ryot sets up a title hostile to
his landlord he cannot claim a right of occupancy, "such an act
amounting to a disclaimer and forfeiture of all his rights of occupancy"—
Mirza Nadir Beg v. *Muddurram*, 2 W. R. (Act X), 2. So mere per-
missive occupation does not give a right of occupancy—*Addoyto Churn
Dey* v. *Peter Doss*, 17 W. R., 383. And mere possession in the capacity
of a servant does not create the right—*Woma Moye Burmonya* v.
Bokoo Behara, 13 W. R., 333. In the same way a person occupying
merely as the assignee of the zemindar, and cultivating because of the
opportunity thus afforded, cannot claim the benefit of this section—
Woomanath Tewaree v. *Koondun Tewaree*, 19 W. R., 177. The right
of occupancy acquired under this section must be an occupancy of one
and the same kind; that is to say, it must be occupancy by the person
pleading it, or by his father or some other person from whom he inherits.
Therefore, where A and B jointly obtained a pottah for a period of five
years; afterwards A alone obtained a pottah for another period of
five years, and upon the expiry of this period A held on for two years
longer, when he was dispossessed by the zemindar,—it was held in a suit
by A to recover possession that he had not acquired a right of occupancy—*Sheik Mahomed Chaman* v. *Rampersad Bhagat*, 8 B. L. R., 338.
And the mere fact of a landlord permitting the tenant to hold over
beyond the term of a lease cannot create any right of occupancy in
his favor—*Kabeel Shaha* v. *Radhakissen Moulick*, 16 W. R., 146. It is
now well established that the mere fact of a ryot having a right of
occupancy does not by subletting confer on the sub-lessee such right,
nor can the sub-lessee acquire any such right thereby—*Ketul Gain* v.
Nadur Mistree, 6 W. R., 168; *Moulvie Abdool Jubbar* v. *Kalee Churn
Dutt*, 7 W. R., 81; *Haran Chandra Pal* v. *Mukta Sundari Chowdhrain*,
1 B. L. R., A. C., 81; 10 W. R., 113; *Nilkomul Sein* v. *Danesh
Shaikh*, 15 W. R., 469; *Unopoorna Dossee* v. *Radha Mohun Pattro*,
19 W. R., 95. Middlemen do not come within the provisions of this
section—*Gopee Mohun Roy* v. *Sibchunder Sein*, 1 W. R., 68.

Tenants-at-will can acquire a right of occupancy—*Hyder Buksh* v. Who are entitled
Bhoopendro Deb Coomar, 15 W. R., 231. And the mere fact of a ryot to a right of occu-
paying rent for some years to a person who had no title to the land pancy.
cannot prevent his counting those years towards his right of occupancy—
Syud Ameer Hossein v. *Sheo Suhae*, 19 W. R., 338. A holding for
twelve years under one of several co-proprietors gives a right of occupancy
provided the tenant has paid the rent—*Mookhtakeshee Dossee* v. *Koylash
Chunder Mitter*, 7 W. R., 493. And a mere change in the proprietary
title does not affect the right of occupancy—*Ram Ghose* v. *Radhachurn
Gangooly*, 15 W. R., 417. So a purchaser of a tenure sold under
Act VIII of 1865 (B.C.) for arrears of rent cannot, under section 16,
eject a ryot who has acquired a right of occupancy under this section—
Nilmadhab Karmokar v. *Shibu Pal*, 5 B. L. R., App., 18; 13 W. R.,
410. A tenant under a *bye-howladaree* tenure can claim a right of

18   THE LAW OF LANDLORD AND TENANT.

SECTION 6.

occupancy—*Rutton Monee Dabee* v. *Kumolakant Talookdar*, 12 W. R., 364. So can one under a *bhagdaree* tenure (*i.e.*, upon a tenure consisting of a portion of the produce)—*Hureehur Mookerjee* v. *Biressur Banerjee*, 6 W. R. (Act X), 17. So can one under an *ootbundee* tenure, that is to say, where by the custom of the particular locality the ryot is only bound to pay rent when the land can be cultivated, as under such circumstances he is to be considered as having paid the rent when it cannot be cultivated—*Remanund Ghose* v. *Shorendronath Roy*, 20 W. R., 329. From 1824 to 1832 the defendant held lands as a cultivator; from that year to 1839 he obtained a lease from the zemindar of the village in which the lands were situate; from 1839 to 1843 he continued to hold these lands as a cultivator; from that time to 1862 he again obtained a lease of the village retaining these lands for his own cultivation; after the expiry of the lease he continued to cultivate the lands. Held that he had acquired a right of occupancy—*Mukandi Lal Dubei* v. *Crowdy*, 8 B. L. R., App., 95. But generally as to the right of occupancy where the tenant has held under a pottah or under several pottahs, see *Pandit Sheo Prokash Misser* v. *Ram Sahoy Singh*, 8 B. L. R., 165, 17 W. R., 62, where it was held that a ryot, who has held or cultivated a piece of land for more than twelve years, but under several written leases or pottahs, each for a specific term of years, is entitled to claim a right of occupancy in that land, unless there is any express stipulation to the contrary. This case is more fully set out in the notes to section 7, p. 23. If a tenant from year to year receive no notice determining the tenancy at the end of eleven years, and is allowed to remain on the land after the beginning of the twelfth year, he cannot be ejected until the end of the twelfth year when he has acquired a right of occupancy—*Dariao* v. *Dowluta*, 5 All., 9 ; and a ryot whose holding has commenced or continued under a mortgagee in possession can acquire the right—*Heeroo* v. *Dhobee*, 2 All., 129.

Loss or determination of right.

The right of occupancy under this section is a right to occupy and hold the land, so when a ryot leaves his home he ceases to be a *khoodkhast* ryot, and if he refuses to come back and cultivate, the zemindar may settle the land with others—*Haro Das* v. *Gobind Bhuttacharjee*, 3 B. L. R., App., 123; 12 W. R., 304. The relinquishment need not be in writing—*Munerooddeen* v. *Mahomed Ali*, 6 W. R., 67. But a ryot does not lose his right because he cannot produce a written lease—*Doorgachurn Mullick* v. *Bhoormon Manjee*, 6 W. R., 195. Nor does he lose his right by subletting his land—*Kaleekishore Chatterjee* v. *Ramchurn Shah*, 9 W. R., 344. Nor apparently by making an invalid transfer—*Sudye Purrira* v. *Boistun Purrira*, 3 W. R., 261. Nor by subsequently taking the land in farm—*Watson and Co.* v. *Koer Jogendronarain Roy*, 1 W. R., 76. Nor will a ryot lose his right merely by making an arrangement to pay a certain rent for his holding for a certain number of years; but if he surrenders his rights in return for an enlarged holding, his occupancy right will be destroyed—*Dirganj Singh* v. *Foorsut*, 1 All., 53.

Right to sublet.

 .An occupancy ryot can sublet the whole of his land—*Kaleekishore Chatterjee* v. *Ramchurn Shah*, 9 W. R., 344. He can even grant a mokururee lease without the consent of his landlord, but such lease is only binding between him and the lessee, and if the landlord is not thereby deprived of any legal right which he possesses, and if he

dispossesses the lessee without the assistance of the law, he is guilty SECTION 6.
of trespass—*Dhomree Sheikh* v. *Bissessur Lall*, 13 W. R., 291.

A right of occupancy is an hereditary right, but it is not necessarily a transferable right. It was not the intention of the Legislature, when passing Act X, 1859, to alter the nature of a jote, and convert a non-transferable jote into a transferable one, merely because a ryot had held it for twelve years, and thereby acquired a right of occupancy—*Ajoodhya Pershad* v. *Mussamut Emam Bundi Begum*, 7 W. R., 528 (F. B.); 2 Ind. Jur., 192. To the same effect is *Ranee Durga Sundari* v. *Brindaban Chandra Sirkar*, 2 B. L. R., App., 37; 11 W. R., 162. A ryot's right of occupancy resting upon legislation and custom alone is not derived from the general proprietary right given to the zemindar by the Legislature, but derogates from and qualifies that right. Whatever the ryot has, the zemindar has all the rest which is necessary to complete ownership of the land; and amongst other rights he must have such a right as will enable him to keep possession of the soil in those persons who are entitled to it. The ryots have no power to transfer *their* right to have possession of, and to use the soil, for their own benefit—*Bibee Sohodwa* v. *Smith*, 12 B. L. R., 82; 20 W. R., 139. Again, in order to make a right of occupancy transferable it must be shown that it is so transferable according to the custom of that part of the country in which the tenure is situated. Where no mention is made in the *dowl* of any right to transfer, the existence of such right cannot be presumed—*Unopoorna Dossee* v. *Oomachurn Doss*, 18 W. R., 55; see also *Sreeram Bose* v. *Bissonath Ghose*, 3 W. R. (Act X), 3; and the *dictum* of Glover, J., in *Nanku Roy* v. *Mahabir Prasad*, 3 B. L. R., App., 35; 11 W. R., 405. It has also been held that, though the law recognised the holding of the father, or other person through whom the ryot inherits as the holding of the ryot, it does not recognise the right of a transferree to be identical with that of the transferror. It is only when occupancy is inherited that the occupancy of the predecessor is considered as the occupancy of the tenant in possession. Unless, therefore, the tenant held a transferable tenure, the sale by him of his jote to another party, without the consent of the landlord, would not transfer to the purchaser any right of occupancy which the seller might have possessed, or enable the present occupant to plead that the period of his own possession joined to that of the former tenant gave him a prescriptive right of occupancy—*Watson and Co.* v. *Ranee Shurat Soonduree Dabee*, 7 W. R., 395. So that when a man and his father before him had held the land for many years a right of occupancy was created—*Naim Chand Borooah* v. *Mooraree Mundul*, 8 W. R., 127. So far then it seems that a right of occupancy is hereditary, that it is not necessarily transferable, but that it may be transferred according to the custom of the part of the country in which the tenure is situated.

A right of occupancy hereditary, but not necessarily transferable.

It seems, however, that if at the time of the transfer the transferror had a right of occupancy, such right is transferable with the consent of the zemindar. This is suggested in *Watson and Co.* v. *Ranee Shurat Soonduree Dabee* just referred to. The same point seems also decided in *Huro Chunder Goho* v. *Dunn*, 5 W. R. (Act X), 55. But if at the time of the transfer the transferror had no right of occupancy, the transferree is not entitled in order to claim such right to add the time during which his predecessor held the jote, even though the zemindar consented to the transfer—*Tara Pershad Roy* v. *Soorjukant Acharjee*

Right of occupancy may be transferred with consent of zemindar.

20   THE LAW OF LANDLORD AND TENANT.

SECTION 6. *Chowdry*, 15 W. R., 153. To the same effect is *Hyder Buksh* v. *Bhudendro Deb Koonwar*, 17 W. R., 179, where it seems the transferror was a mere tenant-at-will. A zemindar, however, does not by the mere receipt of rent from a purchaser from a tenant having a right of occupancy sanction the sale to the purchaser so as to give him a right of occupancy—*Gaur Lal Sirkar* v. *Rameswar Bhumik*, 6 B. L. R., App., 92. But where a ryot succeeded to the holding of his uncle, who had a right of occupancy, and was allowed by the zemindar to continue in the holding for eleven years, it was held that though the plaintiff was not strictly entitled to succeed by inheritance, yet he must be taken to have succeeded to the holding by the consent of the zemindar, and acquired a right of occupancy—*Mussamat Hukeem-oon-nissa* v. *Bhooria*, 5 All., 23.

Under what circumstances a right of occupancy can be acquired in *Neej-jote* land. *Neej-jote* passes to purchaser on sale of zemindaree.

A ryot who cultivates *neej-jote* land belonging to the proprietor of an estate acquires no right of occupancy against his landlord if the land is leased to him for a term, or year by year; but he does acquire a right of occupancy where it has not been so leased to him—*Gour Huree Sing* v. *Beharry Raut*, 3 B. L. R., App., 138; 12 W. R., 278. It may be remarked here that when a zemindaree is sold, *neej-jote*, like other land, passes to the purchaser. A zemindar cannot plead that it is not included in the purchase, on the ground that he has a right of occupancy in it—*Joy Dutt Jha* v. *Bayeeram Singh*, 7 W. R., 40. To the same effect is *Reed* v. *Sreekishen Singh*, 15 W. R., 431.

A ryot who relies on a pottah, which he fails to prove, can plead a right of occupancy.

Under this section, a defendant whose pottah has been rejected, is still entitled to show that he has held for twelve years, and thereby acquired a right of occupancy—*Bydnath Shaha* v. *Jadub Chunder Shaha*, 3 W. R., 208.

Court to determine rates of rent.

And where a tenant suing for a renewal of his lease proves a right of occupancy, the Court should proceed to determine what rates of rent should be imposed even though he fail to make good his claim to fixed rates—*Sheodie Mahtoon* v. *Hurreekishen*, 9 W. R., 81.

With reference to the question of transferable tenures Mr. Bell in the first edition makes the following remarks:—

Questions discussed, 1st—Is a right of occupancy transferable by inheritance, or transferable by inheritance and sale?

I cannot conclude my remarks under this section without observing, with great submission, that the law relating to the right of occupancy has been somewhat misinterpreted and misunderstood. It seems to be taken for granted that the right of occupancy is transferable by inheritance, but in no other way. With all submission, I maintain that the law makes no such distinction. It would indeed be strange if the law allowed transfers after a man's death, which it did not permit in his lifetime. A tenure must be transferable in all cases, or not at all. If a landlord is entitled to object to a transfer by purchase, he must equally be entitled to object to a transfer by inheritance. If he can refuse to recognize the purchaser, he must be equally entitled to refuse to recognize the heir. The question is, does the law make any distinction between the two cases? I think not. Section 6 says, that "any ryot who shall have cultivated or held land for a period of twelve years, shall have a right of occupancy in the land so cultivated or held by him;" and it is added that "the holding of the father, or other person from whom the ryot inherit, shall be deemed to be the holding of the ryot within the meaning of this section." The clear meaning of this is, that in computing the period of twelve years, the ryot who succeeds to his father's land shall be permitted to reckon the period of his father's occupation as his own. The section does not refer to cases

in which occupancy rights have been acquired; it merely lays down SECTION 6.
the conditions under which they are to be acquired. The law is
absolutely silent as to the manner in which these rights, when once
acquired, are to be transferred. If occupancy rights are not transferable by purchase, there is nothing in the law to make them transferable
by inheritance.

Speaking from the limited experience I possess of several districts
in Bengal, I should say that a right of occupancy was transferable
by purchase and inheritance alike. Local custom in such a matter
supplements the law. There is not a district in which I have resided,
in which ryots' holdings are not daily sold by the Courts in execution
of decrees; and no objections, as far as I am aware, have ever been
made by the zemindars to these sales. It has even been held—
Nyamutulla Ustagur v. *Gobind Churn Dutt*, 6 W. R. (Act X), 40—
that an occupancy-ryot can build a *pucka* house upon the land even
if the zemindar objects; and it would, indeed, be hard if he were
not permitted to leave this house to his children, or dispose of it by
sale.

I have said that the law makes no distinction between transfers by
inheritance and transfers by sale. If a ryot's jote is transferable by
inheritance, my contention is that it must equally be transferable by
sale. If a transfer can be made without the zemindar's consent, it
matters not whether it is made by inheritance or sale. Now it is
admitted, and rightly admitted, that a right of occupancy can be
inherited. If a right of occupancy could not be inherited, all rights in
the land which a ryot possessed would die with him. No ryot could
succeed to the rights of his father; each man would have to acquire
de novo rights of occupancy for himself. There could in that case be
no holding from the time of the Permanent Settlement, for no ryot
could go further back than the commencement of his own tenancy.
I need hardly say that any such construction would be opposed to
existing practice and the clear intention of the law. Fathers daily
transmit their holdings to their children, and if they are able to do this,
it surely follows that they have the power of transferring them by sale
to strangers. I say it follows, because if we admit that a holding is
transferable at all, we have no right, in the absence of an express
enactment of the law, to say that it is transferable in one way and
not in another. In my opinion, therefore, the Courts are bound to
presume that occupancy rights are transferable by sale, unless the
contrary is shown.

There is another point in which, as it appears to me, this section 2nd—Does a lease
seems to be misunderstood. It has been held in several cases that ryots for a fixed term, in the absence of
who hold under fixed leases can acquire no right of occupancy in the an express stipu-
land—*Domunulla Sirkar* v. *Mahmondie Nushyo*, 3 B. L. R., A. C., 178; lation, bar a right of occupancy?
11 W. R., 556. If we look at section 6, we shall see that there is a
distinction made between land let out generally to ryots, and *Khamar*,
Neej-jote, or *Seer* land, belonging to the proprietor of the estate. In
the first case a ryot who has held for twelve years, acquires a right of
occupancy whether he has held under a pottah or not; in the second
case, he does not acquire the right if the land has been leased to him
for a *term*, or *year by year*. The law clearly makes a distinction between
the two cases; and it is only when a ryot cultivates *Khamar* and *Neej-
jote* land, that a lease for a term, or year by year, necessarily bars his

SECTION 7. right of occupancy. The object of the Legislature in making this distinction is obvious. *Khamar* or *Neej-jote* land is land which the zemindar presumably keeps for his own cultivation; and even if circumstances compel him to let it out for a few years to ryots, he is still supposed to have reserved to himself the right of taking it back again into his own occupation. But there is no necessity to make any such reservation in the case of land which the zemindar has never cultivated, and has no intention of cultivating, and the law therefore grants to a ryot who holds such land for twelve years, whether by lease or otherwise, a right of occupancy in it.

3rd.—Ought not an occupancy-ryot, who permanently leases out his land to under-tenants, to be treated as a middleman?

It is worthy, too, of observation, that the ryot of an occupancy-ryot, like the ryot who cultivates *Neej-jote* land, acquires no right of occupancy, if the land is only let to him "for a term, or year by year; and from the analogy of the case of *Gour Huree Sing* v. *Beharee Raut*, 12 W. R., 278, it would follow that the tenant of an occupancy-ryot does acquire a right of occupancy when he is neither a term nor a yearly tenant. Now two persons cannot have a right of occupancy in the same land; and it seems therefore to follow that an occupancy-ryot, who leases out his land permanently to under-tenants, forfeits his own rights of occupancy, and becomes, instead of a cultivator, the holder of an intermediate tenure, which he is bound to register in the zemindar's sheristah. So long as a ryot with a right of occupancy cultivates the land himself, the zemindar has a right to distrain the crop; but when the land is leased out to under-tenants, the zemindar loses his right of distraint; for, under section 68 it is only the crop of the actual cultivator that can be distrained. It would be most unreasonable to hold that a tenant, who by subletting deprived his landlord of the right of distraint, could retain his holding as an intermediate tenure, free from all the obligations which attach to intermediate tenures. This opinion is offered with great submission, because it is, I am aware, opposed to the judgment delivered in the case of *Karoo Lall Thakur* v. *Lutchmeput Doogur*, 7 W. R., 15. That judgment, however, if it correctly interprets the law, is exceedingly unfair to the zemindars. Though section 63 says, that no transfer of a transferable intermediate under-tenure shall be recognized, unless registered in the zemindar's sheristah, yet this ruling lays down the principle that an under-tenure, admittedly permanent, intermediate and transferable, need not be registered if it was in its inception ryottee.

4th.—Is it absolutely necessary that a ryot should hold for twelve years to acquire a right of occupancy?

It is generally assumed that a ryot must have been in possession of his holding for twelve years to acquire a right of occupancy. This, I think, is a very doubtful proposition. There is no magic in the number twelve; and it is submitted that a *khood-khast* ryot, who settles and builds his house upon the land, possesses from the commencement of his tenancy a right of occupancy in it. The law merely says that a ryot who has not held for twelve years shall not have a right of occupancy.

I have thought it right to submit, though with great diffidence, my opinion upon these points, because they involve questions of great importance, though of considerable intricacy.

Act X, 1859, section 7.

Saving of terms of written contracts.

VII. Nothing in the last preceding section shall be held to affect the terms of any written contract for the cultivation of land

entered into between a landholder and a ryot, when it **Section 7.**
contains any express stipulation contrary thereto.

As to the meaning of the words "any express stipulation contrary General effect of thereto," the following Full Bench decision may be considered as explanatory of many of the former difficulties which may have arisen with regard to the meaning of the words quoted. The plaintiff had held for nearly thirty years under three successive leases, and was ejected by the defendant about four years after the expiration of the last lease. There was no express stipulation for re-entry in the leases, and the question referred was—" Whether a ryot who has held or cultivated a piece of land continuously for more than twelve years, but under several written leases or pottahs, each for a specific term of years, is entitled to obtain a right of occupancy in that land or not." Couch, C.J., in delivering judgment says as follows :—

"The whole question turns upon what is the meaning of an express stipulation contrary to the ryot acquiring a right of occupancy. Now when there is a pottah for a fixed term, no doubt, at the expiration of that term, the landlord has a right of re-entry upon that land, and if the ryot does not give up possession, the landlord may recover the land from him. The landlord need not re-enter upon the land if he does not think fit; he may and often does (in this case he did) allow the tenant to remain in possession of the land. I cannot consider that the right of re-entry which arises by reason of the expiration of the term named in the pottah can be regarded as an express stipulation that the ryot shall not, if he occupies the land for more than twelve years, acquire the right of occupancy given by section 6. An express stipulation must mean something more than that. It is not necessary in this case to define precisely what would be an express stipulation. Of course the clearest express stipulation would be an insertion in the pottah or written contract of a clause that the ryot shall not, by reason of his holding under that instrument, acquire any right of occupancy in the land, or it might be that something less would suffice, when, for instance, the term in the pottah exceeded twelve years, if the ryot agreed expressly to give up the land at the expiration of the term, that would be regarded as an express stipulation contrary to the right of occupancy, because an agreement that he would give up the land would be inconsistent with his having right of occupancy, the right to detain possession of it. In this case, the question as put to us is that of a man holding under a pottah which does not contain any contract or agreement of that nature. I think, as the question is put, that the fact of a simple holding under a pottah which does no more than fix the term of the holding, cannot be considered as a written contract which contains an express stipulation contrary to the right given by section 6, and that this question should be answered in the affirmative. It appears to me that the cases, in which it has been held that a ryot did not acquire a right of occupancy, have turned very much upon what was the effect of the right of re-entry on the part of the landlord. I think that the mere existence of the right of re-entry, the mere fact that at the end of the term agreed upon, the landlord can turn out the tenant and get possession of the land is insufficient to bring the case within section 7"—*Pandit Sheo Prokash Misser* v. *Ram Sahoy Singh*, 8 B. L. R., 165 ; 17 W. R., 62.

SECTION 8.
Act X, 1859, section 8.

VIII. Ryots not having rights of occupancy are entitled to pottahs only at such rates as may be agreed on between them and the persons to whom the rent is payable.

Pottahs to which ryots not having rights of occupancy are entitled.

A ryot who has no right of occupancy cannot sue for a pottah.

"The meaning of this section," observed Peacock, C.J., in the case of *Sheik Moheem* v. *Raheem Oollah*, Marsh., 341, " is, that if a party wants a pottah and has no right of occupancy, he must come to some agreement with his landlord as to the amount of his rent. In this case the ryot has made no agreement as to the rate of rent, but he wants us to fix the rent, which he has no right to ask the Court to do, and which would be equivalent to ordering that he should get a pottah for one year at the rate contended for. If he has no right of occupancy, and the landlord has demanded too much rent and distrained his goods, he might have brought a suit for excessive demand of rent; or if the landlord had sued him for the full amount mentioned in the notice, he might have resisted that suit, and maintained that the amount demanded was larger than he ought to pay. Not having a right of occupancy, the tenant has no right to remain on the land, unless he can agree with the landlord as to the amount of rent." To the same effect are *Sree Nubudeep Chunder Sirkar* v. *Lalla Sheeb Loll*, Marsh., 325; *Syed Ahmed Riza* v. *Agore*, 2 B. L. R., S. N., 15. But if the tenant does remain upon the land, the landlord can only recover from him a fair and equitable rate of rent. "The defendant," observed the Court in a recent case, "has no right of occupancy; but when the plaintiff, instead of giving him notice to quit the land, chooses to retain him as a tenant, and asks the Court to compel the tenant to enter into an engagement to pay rent, the Court is bound to see that it does not enforce the payment of any rates but such as are just and equitable"—*Ram Mohon Ghose* v. *Modhoo Soodan Chowdhry*, 11 W. R., 304. This decision was in accordance with a Full Bench Ruling, which, after many conflicting decisions, finally settled the law upon the subject. "It was contended," said Peacock, C.J., in delivering the judgment of the Court, "that the landlord may enhance the rent of a ryot not having a right of occupancy to any amount he pleases, and specify any grounds that he pleases for such enhancement; and that he is not bound to prove that any of such grounds exist, and that it is for the ryot to prove that no such grounds exist. It appears to me that a landlord cannot enhance the rent, unless he states the grounds on which he seeks to enhance; and if those grounds are disputed it will be for the Court to determine whether they exist, and whether they are such as to justify the enhancement. Section 8 has been referred to, but it appears to me to have nothing to do with the question. It merely says that a ryot not having a right of occupancy is not at liberty to compel his landlord to give him a pottah at any rent he pleases"—*Bakranath Mundle* v. *Binodram Sen*, 1 B. L. R., 25.

But the landlord can only demand a fair and equitable rent from such tenant.

And can only enhance the rent after notice.

General conclusions.

The following deductions may be drawn from these decisions :—

1. A zemindar can eject a ryot not having a right of occupancy, who refuses to pay the rent demanded of him.

2. But if the zemindar permits the ryot to stay on, he can only recover from him a fair and equitable rent.

3. A ryot not having a right of occupancy cannot sue his landlord for a pottah; but if he is sued by his landlord for an enhanced rate of rent, he can plead that the amount claimed is not fair and equitable; or if his goods have been distrained, he can bring a suit against his landlord for an excessive demand of rent. SECTION 9.

IX. If on the trial of a suit for the delivery of a pottah instituted by a ryot having a right of occupancy, the parties do not agree as to the term for which the pottah is to be granted, the Court shall fix such term as under the circumstances of the case may seem just and proper: Provided that the term shall not in any case be longer than ten years, and, in estates not permanently settled, shall not extend beyond the period for which the proprietor of the estate has engaged with Government: Provided, also, that if the defendant be a farmer or other person having only a temporary interest in the land, the term of the pottah shall not extend beyond the period of the continuance of such interest. For cultivators not having a right of occupancy the term of pottah shall be exclusively in the discretion of the person entitled to the rent of the land. Act X of 1859, section 76.

If on trial of suit for delivery of pottah, parties do not agree as to the time for which the pottah is granted, Court to fix the time.

Proviso.

It will be observed that this section merely applies to suits by occupancy ryots against their landlords for pottahs. It does not extend to cases in which a land-owner sues a ryot for a kabuliat. The difference between the two cases is this, that a right of occupancy is the right of the ryot. It does not give the landlord a right to compel him to continue his occupation—*Hills* v. *Ishur Ghose*, W. R., Sp., 141.

It is obvious that a ryot who is suing for a pottah is in a very different position, so far as the pleadings are concerned, to a ryot who is being sued by his landlord for rent. We have seen in the cases quoted under section 6, that when a ryot, in answer to a claim for enhanced rent, failed in proving that he was entitled to hold at a fixed rate, he was, nevertheless, allowed to fall back upon the plea that he had a right of occupancy, and was only liable to pay a fair and equitable rate. But when a ryot comes forward to sue his landlord for a pottah, he must stand or fall by the allegations of his plaint. Thus, when a ryot claimed a pottah at a fixed rent, on the plea that the land had been held from generation to generation, and failed to prove his right to a pottah at those rates, it was held that he was not entitled to have a decree for a pottah at fair and equitable rates under section 6—*Doorga Mohtoom* v. *Kannye Lall Ajha*, Marsh., 371. The opposite view was held in the case of *Sheodie Mahatoon* v. *Huree Kishen*, 9 W. R., 81.

But where a landlord sues for a kabuliat and fails to make out a right to a kabuliat of that description, he is not on principles of justice entitled to a decree—*Golam Mahomed* v. *Asmut Alee Khan Choudhry*,

Section only applies to suits for pottahs.

A ryot who sues for a pottah must stand or fall by his pleadings.

Equitable rates cannot be decreed to a ryot who claims fixed rates.

5

SECTION 10. 10 W. R., F. B., 14. This case is further alluded to under the following section.

Act X, 1859, section 9.

Person granting pottah entitled to a counterpart engagement.

X. Every person who grants a pottah is entitled to receive, from the person to whom the pottah is granted, a kabuliat or counterpart engagement in conformity with the terms of the pottah. The tender to any ryot of a pottah, such as the ryot is entitled to receive, shall be held to entitle the person to whom the rent is payable to receive a kabuliat from such ryot.

Landlord cannot sue a trespasser for a kabuliat;

In order to maintain a suit for a kabuliat, the plaintiff must show that the relationship of landlord and tenant subsists between himself and the defendants—*Ramessur Audhikaree* v. *Watson and Co.*, 7 W. R., 2. A mere trespasser cannot be sued for a kabuliat—*Mohunt Jalha* v. *Koylash Chunder Dey*, 10 W. R., 407. A suit for a kabuliat cannot be maintained when there is no evidence of defendant having ever agreed to hold the land of the plaintiff or ever paid him rent—*Chunder Nauth Nag Chowdhry* v. *Assanoolla Mundul*, 10 W. R., 438. As to cases of the relationship of landlord and tenant, see p. 1 and 2.

nor the holder for lakhiraj land.

A suit for a kabuliat will not lie against the holder of an alleged rent-free tenure, until the landlord has established his right to assess the land—*Maharajah Ramnath Sing* v. *Huro Lall Pandey*, 8 W. R., 188—the *onus* being on the landlord—*Umbika Churn Mundle* v. *Ramdhun Mohurrir*, 11 W. R., 33; see also *Hill* v. *Khowaj Sheikh Mundle*, Marsh., 554; *Mahomed Myanoboo Hek* v. *Mahomed Syud Khan*, 1 W. R., 15; *Nund Kishore Lall* v. *Kureem Buksh Khan*, 5 W. R. (Act X), 62. A suit for a kabuliat is not the correct mode of establishing a title; and when no receipt of rent from the party from whom the kabuliat is required is proved, the question of title must be decided before a suit for a kabuliat can proceed—*Syed Jeshon Hossein* v. *Bakur*, 3 W. R. (Act X), 3. Of course, the mere allegation on the part of the defendant that the relation of landlord and tenant does not exist, would not bar the jurisdiction of the Court. In such a case, the Court is bound to ascertain by judicial investigation, if the position of landlord and tenant is proved to exist or not, and to exercise jurisdiction or not, according to the result—*Huree Pershad Malee* v. *Koonjo Behari Shaha*, Marsh., 99. So it is more than doubtful whether a suit for a kabuliat would lie on the mere allegation that the defendant is holding a specific quantity of land under the plaintiff—*Yakoob Ali* v. *Kaernollah*, 8 W. R., 329; see also *Shib Chunder Bose* v. *Ram Chand Chand*, 9 W. R., 521.

Tender of pottah.

A landlord cannot bring a suit to compel a ryot to execute a kabuliat unless he first tenders a pottah to the ryot such as he is entitled to receive under this section, and a suit for a kabuliat at an enhanced rate of rent cannot be supported without a previous notice under section 14 of this Act—*Akhoy Sunker Chuckerbutty* v. *Indro Bhoosun Deb Roy*, 4 B. L. R., F. B., 58; 12 W. R., F. B., 27. With respect to the first point, Peacock, C.J., in his judgment in this case, remarks:—" It appears to me that a suit cannot be brought to compel the tenant to execute a kabuliat unless the landlord has tendered a pottah to him such as he is entitled to receive. Whether, after the expiration of the notice to Section 10. enhance, a suit could be commenced to declare what were the fair and reasonable rents, and that the tenant would be bound to execute a kabuliat at those rents upon the landlord executing or tendering him a pottah, is a matter on which it is not necessary for me to express any opinion." In the great Rent Case, where the same question was raised, Peacock, C.J., said as follows :—" Such a suit has in substance a twofold aspect: 1st, to enhance the rent and to declare the rate to which it is liable to enhancement; and 2nd, for a kabuliat at that rent. I think the suit may be maintained if notice of enhancement has been given for the purpose of determining the amount to which the rent may be enhanced. A decree in such a suit will have the effect given to it by section 81, Act X of 1859 (section 56 of this Act), which declares that if a person who is required by a decree to execute a kabuliat refuse to execute the same, the decree shall be evidence of the amount claimable from him, and that a copy of the decree under the hand and seal of the Collector shall be of the same form as a kabuliat executed by the same person"—*Thakooranee Dossee* v. *Bisheshur Mookerjee*, B. L. R., 1 Sup. Vol., 22; 3 W. R. (Act X), 29. It is doubtful therefore whether under these decisions it would not be possible in some cases to obtain a decree without first tendering a pottah ; it would be far safer, however, to tender a pottah previous to filing the plaint; see the remarks of Paul, J., in *Romanauth Ruckit* v. *Chand Huree Bhooya*, 6 B. L. R., 356 ; 14 W. R., 432.

It had long been doubtful whether a landlord, who sued a ryot for If landlord fails a kabuliat at a given rate of rent, and failed to prove upon the is entitled to the evidence that the rate demanded was fair and equitable, was entitled rent claimed, the to ask the Court to decree a kabuliat at a lower rate. The Court, missed. however, held that the plaintiff must stand or fall by his pleadings, and that his suit must be dismissed if he did not make good his right to the rent asked for in his plaint. "It appears to me," said Peacock, C.J., "that where the plaintiff seeks to compel a tenant to execute a kabuliat of a particular description, and fails to make out a right to a kabuliat of that description, he is not entitled to have a decree ordering the ryot to execute a kabuliat of the description to which he is entitled. This opinion is not founded upon mere technicality, but upon principles of justice. A man ought not to have a decree to compel a ryot to execute a kabuliat, unless, at the time he commences the suit, he is willing to execute a corresponding pottah"—*Golam Mohamed* v. *Asmut Alee Khan*, 10 W. R., F. B., 14. So also where the suit was for a kabuliat for resumed *lakhiraj* land—*Soudaminee Debee* v. *Mohesh Chunder Mookerjee*, 19 W. R., 262; see also *Imdad Hossein* v. *Stack*, 12 W. R., 454. The principle applies whether the difference was in the quantity of land or in the rate at which the kabuliat is asked for—*Shib Ram Ghose* v. *Pran Pria*, 4 B. L. R., App., 89 ; 13 W. R., 280. The Court however is not bound in every case to dismiss a suit for a kabuliat in which the plaintiff has failed to prove the specific rate claimed by him—*Nizamat Ali* v. *Romesh Chunder Roy*, 3 B. L. R., A. C., 78 ; 11 W. R., 430. Where for instance a tenant has had full and timely notice of the grounds on which his landlord claims a kabuliat at enhanced rates, the landlord is entitled to a decree for a kabuliat for what he may prove to be a fair and legal demand, notwithstanding his failure to prove his right to a kabuliat at the rate

SECTION 10. fixed by him—*Gopeenauth Jannah* v. *Jeteo Mollah*, 18 W. R., 272. An objection taken under the above Full Bench Ruling for the first time in special appeal cannot be entertained—*Nizamat Ali* v. *Ramesh Chunder Roy*, 3 B. L. R., A. C., 78; 11 W. R., 430. The Court can, however, of its own motion, take the objection, although it does not appear on the grounds of appeal—*Hameed Ali* v. *Afaodeen*, 1 B. L. R., S. N., 14; 10 W. R., 213.

No suit for kabuliat for portion of holding.   A landlord is not entitled to ask the tenant for a kabuliat for a portion of the land included in one holding—*Abdool Ali* v. *Yah Ali Khan*, 8 W. R., 467. A separate kabuliat cannot be claimed for uncultivated lands already comprised on a lease, on the ground that such uncultivated lands have now been brought into cultivation—*Sheikh Mahomed Kaloo Chowdhry* v. *Fedaye Shikdar*, 8 W. R., 219.

A shareholder cannot sue joint-tenant for a kabuliat.   Where a number of co-sharers have given a joint lease, it is not competent for one of the shareholders to bring a separate suit for his share of the rent—*Ramjoy Singh* v. *Nagar Gazee*, 5 W. R. (Act X), 68. A proprietor of a fractional share of an undivided estate, though receiving a definite portion of the rent from the ryot, is not entitled to maintain a suit for a separate kabuliat in respect of such undivided share—*Rani Sarat Soondari Debi* v. *Watson*, 2 B. L. R., A. C., 159; 11 W. R., 25; *Woodoy Churn Dhur* v. *Kalee Tara Dasi*, 2 B. L. R., App., 52; *Indromonee Burmonee* v. *Sooroop Chunder Paul*, 15 W. R., 395. In another case, where the question referred to a Full Bench was "whether a suit by the owner of a fractional share of an undivided estate for a kabuliat will lie," Norman, J., said—"A tenure is an entire thing. The obligation to pay the rent reserved upon the letting of land, or in respect of the tenure of land by a ryot, is either a contract or an obligation in the nature of a contract to pay the rent. The obligation is single and entire. A tenant is not liable to have an entire tenure subdivided and split up against his own will and to his own prejudice by any act on the part of persons to whom he is liable to pay rent. Again the contract or obligation to pay rent as a single sum cannot be split up and subdivided and converted into several obligations to pay different proportionate parts of the sum to different individuals, at the will of the party to whom the rent is payable. But if all the obligors to whom the entire rent is payable could not, against the will of the tenant, increase the burden of the obligation by compelling the ryot to pay to several persons at different places, and in separate proportion, much less can one shareholder, who could not in the absence of the others even sue alone to enforce the original obligation, maintain a suit to compel the ryot to pay him a proportion of the debt. If such suit could be maintained the greatest injustice would be done the ryot." The rest of the Court did not answer the question on the ground that it did not arise in the suit—*Indur Chunder Dugar* v. *Brindaban Bihara*, 8 B. L. R., 251; 15 W. R., F. B., 21. The same case also decides that payment to each shareholder of his quota of the rent is of itself no evidence of the consent on the part of the tenant to the division of the tenure.

Unless by special agreement the rent has been separately paid.   But where the plaintiff, though a joint-proprietor, can prove that the defendants have always recognized him as being the proprietor of a particular share of the property, and have paid to him separately a certain proportion of the rent, then the suit will lie against them without the other joint-proprietors being made parties. But unless the plaintiff either proves that the defendants have paid rent to him separately, or

proves an express agreement on their part to pay to him separately, the **Section 10.**
suit will not lie in the absence of the other shareholders—*Gunga Narain Dass* v. *Sharoda Mohun Roy*, 3 B. L. R., A. C., 230 ; 12 W. R., 30; *Doorga Churn Surmah* v. *Jampa Dassee*, 21 W. R., 46. A proprietor of a fractional share of undivided estate may sue to obtain a kabuliat from the ryot without making his co-sharers parties when there is no dispute as to his share, and when the tenant has paid him rent separately for his share. It is said :—" The first point taken in appeal is that the plaintiff (who is the appellant) as proprietor of a fractional share of an undivided estate could not sue the defendant for a kabuliat, and that therefore his suit has been improperly dismissed. On this point I really have no doubt whatever that the plaintiff could sue for a kabuliat, his action being simply one intended to put upon paper a separate engagement and contract already existing between himself as landlord and the defendant as tenant. It is moreover the general custom of this country, as far as I know, to collect rents in certain specific shares and to grant receipts for such fractional shares"—*Romanath Rakhit* v. *Chand Hari Bhuya*, 6 B. L. R., 356; 14 W. R., 432 ; see also *Mohamed Singh* v. *Mussamut Mughy Chowdhrain*, 1 W. R., 253. When there is no joint lease, and the plaintiff's share is not disputed, a suit for a kabuliat at an enhanced rate will lie ; the suit however must be for the enhancement of the rent of the whole of the defendant's tenure—*Dookee Ram Sirkar* v. *Gowhar Mundul*, 10 W. R., 307.

A landlord cannot sue a ryot who has no right of occupancy for a **Miscellaneous.** kabuliat. A suit for arrears of rent on the footing of the notice of enhancement might lie—*Rammonee Chuckerbutty* v. *Alla Buksh*, 4 W. R. (Act X), 46 ; see also *Khoda Buksh* v. *Akoot Ghazee*, 9 W. R., 595. A suit for a kabuliat will not lie for a right to fish in certain waters—*Mohun Gobind Sein* v. *Nittaye Holdar*, 6 W. R. (Act X), 101. It seems, however, that a suit for a kabuliat for the payment of the rents of a fishery is cognizable—*Koylash Chunder Dey* v. *Joy Narayan Jalooah*, 7 W. R., 93. In a suit under this section, if the plaint does not specify the date from which the kabuliat is to commence, it should be returned by the Court; but if the plaint has been admitted, and the case heard, the Judge should supply the omission in the decree by specifying the time from which the kabuliat is to take effect—*Golam Mohamed* v. *Asmut Ali Khan*, 10 W. R., F. B., 14 ; see also *Poorno Chunder Roy* v. *Stalkart*, 10 W. R., 362. When, however, a suit for a kabuliat at an enhanced rate is decreed without any term being fixed by the Court, the kabuliat executed is inoperative beyond the year of demand—*Raja Kristo Chunder Mundraj* v. *Poorosuttun Doss*, 15 W. R., 424.

It must be remembered that the definition of a lease given in the **Registration of** Registration Act (Act VIII of 1871) includes a kabuliat ; and when **kabuliat.** a lease must be registered, the kabuliat must be registered also.

Kabuliats given in exchange for a lease by cultivators are exempt **Stamps upon** from stamp-duty, unless a fine or premium has been paid in consider-**kabuliats.** ation of the lease—Act XVIII, 1869, s. 15, cl. 10. Such kabuliats, however, are not exempt from stamp-duty, unless a lease has been granted—*Id.*, s. 3, cl. 12. Kabuliats executed by under-tenants are chargeable, under Schedule II, No. 16, with a stamp-duty of one rupee, " provided that the counterpart shall not be available, unless the Collector, or such other officer as he may authorize in that

30 THE LAW OF LANDLORD AND TENANT.

SECTION 11. behalf, shall certify that the proper stamp-duty on the original instrument has been paid. Such certificate shall be endorsed on the counterpart, on the same being produced together with the original instrument, and on the whole being duly executed and stamped in other respects." Where stamp-duty is chargeable on a kabuliat, the cost of the stamp is, in the absence of express agreement, to be borne by the lessor—Act XVIII, 1869, s. 6.

Act X, 1859, section 10.
Damages for exactions in excess of rent, or for receipt withheld.
Form of receipt.

XI. Every under-tenant or ryot, from whom any sum is exacted in excess of the rent specified in his pottah, or payable under the provisions of this Act, whether as abwab or under any other pretext; and every under-tenant, ryot, or cultivator, from whom a receipt is withheld for any sum of money paid by him as rent, shall be entitled to recover from the person receiving such rent, damages not exceeding double the amount so exacted or paid. Receipts for rent shall specify the year or years on account of which the rent is acknowledged to have been paid ; and any refusal to make such specification shall be held to be a withholding of a receipt.

Cesses cannot be recovered over and above rent.

By Regulation VIII, 1793, sections 54 and 55, all abwabs or cesses then existing were to be consolidated into one specific sum; and the imposition of any fresh cess under any pretence whatever was made "punishable by a penalty equal to three times the amount imposed." No cess, therefore, whatever may be its nature, can be received over and above the rent, unless the ryot has agreed to pay it. Thus, where a landlord sued for certain cesses called Bukoomat, it was held that the plaintiff could " recover from the ryot nothing but the rent, except on the ground of some express contract to pay it"—*Orjoon Sahoo* v. *Anund Singh*, 10 W. R., 257. Similarly, when a landlord, who had leased a mehal, called Bainsoondah, from Government, claimed from all the jotedars a cess for grazing their cattle within the mehal, the Court decided that the cess was not recoverable. If the ryots' cattle, it was said, trespassed upon his land, he had his remedy against them under the Trespass Act ; but he could levy no cess which the ryots had not contracted to pay—*Bhogeeruth Shikdar* v. *Ram Narain Mundur*, 9 W. R., 300. Where a cess is illegal, a contract for the collection and payment of such cess is also illegal, on the ground that " any contract made for or about anything which is prohibited by statute is a void contract"—*Kumala Kant Ghose* v. *Kalu Mahomed Mandal*, 3 B. L. R., A. C., 44 ; 11 W. R., 395. And the mere fact of payment of rent, including an illegal cess, for three years, does not legalize the cess—*Dhalee Paramanick* v. *Anund Chunder Tolaputtur*, 5 W. R. (Act X), 86.

Contract to collect an illegal cess invalid.

What are illegal cesses.

The following have been held to be illegal cesses :—*Najai*, see *Dhalee Paramanick* v. *Anund Chunder Tolaputtur*, 5 W. R. (Act X), 86. *Putwareean*, see *Burmah Chowdry* v. *Sreenund Singh*, 12 W. R., 29. *Purvi-bhika*, or a present to the zemindar on the *Unnoprashun* ceremony (first eating of rice after birth), see *Nobin Chunder Chowdry* v. *Gooroo*

THE LAW OF LANDLORD AND TENANT. 31

Gobind Surmah Mojoomdar, 14 W. R., 447. But *bhihya,* or a sum of money paid by ryots to the zemindar under compromise instead of suits for enhancement, is not, see *Bholanath Mookerjee* v. *Brijo Mohun Ghose,* 14 W. R., 351. SECTION 11.

Where a zemindar, after granting a ticca lease, collects the rents direct from the ryots, and the amount so received exceeds the rent due from the ticcadar, the excess amount so collected is an exaction, and is recoverable under this section—*Rampershad Vogut* v. *Ramtohul Singh,* Marsh., 655. In other words, any sum which is collected by a landlord in excess of the amount due to him under the agreement with his ryot, is an exaction, for the recovery of which a suit will lie under this section. It is not, however, an exaction when the excess is recovered by legal process. Where, for instance, a tenant supplied the zemindar with rice, on the agreement that the value of the rice was to be deducted from the rent, and the zemindar, without making the deduction, sued the tenant under Regulation VIII, 1819, and recovered the full amount of the rent, it was held that this was not an exaction under this section. "The tenant," observed the Court, "might have contested his liability to pay the amount, and might have demanded a summary investigation as to the amount due, and he might have stayed the sale of the tenure by depositing the amount claimed. Instead of doing so, he paid the amount claimed to the zemindar. The zemindar having recovered the amount under a proceeding prescribed by law, the question is, whether that is an undue exaction? He possibly might have demanded more than was due after allowing for the rice supplied, but the defendant, instead of demanding an investigation, paid the amount claimed, with knowledge of all the facts. Can this be said to be an illegal exaction of rent within section 10, Act X, 1859? We think that it is not an illegal exaction of rent within the meaning of that Act"—*Chunder Monee Chowdrain* v. *Debendernath Roy Chowdry,* Marsh., 420. And where, on the allegation that the defendant had sublet land to him for the purpose of raising crops under a contract to share the produce between them, plaintiff sought to recover the value of his share of the crop which the defendant had misappropriated, it was held the claim was for a sum exacted in excess of rent—*Gureebollah Puramanick* v. *Fukeer Mahomed Kholoo,* 10 W. R., 203. But a suit for the recovery of money alleged to have been paid by the plaintiff to an ijaradar on account of arrears of rent, when the same has not been applied to the purpose for which it was given, or when a receipt is withheld from the plaintiff, is cognizable under this section—*Brojonath Dey* v. *Shumboo Chunder Chatterjee,* 18 W. R., 25. Illegal exactions.

The present law regarding receipts is merely a re-enactment of section 63, Regulation VIII, 1793. Any landlord who withholds a receipt is liable to pay to the tenant double the amount as damages. It will be observed that the law does not say that double the amount is to be awarded as a *penalty,* but that the ryot is entitled to "*damages not exceeding double* the amount so exacted or paid." The Court must therefore fix the damages within the above limit, according to the circumstances of each case—*Ras Monee Dabya* v. *Ramjay Saha,* 1 Board's Rep., 135. If, however, it is proved that receipts have been withheld, the Court must award some damages. The Judge has no discretion as to the award of damages: his discretion is only limited as to the amount—*Zumeerudnissa Khanun* v. *Phillipe,* 1 W. R., 290. But Receipts.
Damages must be awarded if receipt is withheld.

Section 12. damages under this section are only recoverable in respect of money actually paid as rent. Thus, where an under-tenant, according to agreement, had paid on his landlord's account Rs. 492 into the Dinagepore Collectorate as revenue, and a further sum of Rs. 26 as income tax, it was held that he had no action against his landlord under this section, which "merely contemplated cases of money actually and simply paid as rent"—*Sameena Beebee* v. *Koylas Chunder Roy*, 6 W. R. (Act X), 79.

Stamps on receipts. Receipts for any sum of money in excess of Rs. 20 require a stamp of one anna; but receipts granted to a cultivator for the rent of land paying revenue to Government are exempt from stamp-duty.—Act XVIII, 1869, s. 15, cl. 1.

Appropriation of payments. The receipts must specify the year or years on account of which the rent is acknowledged to have been paid. If, however, the tenants omit to specify on what account the money is paid, the landlord can appropriate it in any way he pleases. In the case of *Ahmuty* v. *Brodie* the plaintiff sued for arrears of rent due in 1266. The defendant proved that he had paid large sums of money at the time of payment to the rent of that year. The plaintiff claimed to apply Rs. 13,000 to arrears of 1865. The Collector dismissed the claim on the ground that as the suit was for the arrears of 1266, it was not within the Court's cognizance to enquire whether the defendants owed rent for 1265 or not. But the High Court reversed the decision, observing that "the defendant was bound to prove not only that he paid money in 1266, but that such payment was in accord and satisfaction of the rents of that year. It is a rule of law, that if a debtor has two distinct debts due to one creditor, and makes a general payment without saying to which debt the money is to be applied, it is in the option of the creditor to appropriate the payment to which account he pleases. If, therefore, there was an arrear in respect of the rents of 1265, the plaintiff had a right to apply such part of the money as was necessary for the purposes for the satisfaction of the arrears of that year: to the extent of such appropriation the defendant will fail in proof of his plea of payment of the rents of 1266"—2 Board's Rep. 20, *per* Loch and Norman, JJ. At the same time the payment of the rent of a particular year affords good *primâ facie* grounds for supposing that the rent of the previous year has been paid. "When," the Court observed, "a tenant shows payment of rent for 1265 and 1266, it is to be presumed that all previous claims have been satisfied; and unless the plaintiff can show that at the close of 1264 there was an arrear due to him, he is not entitled to carry to the credit of 1264 any of the payments made in 1266. He has not given any evidence that any arrear of rent was due to him in 1264; and we hold therefore that he has failed to discharge the burden which lay upon him"—*Ranee Sooruth Soondaree Dabee* v. *Brodie*, 1 W. R., 274.

Act X, 1859, section 11.

Landholder not to compel the attendance of tenant for adjustment of rent or for any other purpose.

Payment of rent to be enforced under this Act.

XII. All power at any time heretofore vested in zemindars and other landholders of compelling the attendance of their tenants for the adjustment of their rents or for any other purpose is withdrawn; and all such persons are prohibited from adopting any means of compulsion for enforcing payment of the rents

XIII. If payment of rent, whether the same be legally due or not, is extorted from any under-tenant or ryot by illegal confinement or other duress, such under-tenant or ryot shall be entitled to recover such damages, not exceeding in any case the sum of two hundred rupees, as may be deemed a reasonable compensation for the injury done him by such extortion. An award of compensation under this section shall not bar or affect any penalty or punishment to which the person practising such extortion may be subject by law.

Sections 13 & 14.

Act X, 1859, section 12. Damages for extorting payment of rent by duress.

XIV. No under-tenant or ryot, who holds or cultivates land without a written engagement, or under a written engagement not specifying the period of such engagement, or whose engagement has expired or has become cancelled in consequence of the sale for arrears of rent or revenue of the tenure or estate in which the land held or cultivated by him is situate, and has not renewed, shall be liable to pay any higher rent for such land than the rent payable for the previous year, unless a written notice shall have been served on such under-tenant or ryot, in districts or parts of districts where the Fuslee year prevails, in or before the month of Jeyt, and in districts or parts of districts where the Bengalee year prevails, in or before the month of Poos, specifying the rent to which he will be subject for the ensuing year, and the ground on which an enhancement of rent is claimed. Such notice shall be served by order of the Collector in whose jurisdiction the lands are situate, on the application (which may be on plain paper) of the person to whom the rent is payable, and shall, if practicable, be served personally upon the under-tenant or ryot. If for any reason the notice cannot be served personally upon the under-tenant or ryot, it shall be affixed at his usual place of residence; or, if he have no such place of residence in the district in which the land is situate, the mode of service of such notice shall be by affixing it at the mâl cutcherry of such land or other

Act X, 1859, section 12. Enhancement of rent of ryot holding without, or under a written engagement, or after expiry, &c., of written engagements.

6

SECTION 14. conspicuous place thereon, or at the village chowree or chowpal, or at some other conspicuous place in the village in which the land is situate.

Notice must be served before suit for enhancement.
This section is applicable to all ryots whether they have a right of occupancy or not—*Bakranath Mundle* v. *Binodram Sen*, 1 B. L. R., F. B., 25; 10 W. R., F. B., 33. In all cases a notice must be served under this section previous to bringing a suit for enhancement—*Akhoy Sankar Chuckerbutty* v. *Rajah Indraboshun Deb Roy*, 4 B. L. R., F. B., 58; 12 W. R., F. B., 27; *Sobha Mahtoon* v. *Pabaroo*, 2 All., 310; *Thakooranee Mahtab Kooer* v. *Buldeo Singh*, 4 All., 58.

In what cases a notice necessary.
A notice of enhancement according to the rate mentioned in an agreement is necessary as to lands found in excess on measurement where no term is specified in the written agreement—*Rajah Burodakant Roy* v. *Seebsunkerree Dossee*, 4 W. R. (Act X), 35. A suit for arrears of rent of a quantity of land alleged to have been held by the defendant over and above the quantity of land covered by his pottah was held to be in substance a suit for rent at an enhanced rate requiring a notice—*Thekmee Beldar* v. *Ramkishen Lall*, 15 W. R., 71. Where a decree of 1848 gave the plaintiffs the right to assess and receive the rents for each year according to the assessment made for that particular year a notice was held not necessary when the rent found assessable for the years for which rent was claimed varied from what was found assessable in 1848—*Saleeboonissa Khatoon* v. *Mohesh Chunder Roy*, 17 W. R., 452. Nor is any necessary in a suit for arrears of rent at a rate fixed by arbitration, where the parties had agreed to submit their claims to arbitrators—*Mudhoo Manjee* v. *Rajah Nilmoney Singh*, 18 W. R., 533.

Notice must specify the grounds of enhancement.
No landlord can enhance the rent of a tenant, whatever may be his position, without notice, and the notice must state the grounds of enhancement. "When section 13," observed Peacock, C.J., "required that the notice of enhancement should specify the grounds on which the enhancement should be claimed, the Legislature could not have intended to compel the land-owner to do that which they considered to be superfluous; still less could they have intended to compel him to do something worse than superfluous, namely, to specify grounds of enhancement by which he was not to be bound. Section 14 authorizes the tenant to contest his liability to pay the enhanced rent demanded of him; and it is clear that the meaning of the Legislature was, that the grounds specified for enhancement should be such as to justify the enhancement, and that their existence should be proved in the suit in which the tenant should contest his liability to enhancement"—*Bakranath Mundle* v. *Binodram Sen*, 1 B. L. R., F. B., 25; 10 W. R., F. B., 33. This decision, therefore, clearly lays down:—

1st.—That no ryot, whether he possesses a right of occupancy or not, is liable to pay an increased rent, unless he has been served with a notice of enhancement under this section.

2nd.—That the grounds of enhancement must be stated, and if these grounds are disputed by the ryot, the Court will have to determine whether they exist, and whether they are such as to justify the enhancement.

In the case of occupancy-ryots, the grounds must be those stated in section 18.
So far then all ryots are upon an equal footing, but there is this difference between an occupancy and a non-occupancy ryot: that in the case of the former, *the grounds of enhancement* are restricted to the

grounds mentioned in section 18, whereas other grounds may be stated SECTION 14. in the case of a non-occupancy ryot; and if these grounds are disputed, it is for the Court to determine whether they are just and reasonable. It is therefore very necesssary that the grounds of enhancement should be carefully stated; and in the case of an occupancy-ryot, that they should agree with one or other of the grounds given in section 18. The notice must be clear and distinct and worded in such a manner that Requisites of the tenant is able to understand the grounds on which the enhancement notice. is sought. When it was objected that the notice was not in the exact words of clause 2, section 17 of Act X of 1859 (section 18 of this Act), it was held that if the ryot knew to what provision in the law of enhancement he was pleading, then although the notice was not in the exact words of the law, yet it was sufficient because the object of the notice, viz., that the ryot might know the exact grounds on which enhancement was sought had been obtained—*Radha Bullub Ghose* v. *Beharee Lall Mookerjee*, 12 W. R., 536. Again Ainslie, J., says:—"There is no doubt that the great strictness with which questions involving questions of such notices were dealt with has been much relaxed in the later practice of this Court, and it has been held in the later rulings that a notice is good, if, without containing the exact terms of the law, it states with sufficient precision the nature of the claim, the amount asked for, and the grounds on which the enhancement is sought, so that the ryot served with the notice may not be misled and can clearly comprehend the case which he has to meet—*McGiveran* v. *Hurhkoo Singh*, 18 W. R., 203. As to this question see also *Wooma Churn Dutt* v. *Grish Chunder Bose*, 17 W. R., 32; and *Tirth Nund Thakoor* v. *Mohur Mundel*, 17 W. R., 279. So that if the notice is such as that it is impossible for the ryot to know what case he has to meet the notice is bad—*Banee Madhub Chowdry* v. *Tara Prosunno Bose*, 21 W. R., 33.

In the following cases the notices have been held to be good: Where Good notices. the notice was to the effect that the rent was liable to be enhanced on the ground that the ryot was paying at a rate lower than that paid by "equal ryot," the Bengalee words being *toollo projah*, such being sufficient to show that the enhancement was one under clause 1, section 17, Act X of 1859 (section 18 of this Act)—*Kumar Paresh Narayan Roy* v. *Gour Sundar Bhomik*, 6 B. L. R., App., 154; 15 W. R., 391. Where the notice omitted the words "ryots of the same class" it was held that such clerical omission in no way prejudiced the defendant, he being well aware of the grounds upon which the enhancement was demanded— *Ryesunnissa Begum* v. *Bydonath Shaha*, 17 W. R., 355; see also *Srimati Jannoba* v. *Grish Chandra Chuckerbutty*, 7 B. L. R., App., 44; 15 W. R., 335; *Watson and Co.* v. *Ramdhan Ghose*, 17 W. R., 496.

In the following cases the notices have been held to be bad:—A Bad notices. notice which stated that "there had been a measurement, and that the productive powers of the lands had increased, and that, therefore, Rs. 39 would be a proper jumma according to the village nirick," was held to be indistinct and bad: as it was impossible to say whether the enhancement was meant to be on account of increased productive powers, or of the rent being less than that paid for similar land in the neighbourhood, or on account of its having been shown by measurement that the tenant held more land than he was supposed to hold— *Khoondkar Abdur Ruhman* v. *Wooma Chunder Roy*, 8 W. R., 330. Similarly, a notice which stated that the productive powers of the

SECTION 14. land had increased, was held to be defective, because it did not add that the increase had been brought about "*otherwise than by the agency or expense of the ryot himself*"—*Syud Soojat Ally* v. *Huree Thakoor*, 6 W. R. (Act X), 44. Where a notice of enhancement was served on an occupancy-ryot, on the ground that he was holding at a rent lower than *surrounding* rates, the Chief Justice decided that the notice was insufficient, "as it did not show that the tenant was holding at a rate lower than the prevailing rate payable by the same class of ryots for land of a similar description, and with similar advantages in the places adjacent. The words 'surrounding rates' are not at all tantamount to the ground of enhancement specified in the 1st clause of section 18"—*Boydonath* v. *Ramjoy Dey*, 9 W. R., 292. Where the notice merely stated that the defendant was holding "excess lands" in his possession, but was altogether silent as to the amount of the "excess lands," no information being given as to the quantity of land for which the defendant was already paying rent, or as to the quantity he was found to be in possession of by actual measurement, such notice was held to be insufficient to meet the requirements of section 13 of Act X of 1859 (section 14 of this Act)—*Grish Chandra Ghose* v. *Iswar Chandra Mookerjee*, 3 B. L. R., A. C., 337; 12 W. R., 226. A notice in the following words:—"As the rate of rent of the said land is below the rate prevailing in the pergunnah and in adjacent places, and as the productive powers of the land and the value of the produce have increased, and as the *patit* land has been cultivated, I am entitled to receive from you Rs. 794-5-7-11½ per annum, according to the rate specified in the schedule," was held bad for indefiniteness and uncertainty—*Gobind Kumar Chowdhry* v. *Haro Chandra Nag*, 4 B. L. R., App., 61. A notice based on the following grounds: "*Firstly*, that the productive power of the land had increased otherwise than by the agency of the ryot; *secondly*, that the quantity of land held is in excess of that for which rent has been paid; and *thirdly*, that the rates paid are below those paid for similar lands in adjacent places," was held to be bad—*Shib Narain Dutt* v. *Ekra Moonissa Begum*, 17 W. R., 356.

Section applies to intermediate tenures.
The provisions of this section apply not only to ryots but also to the holders of intermediate tenures. The Act throughout contemplates under-tenants as distinct from ryots, and contains provisions relating to both classes. A notice of enhancement, therefore, must be in accordance with the terms of this section, and the enhancement must be made according to the pergunnah rate of rents payable not by the ryots but by the holder of similar tenures—*Baboo Dhunput Singh* v. *Gooman Singh*, 11 Moo. I. A., 432; 9 W. R., P. C., 3. It may be that section 17 of Act X of 1859 or section 18 of this Act is not applicable to holders of intermediate tenures; but under sections 13 to 16 of Act X of 1859, or sections 14 to 17 of this Act, it is evident that a tenant who is a middleman may be enhanced on notice on the same grounds (except as provided in these sections) on which he was liable to enhancement prior to the passing of Act X of 1859—*Grish Chunder Ghose* v. *Ram Tano Biswas*, 12 W. R., 449. The notice therefore must be clear and distinct as in the case of ryots, and must state the grounds of enhancement—*Kalee Nauth Chowdhry* v. *Humee Bibee*, 7 B. L. R., App., 47 (Note); 12 W. R., 506; *Burodakant Roy Bahadur* v. *Rada Charan Roy*, 13 W. R., 163; *Sri Gopal Mullick* v. *Dwarkanauth Sein*, 15 W. R., 520; *Dinonauth Doss* v. *Gogan Chandra Sen*, 7 B. L. R., App., 45 (Note).

THE LAW OF LANDLORD AND TENANT. 37

Glover, J., however, says "it may very well be doubted whether a SECTION 14. zemindar seeking to enhance an intermediate tenure such as this (a *tukshishi* talook) is bound to give any other notice than the one contemplated by section 51, Regulation VIII of 1793. There is no rule laid down in Act X of 1859 for the enhancement of rents of under-tenants, and the notice would, we think, have been a good notice if it had merely stated the plaintiff's right to enhance according to the special custom of the district." In the same case it was further held that a clerical omission which in no way prejudiced the talookdars should operate to make a notice bad for incompleteness, the defendant having perfectly understood why he was called upon to pay more than he used to—*Srimati Jannoba* v. *Grish Chandra Chuckerbutty*, 7 B. L. R., App., 44; 15 W. R., 335.

A notice of enhancement should not be prospective, the principle Effect of notice. being that the ryot should be prepared to meet the claim on grounds existing at the time the notice is received—*Byjnauth Koonwar* v. *Saheb Koonwar*, 12 W. R., 532. Nor can it be retrospective. The notice must refer to enhanced rates for some period succeeding the giving of the notice—*Dinonauth Doss* v. *Gogan Chandra Sen*, 7 B. L. R., App., 45 (Note). So that a decree for enhancement can have no retrospective effect—*Chunder Mun Chowdhry* v. *Sriman Chowdhry*, 15 W. R., 119.

A judgment passed against a ryot in a contested suit operates as a Judgment oper-notice of enhancement to him taking effect from the commencement ates as notice. of the year following that in which the decree was passed—*Modhoosoodun Koondoo* v. *Gopee Kishen Gossain*, 6 W. R. (Act X), 81; *Romanauth Dutt* v. *Joy Kishen Mookerjee*, 11 W. R., 3; see also *Ram Jeebun Bose* v. *Tripoora Dossee*, Marsh., 396; but when a notice of enhancement is served during the pendency of a declaratory suit to enhance rent, the notice is inoperative—*Romanauth Dutt* v. *Joy Kishen Mookerjee*, 6 W. R. (Act X), 80.

When in a suit for enhancement the plaintiff fails to prove the notice, Failure to prove the suit should be dismissed—*Anund Moyee Chowdhrain* v. *Chunder Monee* notice. *Dossia*, 3 W. R. (Act X), 139; *Kristo Motee Debia* v. *Fukeer Chunder Khan, ib.*, 140; *Ram Chunder Chowdhry* v. *Hurish Chunder Chowdhry*, 5 W. R. (Act X), 14; *Radha Monee Dossia* v. *Moharani Shibessuree Debia*, 6 W. R. (Act X), 25; *Nara Kant Mozumdar* v. *Raja Baroda Kant Roy Bahadur*, 3 B. L. R., App., 31.

The notice is to be served on the application of the person *to whom* By whom to be *the rent is payable.* A zemindar who has leased out his property to a issued. farmer cannot serve a notice of enhancement during the continuance of the lease: the notice must be served by the farmer to whom, for the time being, the rent is payable—*Binodee Lall Ghose* v. *Mackenzie*, 3 W. R. (Act X), 157; *Hem Chunder Chatterjee* v. *Poornu Chunder Roy*, 3 W. R. (Act X), 162; *Gubdoo Mull* v. *Hoolasee*, 2 Agra, 247. And where a zemindar served a notice on the ryots of a mauza, and after-wards granted a lease of the mauza to the plaintiff, it was held that the notice was good, and the plaintiff was entitled to sue for enhancement upon it—*Khaski Roy* v. *Farzand Ali Khan*, 9 B. L. R., 125; 18 W. R., 144. It is almost needless to observe that farmers and other lease-holders, unless precluded by the terms of their lease, are entitled to enhance the rents of the ryots holding under them—*Rushton* v. *Girdharee Tewaree*, Marsh., 331. It is not, of course, necessary that the landlord

SECTION 14. should himself sign, and personally apply for the issue of the notice. The signing and issuing of notices is entirely within the scope of the ordinary duties of a mofussil *naib*; and no proof is required that the landlord authorized the agent to sign the notice—*Degumber Mitter* v. *Gobindo Chunder Haldar*, Marsh., 354.

On whom notice is to be served.

The notice, it will be observed, must be in writing, and must state not only the grounds of enhancement, but the amount of rent demanded; and it must be served in the manner prescribed by the law. The service of a notice upon the *gomashtah of a purdah nisheen lady* was held to be no service within the meaning of this section. "The Act," observed Peacock, C.J., "does not say that the notice shall be served personally upon the under-tenant, the ryot, *or his agent*, but upon the under-tenant or ryot. The notice in this case was not served personally on the under-tenant or ryot; and if for any reason it was shown that it could not be served personally upon her, then it ought to have been served by being affixed to her usual place of residence in the district, or if she had no such residence, in the manner prescribed by the Act. That not having been done, I do not think that the notice can render the tenant liable to be enhanced"—*Chunder Monee Dassee* v. *Dhuroneedhur Lahory*, 7 W. R., 2.

Separate notice to be served for each holding.

A ryot is entitled to a separate notice for each separate holding he possesses; not only because some of his holdings may be protected from enhancement, while others are not, but because he may be ready to pay the enhanced rent upon some, while he may prefer to relinquish the others. If the whole of his jummas are lumped together and treated as one holding, he has no means of exercising his discretion—*Bejoy Gobindo Bural* v. *Junnobee Bromonya*, 8 W. R., 252; *Dinobundhoo Bhadooree* v. *Prankishen Sircar*, 20 W. R., 146; *Dwarkanath Haldar* v. *Huree Mohan Roy*, 20 W. R., 404. But the notice need not be on a separate piece of paper for each holding. It is sufficient if the tenant is able to distinguish the separate holdings on the notice—*McGiveron* v. *Duriaw Chowdhry*, 20 W. R., 479. When, however, a number of holdings had been treated as one consolidated holding, and the ryots had paid their rent in one entire sum as a consolidated jumma, it was held that one notice was sufficient. "Had the jumma," observed the Court, "not been treated as a consolidated jumma, we should have been disposed to declare that one notice to enhance the aggregate jumma was insufficient; because in cases where a ryot holds several tenures, or separated jummas, he may, on receipt of notice, use his discretion as to which to retain and which to relinquish. If his several tenures are lumped together and treated as one tenancy, and he is served with the one notice, he is precluded from using this discretion. Under such circumstances, we think we ought not to infer from the fact that the jumma has, for purposes of convenience, been treated as one in the summary suits and other proceedings, that the original separate tenures have been surrendered, and that a fresh taking at an entire rent must have been made; because to do so would seriously prejudice important rights, which the plaintiff may have acquired under the original holdings. Therefore, though we hold that under the circumstances disclosed in this case one notice was sufficient, we must declare that the ryots are entitled to relinquish or retain all or any one of the separate holdings occupied by them at their option under section 20; and the Lower Court in deciding the case must ascertain what are the separate holdings, and assess a

Unless the holdings have been consolidated.

separate rent on each distinct holding"—*Jadub Chunder Holdar* v. SECTION 15.
Etwaree Lushkur, Marsh., 498. But though a separate notice is
necessary for each separate holding, it is not necessary that the landlord
should serve a separate notice on each person interested in such holding.
Thus, when a holding had been subdivided without the consent of the
landlord, it was held that it was quite sufficient if notice was served on
the recognised and recorded tenants—*Mothooranath Chatterjee* v. *Khetter-nauth Biswas*, 2 W. R. (Act X), 93.

Where an objection as to the sufficiency of notice has not been taken Objection taken in
in the Courts before it will not be allowed to be taken in special appeal— special appeal.
Kashee Nath Deb v. *Moharanee Shibessuree Debea*, 8 W. R., 503 ; *Sri
Gopal Mullick* v. *Dwarkanath Sein*, 15 W. R., 520; *Shaikh Husmut
Ali* v. *Onree Thakoor*, 20 W. R., 232. The same rule will apply when
no objection has been taken to the proof of the notice in the Courts
below—*Dumaine* v. *Attam Singh*, 5 B. L. R., App., 44; 13 W. R., 462.

The ryots of a Government khas mehal are in exactly the same posi- Ryots in Govern-
tion with regard to enhancement as the ryots of ordinary zemindars. ment and resum-
Their rents can only be *enhanced* after notice under this section—*The* ed estates.
Nawab Nazim v. *Ram Lal Ghose*, 6 W. R. (Act X), 215. When the
revenue authorities resume and assess invalid lakhiraj land, the act of
resumption and settlement creates the legal relation of landlord and
tenant; and the ex-lakhirajdar is bound to pay rent according to the
jummabundee, " as the law distinctly provides that such proceedings of
settlement officers shall be valid and binding until set aside by the Civil
Court "—*Hurro Prosad Chowdry* v. *Shama Persaud Roy Chowdhry*,
6 W. R. (Act X), 107 ; see also *Woomanauth Roy Chowdhry* v. *Deb Nath
Roy Chowdry*, 14 W. R., 471. The effect of these latter cases, however,
seem modified, as it has been held that the provisions of sections 7 and 9
of Regulation VII of 1822 must now be read as qualified by this section,
so that unless the under-tenant or ryot enters into a fresh engagement
at the time of the re-settlement he is entitled to a notice under this
section—*D'Silva* v. *Raj Coomar Dutt*, 16 W. R., 153.

It would seem that a declaratory decree can be given even though Declaratory
no notice to enhance has been proved, where the liability of the tenure decree under this
to enhancement is in issue—*Nufferchunder Paul Chowdry* v. *Poulson*, section.
12 B. L. R., 53 ; 19 W. R., 175. A higher rent cannot be recovered
than the sum mentioned in the notice of enhancement—*Hills* v. *Panch
Cowrie Sheikh*, 1 W. R., 3.

XV. Any under-tenant or ryot, on whom such notice Act X, 1859,
Mode of contesting as aforesaid has been served, may Section 14.
enhancement of rent. contest his liability to pay the enhanced
rent demanded of him, either by complaint of excessive
demand of rent as hereinafter provided, or in answer to
any suit preferred against him for recovery of arrears of
the enhanced rent.

There are two courses open to a ryot, who, after being served with a Complaint by ryot
notice under the preceding section, disputes his liability to pay the of excessive
enhanced rent claimed :— demand of rent.

1*st*.—He can take the initiative, and complain that the rent demanded
of him is excessive.

SECTION 16.

Right of taking initiative does not apply to non-occupancy ryots.

In suit under this section, Court cannot fix the rates of rent.

When sufficiency of notice can be contested by suit.

2nd.—He can wait until sued by the landlord for the enhanced rent, and then plead in answer to the claim that the amount is higher than the landlord is entitled to demand.

The right of taking the initiative will not apply to a ryot without a right of occupancy, if he is served with a notice, he must wait either until the landlord proceeds to levy the excessive rent by distraint, or until he brings an action for the rent specified in the notice—*Sheikh Moheem* v. *Sheikh Raheemotollah*, Marsh., 341.

When a ryot, on whom notice of enhancement has been served, sues under this section and fails to prove his case, the suit ought to be dismissed, and the Court ought not to go on to try the defendant's case as if he was suing for enhancement—*Gunga Narain Chowdry* v. *Kofa Pali*, 11 W. R., 376. For such a suit is sometimes brought to resist the notice altogether on the ground that the plaintiff is not liable to enhancement, and not to try whether the ground of enhancement exists, or whether the rate of enhancement is fair—*Gunga Pershad Singh* v. *Ramloll Singh*, Marsh., 185. The case of *Sheikh Gholamee* v. *Iman Buksh*, 2 W. R. (Act X), 91, seems to be contrary to this decision, but in that case the proper rates of rent were fixed by the Court of first instance, and the plaintiff had made no objection until the suit had been heard four different times. And to the same effect is *Gora Chund* v. *Gudadhur Chatterjee*, 7 W. R., 470.

A ryot who has received a notice of enhancement may be in a somewhat different position relative to the sufficiency of the notice according as he waits until a suit has been brought against him, or comes into Court of his own accord to attack the notice. Where he does the latter and shows that he thoroughly understood the notice, he cannot contest it on the ground of insufficiency—*Ram Bhurosee Singh* v. *Syud Mahomed Asguree Khan*, 19 W. R., 205.

Act X, 1859, section 16.

Dependent talookdar, &c., holding land at fixed rent without change since Permanent Settlement, not liable to enhancement of rent.

XVI. No dependent talookdar, or other person possessing a permanent transferable interest in land intermediate between the proprietor of an estate and the ryot, who, in any province to which the provisions of this Act may apply, holds his talook or tenure (otherwise than under a terminable lease) at a fixed rent which has not been changed from the time of the Permanent Settlement, shall be liable to any enhancement of such rent, anything in Section 51, Regulation VIII of 1793, or in any other law, to the contrary notwithstanding.

Application of the section.

This section will only apply to dependent talookdars and other persons possessing permanent transferable and intermediate interests in land which has been held at a fixed rent, which has not been changed from the time of the Permanent Settlement,—that is to say, not the Permanent Settlement of Bengal, Behar, and Orissa, and not the Permanent Settlement of any particular year which was afterwards made; see *Sheoburn Lal* v. *Ram Pertab Singh*, 3 W. R. (Act X), 20. And it will, in such cases, have effect even although there has been a decree for

THE LAW OF LANDLORD AND TENANT. 41

enhancement before the passing of Act X, provided that such decree has never been executed—*Gobindchunder Dutt* v. *Baboo Hurronath Roy*, 5 W. R. (Act X), 10; 1 Ind. Jur., 52.

Section 16.

A zemindar wishing to enhance the rent of a dependent talookdar, who has not held at a fixed rent which has not been changed from the time of the Permanent Settlement, must proceed on the grounds mentioned in section 51 of Regulation VIII of 1793; he cannot proceed on the grounds laid down in section 17 of Act X of 1859, or in section 18 of this Act—*Hurronath Roy* v. *Bindo Bashinee Debia*, 3 W. R. (Act X), 26; *Nobokishore Bose* v. *Pandul Sircar*, 8 W. R., 312; *Brojo Soondur Mitter* v. *Kalee Kishore Chowdry*, 8 W. R., 496; *Tarinee Kant Lahoree* v. *Koonj Beharee Awusty*, 12 W. R., 112; *Kristo Chunder Goopto* v. *Elahee Buksh*, 20 W. R., 459.

Enhancement of rent of dependent talookdars.

Section 51 of Regulation VIII of 1793 is as follows:—" No zemindar or other actual proprietor of land shall demand an increase from the talookdars dependent on him, although he should be subject to the payment of an increase of jumma to Government; except upon proof that he is entitled to do so, either by the special custom of the district, or by the conditions under which the talookdar holds his tenure, or that the talookdar by receiving abatements from his jumma has subjected himself to the payment of the increase demanded, and that the lands are capable of affording it."

Section 51 of Regulation VIII of 1793.

This section of the Regulation, it will be seen, applies only to dependent talookdars; it does not apply to those whose talooks are held under writings, sunnuds, or other documents granted by proprietors of lands which do not expressly transfer the property in the soil—*Rajah Suttyanund Ghosal* v. *Huro Kishore Dutt*, 12 W. R., 474. Nor does the section apply to ryottee kudeemee tenures—*Ram Chunder Dutt* v. *Juggeshchunder Dutt*, 19 W. R., 353,—a Privy Council case. It is sufficient to show that the tenure existed, and was capable of being registered at the time of the Decennial Settlement—*Bamasoondery Dassyah* v. *Radhika Chowdhrain*, 13 Moo. I. A., 248; 4 B. L. R., P. C., 8; 13 W. R., P. C., 11.

To what section 51 applies.

By "special custom" may be understood to mean the customary rate of the pergunnah, or, in other words, the rent paid by similar tenures in the same pergunnah. For in the case of *Bamasoondery Dassyah* v. *Radhika Chowdhrain* last referred to, it is said, " a suit to enhance rent proceeds on the presumption that a zemindar holding from the perpetual settlement has the right from time to time to raise the rents of all rent-paying lands within his zemindary, according to the pergunnah or current rates, unless he is precluded from the exercise of that right by a contract binding on him, or the lands in question can be brought within one of the exemptions recognized by Bengal Regulation VIII of 1793; and it also assumes that the defendant has some valid tenure or right of occupancy in the lands which are the subject of the suit." And it has always been laid down that talookdars are to be enhanced according to the rates as paid by talookdars of a similar description, and holding the same quality of land, and with similar advantages, and not according to ryotwaree rates—*Mohima Chunder Dey* v. *Gooroo Doss Sein*, 7 W. R., 285; *Huro Soonduree Chowdhrain* v. *Anund Mohun Ghose Chowdry*, 7 W. R., 459; *Muneekurnika Chowdry* v. *Anund Moyee Chowdry*, 10 W. R., 245. Further as to this point, see p. 45.

Special custom.

SECTION 16.

Rule to be followed when no customary rate exists.

The case of *Bunchanund* v. *Hurgopal Bhadery*, 1 Sel. Rep., 145, lays down the rule which should be followed when it is impossible to ascertain what the pergunnah talookdaree rates are. In that case it was admitted that the lands were held by the talookdar at a variable rent; but as there did not appear to be in the pergunnah any settled rates of rent for similar tenures according to which the proper rent could be adjusted, it was determined that the rent demandable from the talookdar should be settled by an actual survey, and measurement to be made at the expense of the zemindar, unless the parties should come to an adjustment between themselves. In the event of no adjustment being made by them, it was decided that the Zillah Judge should cause a measurement of the lands, and estimate of their produce to be taken; and after deducting from the produce ten per cent. as the customary profit of the talookdar, together with the actual charges of collection, should fix the residue as the annual rent demandable from the talookdar. The principle laid down in this decision was afterwards adopted by the Legislature in Regulation V, 1812, section 8, which was as follows:—" In the case of a dependent talookdar, if the rent of the lands be computed according to the rates payable by ryots or cultivators for land of a similar quality and description, a deduction shall be allowed from the gross rent in the adjustment of the jumma of such dependent talook at the rate of ten per cent. for the talookdar's profit or income, over and above a reasonable allowance for charges of collection according to the extent of the talook." Though this section was repealed by Act X, 1859, its principle has always been recognized in the assessment of such tenures—*Mohamed Aynuddeen* v. *Baboo Rajendra Chandra Neogi*, 2 Board's Rep., 749. In another case, decided in 1813, the assessment was made upon a slightly different principle. The Court, following local custom, held that the talookdar was entitled to hold free of assessment 4 *kanees* in every *drone* as *jeebka*,* and 3 *kanees* 4 *gundahs* per *drone* as *mattan*. As there are 16 *kanees* in a *drone*, the deduction in favor of the talookdar in this case would amount to nearly half the land included in the talook—*Ram Kant Dutt* v. *Gholam Nubby Chowdhree*, 2 Sel. Rep., 55.

Abatement.

In order to constitute the "abatement" mentioned in section 51, it is not sufficient for the plaintiff to allege that the rent by degrees has become less—*Nubokristo Mojoomdar* v. *Tara Monee*, 12 W. R., 320.

What tenures are permanent and transferable.

Whether a tenure is permanent and transferable will depend much either on the name of the tenure, the document under which the undertenant holds, or a variety of other circumstances connected with each particular case. For instance a putnee talook is *primâ facie* hereditary and transferable,—*Tarini Charan Ganguli* v. *Watson*, 3 B. L. R., A. C., 437; 12 W. R., 413. So is a *surborakari* tenure in Cuttack—*Saddanando Maiti* v. *Nourattam Maiti*, 3 B. L. R., 280; 16 W. R., 290. In every district of Bengal there is a different custom. What is the custom in Lower Bengal is not so in the eastern or northern parts, and *vice versâ*. In some parts, even *khoodkast* tenants are allowed to sell without reference to their landlords; in other parts the practice has not been allowed, and the only method by which the question in each case can be decided, is by reference to local custom—*Joy Kissen Mookerjee* v.

---

* Sir William Macnaughten, in a note to this case, describes *jeebka* as "a portion of land granted as an allowance for the maintenance of a family: and *mattan* as a portion of land allotted by a zemindar as a remuneration for bringing waste lands into cultivation."

Rajkissen Mookerjee, 1 W. R., 153. It is not, of course, essential that SECTION 16. a tenure should be *mokururee* to make it transferable. There are various descriptions of tenures other than *mokururee* that can be transferred and are transferred every day,—the *howlahs* and *neem-howlahs* of Backergunge and the *jotes* of Rungpore for example. Neither of these holdings are, properly speaking, *mokururee*, but they are *mouroosee*, and contain hereditary rights, which are, and always have been, considered transferable—*Hurromohun Mookerjee* v. *Ranee Lalun Monee Dossee*, 1 W. R., 5. Again where the words *mokururee* (fixed) and *istemrari* (permanent) are both used in a pottah, such pottah must be considered as conveying an hereditary right in perpetuity—*Mussamut Lakhu Kowar* v. *Roy Hari Krishna Sing*, 3 B. L. R., A. C., 226; 12 W. R., 3; *Karunakar Mahati* v. *Niladhro Chowdry*, 5 B. L. R., 652; 14 W. R., 107. Though the word *mokururee* of itself does not necessarily import perpetuity—*The Bengal Government* v. *Nawab Jafur Hossein Khan*, 5 Moo. I. A., 467. But even if in the document, which confers the title on the under-tenant, there are no words which import a permanent transferable interest, the omission of such words may be supplied by long uninterrupted usage. This was one of the main points in the case of *Baboo Dhunput Singh* v. *Gooman Singh*, 11 Moo. I. A., 433; 9 W. R., P. C., 3, already referred to. The original pottah, upon the right construction of which that case turned, was granted to one Augham Singh, and was to the following effect:—" In accordance with your application, the lands of Mouzah Cheloone and other villages in the forest of Sukhooa trees, have been assessed with a rental of Rs. 101; everything being consolidated, and a pottah granted to you, it is required that you will in all confidence have the lands of the said forests occupied by Purbuttea and other ryots, and keep paying to the sirkar the rent year by year according to this pottah; and whenever you may be summoned for the purpose of hunting, you will attend, accompanied by all the Purbuttcas." In considering the nature and extent of the interest which this pottah conveyed, their Lordships remarked as follows:—"Their Lordships are not prepared to dissent from the judgment of the High Court, in so far as it found that the pottah taken by itself cannot be held to have granted a *mokururee istemrari* tenure. It does not contain the term *mokururee*, or any equivalent words, from which an obligation on the part of the grantor never to raise the rent is fairly to be inferred; nor does it contain the expressions 'from generation to generation,' or other like words importing that the tenure, whether the rent was to be fixed or variable, was to be hereditary. Again, neither the date nor the nature of the transaction is, on the whole, in favor of the hypothesis, that the intention of the grantor was to create a perpetual tenure at a fixed rent. The whole policy of the Decennial Settlement, as appears by Regulation VIII, 1793, was adverse to *mokururee* tenures. It made them all subject to reassessment, unless they fell within the protection of the 49th section of that Regulation. It is not, therefore, probable that the zemindar would immediately after the completion of that settlement grant such a tenure, except upon special grounds and adequate consideration: and of these there is no proof. But passing from the pottah taken by itself, it is necessary to consider the character of the occupation of the land, as shown by the uncontested facts of the case. These facts afford incontestable proof, that, ever since the death

SECTION 16. of Augham Singh, the hereditary character of his sub-tenure has been recognized by the successive zemindars. There is also evidence that some of them have recognized its transferable nature. This evidence affords ample grounds for inferring either that the tenure was always intended to be hereditary, though not so expressed in the pottah, or that if the original grant was limited, as was suggested, to the life of Augham Singh, his tenure has by subsequent grant become hereditary and transferable. And upon the proof here given of long uninterrupted enjoyment, accompanied by the recognition of its hereditary and transferable character, it is almost impossible to suppose that a suit by the zemindar in the Civil Court to disturb the possession of the respondent could not be successfully resisted. The case of *Joba Singh* v. *Meer Najeeb Oollah*, 4 S. D. A. Rep., 271, is an authority for the proposition, that evidence of this kind will supply the wants of the words 'from generation to generation' in the pottah." Their Lordships, therefore, held that the tenure was, or had become, hereditary and transferable; and that as the rent had not been changed since the time of the Permanent Settlement, the case came under the protection of this section. To a similar effect are *Baboo Gopal Lall Thakoor* v. *Teluck Chunder Rai*, 10 Moo. I. A., 191; 3 W. R., P. C., 1; *Rajah Satyasaran Ghosal* v. *Mohesh Chunder Mitter*, 12 Moo. I. A., 263; 2 B. L. R., P. C., 23; 11 W. R., P. C., 10; *Kolodeep Narain Singh* v. *The Government of India*, 14 Moo. I. A., 247; 11 B. L. R., 71.

Construction of leases.

Where a lease contained the following words:—"You shall continue to pay the sum of Rs. 5 fixed on the whole as ticca jumma of the said mouzah every year, and having cleared the village of jungle, and having brought the lands under cultivation, yourself and through others, as usual, enjoy and occupy the same, with your sons and grandsons in succession," it was held that this was a lease of which the rent was permanently fixed at Rs. 5, and that it descended from the grantee to his heirs. Being an absolute interest, the grantee and his heirs were entitled to transfer it, and to vest in the transferree the full benefit of the lease. A lease, however, of this nature granted since the time of the Permanent Settlement, would not be binding upon a purchaser at a sale for arrears of revenue—*Watson and Co.* v. *Juggeshar Atta*, Marsh., 330. A lease which does not contain the words "*mokururee istemrari*," or anything to show that it is intended to be hereditary, but simply the words "*year by year*," creates merely a yearly tenancy, determinable every year at the option of either party—*Punchanun Bose* v. *Peary Mohun Deb*, 2 W. R., 225. And the words "*tikka mohto*" in a lease are not tantamount to "*mouroosee*" or "*istemrari*"—*Nuffer Chunder Shaha* v. *Gossain Jysingh Bharuttee*, 3 W. R. (Act X), 144. And where a pottah stated that the lessee should hold the lands for four years rent-free; that, after measurement, the lands were to be assessed; that then he was to pay 4 annas a bighah in the year 1265, 6 annas in 1266, and 8 annas and 3 gundahs in 1267, and for five years after, it was held this did not constitute a *mokururee* holding at a fixed rate, even though the words "full customary rates" were used in the pottah—*Kasimuddi Khandkar* v. *Nadir Ali Tarafdar*, 2 B. L. R., A. C., 265; 11 W. R., 164. But this decision may now be doubted, see the Privy Council case of *Golam Ali* v. *Baboo Gopal Lal Thakoor*, 19 W. R., 141. A continuous payment of rent for a hundred years gives rise to the presumption that the tenant held under a *mouroosee*

title—*Brojanath Kundu Chowdry* v. *Lakhi Narayan Addi,* 7 B. L. SECTION 16.
R., 211.

No rules are laid in this Act, nor are there any statutory rules as to Grounds of the grounds of enhancement of permanent transferable tenures. The grounds on which such tenures can be enhanced is now pretty clear. In *Dyaram* v. *Bhobindur Naraen,* 1 Sel. Rep., 139, the plaintiff held some lands on a *mouroosee ijarah,* or hereditary farm, and it was considered by the Court that "he was entitled to occupy the lands at the usual rate of rent for similar tenures in the pergunnah, and that the zemindars were not justified in turning him out." Sir William Macnaughten in a note made the following remarks upon the customary rate of the pergunnah:—" The pottah or lease for a *mouroosee ijarah* does not specifically convey more than a hereditary right of occupancy. If it be not *istemrari,* or entitling the tenant to hold at a fixed rent, the amount of the rent payable to the zemindar is variable, and when not settled by mutual agreement, is determinable only by the indefinite standard of the 'customary rate of the pergunnah,' that is 'the rent paid by similar tenures in the same pergunnah.'" The soundness of this opinion was recognized by the Privy Council in *Baboo Dhunput Sing's* case, where their Lordships, after referring to *Dyaram's* case, observed that, " where the suit is against an intermediate tenant, the enhancement ought to be made according to the pergunnah rate of the rents payable not by the ryots, but by the holders of similar tenures. To assess such an intermediate tenant according to the rents paid by ryots, would necessarily deprive him of all beneficial interest in his tenure"—11 Moo. I. A., 433; 9 W. R., P. C., 3. It has more recently been held that a deduction of 15 per cent. from the gross rents is a fair and equitable mode of assessing the rent payable by an intermediate tenant in a suit for enhancement. Intermediate tenures should be assessed at a rate so as to allow the tenant a reasonable profit, and not at a rate at which cultivation are assessed—*Ranee Swarnamayi* v. *Gouri Prasad Das,* 3 B. L. R., A. C., 270.

Where land accretes to an under-tenure, the right of occupancy in Accretions to the land passes to the owner of the under-tenure, and not to the under-tenures. zemindar. The general law upon the subject is contained in clause 1, section 4, Regulation XI, 1825, which is as follows :—" When land may be gained by gradual accession, whether from the recess of a river or of the sea, it shall be considered an increment to the tenure of the person to whose land or estate it is thus annexed, *whether* such land be held immediately from Government by a zemindar, or as a subordinate tenure by any description of under-tenant whatever : provided that the increment of land thus obtained shall not entitle the person in possession of the *estate* or *tenure* to which the land may be annexed, to a right of property or permanent interest therein beyond that possessed by him in the estate or tenure to which the land may be annexed ; and shall not in any case be understood to *exempt* the holder of it from the payment to Government of any assessment for the public revenue to which it may be liable under the provisions of Regulation II, 1819, or of any other Regulation in force. *Nor, if annexed to a subordinate tenure* held under a superior landholder, shall the under-tenant, whether a *khoodkast* ryot holding a *mouroosee istemrari* tenure at a fixed rate of rent per bigah, or any other description of under-tenant, *liable by his engagements* or *by established usage* to an increase of rent for the land

SECTION 16. annexed to his tenure by alluvion, be considered exempt from the payment of any increase of rent to which he may be justly liable." The accretion then will belong to the holder of the jote to whose tenure it has become attached—*Juggut Chunder Dutt* v. *Panioty*, 6 W. R. (Act X), 48; *Attimoollah* v. *Shaik Saheboollah*, 15 W. R., 149. And the jotedar is entitled to hold the accretion on the same principle and under the same legal conditions as he holds the parent estate—*Gobind Monee Debia* v. *Dino Bundhoo Shaha*, 15 W. R., 87. When, therefore, a zemindar desires to assess the accretion, he must show that he is entitled to do so either by law, custom, or special agreement, and accreted lands, when liable to enhancement at the ordinary neighbouring rates, are entitled to a deduction of 10 per cent. for collection charges and 10 per cent. for talookdary profits—*Juggut Chunder Dutt* v. *Panioty*, 6 W. R. (Act X), 48; *Baboo Gopal Lall Thakoor* v. *Kumur Ali*, 6 W. R. (Act X), 85; *Juggut Chunder Dutt* v. *Panioty*, 8 W. R., 427; (in review), 9 W. R., 379. And even a tenant-at-will is entitled to occupy an accretion so long as he retains possession of his original holding—*Bhagabat Prasad Sing* v. *Durg Bijai Sing*, 8 B. L. R., 73; 16 W. R., 95. It will be observed that clause 1, section 4 of Regulation XI of 1825, refers only to under-tenants intermediate between the zemindar and the ryot, and *khoodkast* or other ryots who possess some permanent interest in the land, and not to tenants from year to year—*Zuheeroodeen Paikar* v. *Campbell*, 4 W. R., 57.

Leases with defined boundaries.

It very frequently happens that a lease, which conveys a certain number of bigahs within certain defined boundaries, contains in reality a greater quantity of land than is specified; and the question whether this excess land is liable to assessment furnishes a constant cause of litigation. It seems, however, to be tolerably settled by a number of recent decisions that, where the boundaries are given, the lease covers all the land included within those boundaries, whether in excess of the quantity specified or not. In such cases the lease is not to be construed as a lease of so many bigahs, and no more, but as a lease of certain lands, the number of bigahs being added more by way of description than of limitation; see *Janokee Bullub Chuckerbutty* v. *Nobin Chunder Roy Chowdry*, 2 W. R. (Act X), 33; 2 Board's Rep., 365; *Limond* v. *Gour Soonder Chowdhry*, ib., 121; *Ramnarain Nundee* v. *Toyluck Chunder Biswas*, ib., 19; *Chundra Kanth Mookerjee* v. *Dhun Sing Roy*, 1 Board's Rep., 174; *Modee Hudden Jorwardar* v. *Sandes*, 12 W. R., 439; see also *Herrick* v. *Sixby*, L. R., 1 P. C., 436, 452.

Include all land within those boundaries.

But where boundaries are not specified, the ryot must pay for all excess land he holds.

Where, however, a lease merely conveyed so many bigahs of land without specification of boundaries, the tenant would, under ordinary circumstances, be bound to pay rent for any excess land he might hold—*Bipro Dass Dey* v. *Mussamut Sakermonee Dasse*, W. R. (Act X), 1864, 38; 2 Board's Rep., 57. But a tenant who had held land, though in excess of his lease, at an unvaried rent from the time of the Permanent Settlement, would be protected from enhancement. A certain ghatwal in Beerbhoom was stated, in certain *ismnavissee* papers prepared by the Police in 1811, to hold a 100 bigahs of ghatwalee land; but upon measurement it was found that the land actually held

Unless the land has been held at an uniform rent from Permanent Settlement.

was very much in excess of 100 bigahs, and the zemindar sued to assess the excess. But the Court dismissed the case, on the ground, that the tenure had been held at a fixed rent from the time of the Permanent Settlement observing that "if the payment of the quit-rent to the zemindar is considered as creating the relation of landlord SECTION 16. and tenant, then the land has been held at a fixed rate of rent, which has not been changed from the time of the Permanent Settlement; and therefore either as a ryot under section 3, or as a person possessing a permanent transferable interest intermediate between the proprietor of the estate and the ryot under section 15, Act X of 1859, these defendants are entitled to continue to hold at the same rents, and the plaintiff as *putneedar* has no right to any fresh assessment"—*Farquharson* v. *Dwarkanauth Singh*, 14 Moo. I. A., 259; 8 B. L. R., 504.

Jungle boorie leases are leases for clearing jungle, and are generally Jungle boorie granted on what is called a *russudee* jumma. The following may be lease. taken as a very fair specimen of the terms under which these tenures are held:—A lease was granted to A. B. of 4 *drones* 3 *kanees* 4 *gundahs* of jungle poteet land, situated within certain specified boundaries; a deduction of 4 *gundahs* per *kanee* (in other words, a deduction of ⅛th) was allowed on account of *rukba*, on the condition that the tenant should hold the land rent-free for 1260, and should thereafter pay rent at the following rates :—

   In the year 1261 at Re. 1 per *kanee*.
    „ 1262 at Rs. 2 „ „
    „ 1263 at „ 3 „ „
    „ 1264 at the full customary rate (*pooradus-*

toor) of Rs. 5 per *kanee*, year by year, and month by month, according Where a maxi-to the instalments mentioned. In this case the Court (Bayley and rate is mentioned, Phear, JJ.) held that the lease conveyed a permanent tenure at a fixed the rent cannot rate of rent; that as the in-coming tenant was embarking upon an that amount. adventure, in which all the labor and expense would be his, it was but fair to assume that an interest such as might become beneficial to the lessee was intended to be passed, rather than merely a right of occupation, which might, after 1264, at the option of the landlord, be screwed down by process of law to a simple rack-rent tenure—*Golam Ali* v. *Baboo Gopal Lall Takoor*, 9 W. R., 65, and this decision has been affirmed by the Privy Council, 19 W. R., 141. It apparently over-rules *Puddo Monee Dossia* v. *Puromanund Sein*, 7 W. R., 158; *Bhurut Chundra Aitch* v. *Gourmonee Dosse*, 2 B. L. R., A. C. (note), 266; 11 W. R., 31; *Kasimuddi Khandkar* v. *Nadar Ali Tarafdar*, 2 B. L. R., A. C., 265; 11 W. R., 164. And generally as to the right of the ryot to hold lands at jungle rates, see the remarks of Campbell, J., in *Choudhry Khan* v. *Gour Jana*, 2 W. R. (Act X), 40.

Ghatwalee tenures are principally found in the western districts of Ghatwalee the Lower Provinces. The holders generally pay a small quit-rent to the tenures. zemindar, and are, besides, bound to render certain services to the State. These services have, in many districts, become practically obsolete, and Held upon con-much litigation has of late years arisen from the natural desire of the ditions of service. zemindars to resume and assess these ghatwalee holdings. It is clear, however, from the judgment of the Court in *Koolodeep Singh's* case that this cannot legally be done. "Some cases" observed Peacock, C.J., If the service is in delivering judgment in that case, "were cited to show that, even the ghatwal holds assuming these lands to be subject to a ghatwalee tenure, the zemindar service. has a right whenever he pleases to dispense with the ghatwalee services, and to take back the lands. Now I must say that this is the first time I ever heard such a contention as that a landlord can dispense with the services upon which lands are held, and take back the estate. It is

48   THE LAW OF LANDLORD AND TENANT.

SECTION 16, not because the services are released or dispensed with, or become unnecessary that the estate can be resumed. If a grantor release the services, or a portion of the services, upon which lands are holden, the tenant may hold the land free of the services; but the landlord cannot put an end to the tenure and resume the lands. It might as well be contended that, if lands were granted at a small quit-rent, the landlord might relinquish or dispense with the payment of the rent and take back the lands"—*Koolodeep Narain Sing* v *Mahadeo Sing*, 6 W. R., 199, and this decision is affirmed by the Privy Council—14 Moo. I. A., 247; 11 B. L. R., 71. The rents of a ghatwallee tenure are not liable for the debts of the former deceased holder of the tenure—*Binode Ram Sein* v. *Deputy Commissioner of the Sonthal Pergunnahs*, 7 W. R., 178; *Raja Nilmani Sing* v. *Madhab Sing*, 1 B. L. R., A. C., 195; 10 W. R., 255. A ghatwal is not competent to grant a lease in perpetuity, and his successors are not bound to recognize such an encumbrance—*Grant* v. *Bunkshee Deo*, 6 B. L. R., 652; 15 W. R., 38.

Effect of Government sales upon under-tenures.   The effect of a Government sale for arrears of revenue upon intermediate tenures has now to be considered. Under Act XI, 1859, section 37, the purchaser of an *entire* estate, sold for the recovery of arrears due on account of the same, acquires the estate free from all encumbrances which may have been imposed upon it *after* the time of settlement, and is entitled to avoid and annul all under-tenures, and to eject all under-tenants with the following exceptions:—

1st.—*Istemrari* or *mokururee* tenures which have been held at a fixed rent from the time of the Permanent Settlement.

2nd.—Tenures existing at the time of the Permanent Settlement, which have not been held at a fixed rent; the rent, however, of such tenures is liable to enhancement, though the holders of the tenures cannot be ejected: provided they are willing to pay the enhanced rent. The provisions of Act XI, 1859, of course merely apply to sales which have taken place since that enactment was passed; all previous sales are governed by the laws which were in force when the sale took place.

Scope of the Sale Regulation.   The general scope and object of the Sale Regulations was very fully discussed by the Privy Council in *Ranee Shornomoyee* v. *Maharajah Suttes Chunder Roy*, 10 Moo. I. A., 123; 2 W. R., P. C., 14. "It has been assumed," observed their Lordships, "as the foundation of these Sale Regulations, that the default of the zemindars may have been occasioned by improvident grants of talooks and other subordinate tenures at inadequate rents; and the purchaser, therefore, has been set free from the obligation of these grants with certain limitations and exceptions." It has been contended that, by the

Under-tenures not *ipso facto* void after a sale, but only voidable at the option of purchaser.   operation of the words "stand cancelled from the day of sale," the existing interest of the talookdar *ipso facto* ceased to exist, without any act done by the purchaser; and that where, from the acquiescence of the purchaser, or those claiming under him, the possession has remained in the talookdar, and those claiming under him undisturbed, and the original rent has been received, no matter for how long, or through whatever number of mesne conveyances, it still remained a bare possession at the will of the zemindar for the time being, and the rent always liable to enhancement. In this hard and literal construction of the words, their Lordships do not concur......Words which make a bishop's grant "utterly void and of none effect to all intents, constructions and purposes," have been held not to prevent the grant from

being good and binding on the grantor, and in some cases confirmable SECTION 17.
by the successor; and so a proviso in a lease that it *should be void*
altogether in case the tenant should neglect to do a certain act, has been
held only to make it voidable at the option of the landlord. In the
present case, the object of the Government was that the jumma should
be duly paid, and that the means of paying it should not be withdrawn
by the improvident grants of the zemindars who had made default; but
cases of default might often arise where no improvident grant had been
made, where the talookdars and the ryots held at proper rents, and the
default was owing to extravagance, mismanagement, or other causes; in
such cases Government cannot be supposed to have intended a wanton
and unjust disturbance of vested interests......The conclusion, therefore,
at which their Lordships have arrived as to the construction of the
section is this,—that a power was given by it to a purchaser at a
Government sale for arrears to avoid the subsisting engagements as to
rent, and to increase the rent to that amount at which, according to the
established usages and rates of the pergunnah or district, it would have
stood had the cancelled engagement so avoided never existed." The
auction-purchaser is bound to exercise his right of annulling the under- And the right of annulling the
tenures created by the defaulting zemindar within a reasonable time; under-tenures must be exercised
and it has been suggested that the right must be exercised within within a reason-
twelve years from the date of the confirmation of the sale—*Tara Chand* able time.
Dutt v. *Mussamut Wakamoonissa Bibee*, 7 W. R., 91. In one case the
purchaser of a *putnee* talook, sold under Regulation VIII, 1819, who
had received rent from an under-tenant for fifteen years after the
purchase, was held to have acquiesced in the tenant's possession, and to
have waived his right to evict the tenant under clause 2, section 11,
of that Regulation—*Woomanath Roy Choudhry* v. *Rogoonauth Mitter*,
5 W. R. (Act X), 63.

A shikmee lakhirajdar cannot be disturbed in possession by an Shikmee lakhi-
auction-purchaser at a sale for arrears of revenue—*Ram Gobind Roy* v. disturbed.
Syud Kushuffudooza, 14 W. R., 1.

XVII. Whenever, in any suit under this Act, it shall Act X, 1859, section 16.
Rent of talookdar, &c., be proved that the rent at which a
not changed for twenty
years to be *primâ facie* talook or other tenure is held in the
evidence of occupancy said provinces has not been changed
at that rent since the for a period of twenty years before
Permanent Settlement. the commencement of the suit, it shall
be presumed that such talook or tenure has been held at
that rent from the time of the Permanent Settlement,
unless the contrary be shown, or it be proved that such
rent was fixed at some later period.

This section does not require proof of actual payment of one rate of
rent for twenty years, but that the rent has remained unchanged from
that period. Uniform rent for the twenty years preceding the suit ought
not to be presumed upon evidence which only touches a portion of that
period: on the other hand, it is not necessary to have evidence bearing
directly on *every* one of the twenty years. It is sufficient if the whole
time is included within limits upon which the evidence bears provided

SECTION 18. the evidence leads to the belief of uniform rent—*Foschola* v. *Huro Chunder Bose*, 8 W. R., 284. The real question is not whether the rent has been paid at an uniform rate, but whether it has not been changed within twenty years prior to the institution of this suit—*Ahmed Ali* v. *Golam Gafar*, 3 B. L. R., App., 40 ; 11 W. R., 432. The zemindar can rebut the *primâ facie* presumption that the rent has not been changed for a period of twenty years by showing that the rent has been fixed at some later period such as by producing a decree declaring his right to enhance—*Nuffer Chunder Paul Choudhry* v. *Poulson*, 12 B. L. R., 53 ; 19 W. R., 175. A Privy Council case.

The resumption by Government of a parent estate does not nullify the existing rights of a *howladar* within that estate, or deprive him of presumption arising under this section—*Mothooranath Gungopliadya* v. *Sheeta Monee*, 9 W. R., 354.

XVIII. No ryot having a right of occupancy shall be liable to an enhancement of the rent previously paid by him, except on some one of the following grounds, namely:—

Grounds on which ryot having right of occupancy is liable to enhanced rent.

That the rate of rent paid by such ryot is below the prevailing rate payable by the same class of ryots for land of a similar description and with similar advantages in the places adjacent.

That the rate paid by him is below that prevailing in adjacent places.

That the value of the produce or the productive powers of the land have been increased otherwise than by the agency or at the expense of the ryot.

That the value of the land, &c., has increased independently of the ryot.

That the quantity of land held by the ryot has been proved by measurement to be greater than the quantity for which rent has been previously paid by him.

That the quantity of land held by the ryot is greater than he has paid rent for.

This section applicable only to ryots and agricultural lands.

This section applies only to occupancy-ryots; it does not apply to talookdars or the holders of intermediate tenures—*Hurronath Roy* v. *Bindoo Bashinee Debia*, 3 W. R. (Act X), 26 ; *Nubo Kishore Bose* v. *Pandul Sircar*, 8 W. R., 312 ; *Panioty* v. *Juggut Chunder Dutt*, 9 W. R., 379 ; *Buduroonissa Chowdhrain* v. *Chunder Coomar Dutt*, 10 W. R., 454. Nor will it apparently apply to a ryot without a right of occupancy— *Chunder Coomar Banerjee* v. *Azeemooddeen*, 14 W. R., 100. Nor to land which has been let on lease for the erection of a school or church— *Ranee Shurnomoyee* v. *Blumhardt*, 9 W. R., 552. Nor to land situated in a town or used for building purposes, and not for agricultural or horticultural purposes—*Madan Mohun Biswas* v. *Stalkart*, 9 B. L. R., 97 ; 17 W. R., 441 ; *Ranee Durga Sundari Dassee* v. *Bibee Umdatannissa*, 9 B. L. R., 101 ; 17 W. R., 151 ; *Brojonath Kundu Choudry* v. *Lowther*, 9 B. L. R., 121 ; 17 W. R., 183. *Bastoo* land however, upon which the ryot's house is built, does not fall within the definition of land for building purposes, and is consequently liable to enhancement under this SECTION 18. section—*Naimudda Jowardar* v. *Scott Moncrieff*, 3 B. L. R., A. C., 283 ; 12 W. R., 140. A landlord who allows his tenant to invest capital in erecting buildings on land let for cultivation, and raises no objection for a considerable number of years, will not be allowed to disturb the holding. The fact of the building having been allowed to remain is *primâ facie* proof that the land was let for building purposes—*Brojonath Choudry* v. *Stewart*, 8 B. L. R., App., 51 ; 16 W. R., 216.

The three grounds of enhancement set forth in this section are all Under no circumsubject to the limitation contained in section 5. Under no circumstances occupancy-ryot's can a ryot, with a right of occupancy, be called upon to pay more than rent be enhanced a fair and equitable rent—*Noor Mohamed Mundle* v. *Hurriprosonno Roy*, fair and equitable. W. R., 1864 (Act X), 75, and in determining what is fair and equitable the Court may take into consideration the rise in wages; but it does not necessarily follow that because wages are double what they were, and the necessaries of life have risen, that the old rent is fair and equitable under the altered state of circumstances—*Savi* v. *Jeetoo Meah*, Marsh., 186. And as the existing rent is always presumed to be fair and equitable until the contrary is shown, it follows that a landlord who claims an increase of rent must clearly make out the grounds upon which the enhancement is sought. The grounds, too, must be one or other of those stated in this section.

The term "prevailing rate" means the rate generally prevalent, or Prevailing rate. the rate paid by the majority of the ryots in the neighbourhood—*Shadoo Sing* v. *Ramanoograha Lall*, 9 W. R., 83; and it is for the plaintiff, who seeks to enhance, to show that the rent paid by the tenant is lower than the prevailing rate. A plaintiff, who alleges as his ground of enhancement that the rates at which the defendant holds are lower than the prevailing rates in the neighbourhood, cannot ask for enhancement on the ground that the pergunnah rates are obsolete; or in other words, that the rates of the whole neighbourhood are too low—*Sreeram Chatterjee* v. *Lakhan Magilla*, Marsh., 379; 1 Board's Rep., 116. So where the ground relied on was the prevailing rate paid by the adjacent occupiers of similar land, and such ground could not be established by the probability or even the certainty that, if the rents of the neighbouring occupants were readjusted, they would come to the rate claimed, such ground is not sufficient to make out that the rate claimed is actually being paid by neighbouring ryots—*Brindabun Dey* v. *Bisona Bibee*, 13 W. R., 107. The evidence of three putwarees who put in their jummabundees showing the rates paid by almost all the ryots was held sufficient to prove the prevailing rate—*Priag Lall* v. *Brockman*, 13 W. R., 346. The mere fact of a particular rate of rent having been decreed against two ryots not having a right of occupancy is not enough to show that the rate so decreed was the rate prevailing in the neighbourhood—*Surahutoonissa Khanum* v. *Gyanee Buktur*, 11 W. R., 142. Pergunnah rates are not necessarily "prevailing rates"—*Kallee Chunder Choudry* v. *Rutton Gopal Bhadooree*, 11 W. R., 571. A claim to the "nerikh" rate may be considered to be a claim at the pergunnah rate, that is the rate paid by the same class of ryot for similar lands in the neighbourhood—*Amirto Lall Bose* v. *Arbach Kazee*, 4 W. R. (Act X), 47.

It is not, of course, sufficient for the Court to find what is the pre- Ryots of the vailing rate, it must also ascertain what is the prevailing rate paid by same class. ryots of the same class as the defendant. It has been held that the

SECTION 18. words "the same class" refer exclusively to occupancy-ryots, but this statement must not be taken too widely, for there may be a separate *class* of ryots within the general body of occupancy-ryots—*Ram Coomar Dhara* v. *Bhoyrub Chunder Mookerjee*, 6 W. R. (Act X), 33. They also refer to the division of ryots into two classes, *viz.*, those having rights of occupancy, and those not having rights of occupancy—*Sadhoo Singh* v. *Ramanoograha Lall*, 9 W. R., 83. And when a ryot had taken a jungle-clearing lease on a *russudee* jumma, which gradually rose to 10 annas a bigah, and it was found that this was below the rates prevailing in the neighbourhood, the Court held that the finding was bad in law, as it left undetermined the all important point, whether these rates were paid by the same class of ryots, and by ryots with similar advantages in the places adjacent—*Purmanund Sein* v. *Puddo Monee Dossia*, 9 W. R., 349. But ryots are not necessarily of the same class, because they hold under a similar class of landlords. A ryot of a *ganteedar* is not on that account to pay more than the ryot of a zemindar—*Gouree Nauth Rai* v. *Ramgutty Chunder*, 12 W. R., 102.

Places adjacent. By the words "places adjacent" the Legislature did not intend that the rates with which the comparison was made should necessarily be those of the village or pergunnah in which the land was situated. It often happens that land lying in a different village, or a different pergunnah, affords a better guide than land situated within the limits of the same estate—*Dukhin Mohun Rai* v. *D'Abreau*, 1 Board's Rep., 167.

Increase in the value of the produce, or productive powers of the land. A claim to enhancement based on the increased productive power of the land, or on the increased value of its produce, can only take effect, in cases where the neighbouring rates of rent have not accommodated themselves to the altered state of circumstances, where in short, all the ryots together are paying less than a fair rate of rent; and to such cases the principle laid down in the Great Rent case would apply. But where there already exists a guide as to what is a fair rate of rent, and the suit is for enhancement on the ground of the prevailing rates, the principle will not apparently apply—*Sreeram Chatterjee* v. *Lakhan Magilla*, Marsh., 379. It would seem, therefore, that the procedure, which this clause provides, should only be resorted to when the old pergunnah rates have become obsolete, and a readjustment of the rent is requisite

The principle of proportion to be followed in adjusting obsolete rates. in consequence of a rise in the value of the produce. When such readjustment is made, it must be made on the principle of proportion; in other words, "the old rent must bear to the increased rent the same proportion as the former value of the produce of the soil, calculated on an average of three or five years next before the date of the alleged rise in value, bears to the present value." Per Trevor, J. "In my opinion," observed Mr. Justice Macpherson in the same case, "the rule of proportion—as the old value of the produce is to the old rent, so is the present value of the produce to the rent which ought now to be paid—is the rule which should be adopted in the absence of any recently adjusted pergunnah customary rates. In thus ascertaining the rate, we shall be ascertaining it on a principle similar to that on which the old pergunnah or customary rates were fixed. We shall be doing what was deemed fair and equitable in the case of ryots having a right of occupancy prior to Act X, and what is not less fair and equitable in the case of ryots having a right of occupancy under that Act. Let the zemindar, seeking to enhance the rent, go back to any year he chooses, and let him prove that the proportion was then more favorable to him than it has subsequently become. Either party should be at liberty, in each case, to prove any special circumstances tending to show that the application of the rule of proportion to that particular case would work injustice."—The Great Rent Case, *Thakooranee Dassee* v. *Bisheshur Mookerjee*, B. L. R., 1 Sup. vol., 202 ; 3 W. R. (Act X), 29. {SECTION 18.}

This rule of proportion applies only to cases in which the sole ground of enhancement is an increase in the value of the produce, and to cases in which the rates have not adjusted themselves to altered circumstances. It will not apply to cases where the value of the produce has increased, but where either the productive powers of the land have decreased, and the expenses of cultivation have also increased. In such cases the value of the present decreased average produce per bigah, calculated on the produce of three or five years, must be found : and it must be contrasted with the average value of the produce before the decrease in the productive power, calculated in the same way, and the increased present cost of production, as contrasted with the former cost per bigah, must be ascertained also. When these data are ascertained, the formula to be applied will stand thus :—The average value of the produce before the decrease in the productive powers of the land, will be to the average value of the present decreased produce, minus the increased cost of production, as the rent previously paid will be to that which the land ought now to pay—*Showdamonee Dassee* v. *Shookool Mahomed*, 7 W. R., 94. Nor is it applicable where the rates between the present value of the produce of the soil and the former value at the time of the original taking cannot be ascertained—*Jadub Chunder Haldar* v. *Etburry Lashkur*, 3 W. R. (Act X), 160. {When rule of proportion applies.}

The increase, however, in the value of the produce must be an increase "in its natural and usual value in ordinary years ; the accidental and exceptional high prices of a particular year in consequence of drought and scarcity, cannot be treated as a measure by which rent is to be adjusted. A tenant takes land, not with reference to the exceptional high prices of a past year, but with reference to the prices he may reasonably expect to realize for the crops he will raise in succeeding years"—*Bhagruth Dass* v. *Mohasoop Roy*, 6 W. R. (Act X), 34. The increase does not mean capacity for realizing a higher rent for buildings or other purposes, but an increase of the productive powers of the land itself—*Bissessur Chuckerbutty* v. *Woomachurn Roy*, 9 W. R., 122. Where a considerable portion of a town had been carried away by the Ganges, and the value of the land had consequently increased, it was held that a rise in the value of the land from such a cause was not an increase in the productive powers of the land as contemplated by this section—*Khoondkar Abdur Ruhman* v. *Wooma Chunder Roy*, 8 W. R., 330. {The increase in the value of the produce must be an increase in the natural and ordinary course.}

But it is not sufficient to show that the value of the produce or the productive power of the land has increased, the landlord must also show that the increase has been brought about "otherwise than by the agency or expense of the ryot." Where a ryot had dug a tank for public use, and the garden he rented had been rendered productive by the exertions and outlay of the tenants, the land was held liable to enhancement—*Sreeram Chatterjee* v. *Lakhan Magilla*, Marsh., 379. Again where tenants had held land for some twenty-five years at rents much below the prevailing rates, it was held· they were not entitled at the end of {The increase must have been brought about otherwise than by the agency or expense of the ryot.}

54 THE LAW OF LANDLORD AND TENANT.

SECTION 18. that time to plead the expenditure of their own capital labor as against the landlord's claim to enhanced rent—*Prosunno Coomar Paul Choudhry* v. *Radhanath Dey Choudhry*, 7 W. R., 97. But where the crops had been deficient in quantity, and, owing to the care and labor of the ryot, they had increased in value considerably above that of former years, the ryot was entitled to set off such against a suit for enhancement—*Showdaminee Dassee* v. *Hurrunchunder Surmah*, 6 W. R. (Act X), 103. And where the productive powers have increased by reason of the Government having erected an embankment, the land is liable to enhancement—*Jadub Chunder Haldar* v. *Etwaree Lushkur*, Marsh., 498. But where the tenant erects a distillery it is not so—*Brojonauth Kundu Choudhry* v. *Stewart*, 8 B. L. R., App., 51; 16 W. R., 216. When a defendant allows that the productive powers of the land have increased, it is still incumbent on the plaintiff to show that the agency, which effected the increase, was not that of the ryot. "When," observed the Chief Justice, "a defendant comes into Court, and the Court asks him, 'what do you say to the plaintiff's claim?' and he says, 'I admit that the productiveness has increased, but not otherwise than by my agency,' such an admission must be taken altogether. So it is in the case of a written statement. A written statement put in by a defendant is not a plea by way of confession and avoidance; it is a statement of the grounds of his defence, and he must verify the statement. If you read a man's answer, you must take the whole admission together. Taking the whole admission together in this case, the defendant says that 'the productiveness has increased, but not otherwise than by my agency,' and the plaintiff then has to prove his case. The general rule of evidence is, that, if in order to make out a title, it is necessary to prove a negative, the party who avers the title must prove the title. The plaintiff alleged the right to enhance on the ground that the productiveness had increased otherwise than by the agency of the ryot. I am of opinion, therefore, that the onus lay on the plaintiff to prove the ground of his right to enhance, namely, 'that the productiveness of the land had increased otherwise than by the agency of the ryot' "—*Poolin Beharee Sen* v. *Watson*, 9 W. R., 190.

A ryot who converts arable into orchard land, only liable for arable land rates.
Where a ryot had taken a lease of some land covered with jungle at a low rent, and had afterwards cleared the jungle and made the land into an orchard, it was held that the landlord could not enhance the rent to the rate paid for other orchards in the neighbourhood, inasmuch as the improvements had been effected by the exertion and at the cost of the tenant. It is not, of course, meant that a ryot who takes jungle land is to hold it for ever at jungle rates. When he simply brings jungle land into cultivation, he is liable, after a reasonable time, to pay the full pergunnah rates for cultivated land; but if the land which he originally received was not only uncultivated jungle, but in its then state impracticable for cultivation; if, for instance, it was salt land, which could only be made sweet by special works of the ryot, or rock, which could only be made culturable by special labor, then the ryot who made those works, or expended that labor, would be entitled to hold at exceptionally low rates. So again, if, having received ordinary land, and converted it into land of specially high value, he would only be liable to pay the ordinary rates paid for land of the same quality, irrespective of the special character impressed upon it by himself—*Choudhry Khan* v. *Gour Jana*, 2 W. R. (Act X), 40.

Under clause 3, landlords who have given leases to ryots, without SECTION 18. knowing the exact quantity of land which those leases covered, are enabled to measure and assess any excess land that may be found in their ryots' occupation. In a province, like Bengal, where so few estates have been regularly measured and surveyed, a landlord seldom knows the exact quantity of land which a ryot's holding contains. It is, therefore, absolutely necessary that landlords should from time to time measure their estates, and ascertain that their ryots are not occupying more land than they are paying rent for. In England, if a man holds land in excess of his lease he is, *quoad* the excess land, a trespasser, and must be treated as a trespasser, and not as a tenant; and this doctrine was strictly applied to tenures in this country. The tenant in that case held a certain quantity of land on a jumma of Rs. 5 under a *mokururee* pottah. The plaintiff asserted that the *mokururee* pottah included only 5 *khadas*, whereas the land upon measurement was found to be 8 *khadas:* and he, therefore, claimed rent for the excess 3 *khadas*. But the Chief Justice held that the suit would not lie. " If," observed his Lordship, " the defendant has been paying Rs. 5 rent for the 8 *khadas*, the case does not fall within the 3rd clause of this section, for the quantity of land held by him has not been proved by measurement to be greater than the quantity for which rent has been previously paid. If he has been paying the Rs. 5 for the 5 *khadas*, and nothing for the excess, he may be trespasser as to the excess, but he is not a tenant liable to assessment"—*Rashum Bebee* v. *Bissonauth Sircar*, 6 W. R. (Act X), 57, and this decision has been approved of and followed in *Prankissen Bagchee* v. *Monmohinee Dassee*, 17 W. R., 34, though it seems to have been differed from in *Binode Beharry Roy* v. *Masseyk*, 15. W. R., 493. But if there has been no express contract, a person holding lands in excess of those for which he pays rent need not necessarily be treated as a trespasser—*Sham Jha* v. *Doorga Roy*, 7 W. R., 122. But he can either be treated as a trespasser or can be sued for a kubooleut in respect of the excess lands—*David* v. *Ramdhun Chatterjee*, 6 W. R. (Act X), 97; *Rajmohun Mitter* v. *Gooroo Churn Aych*, 6 W. R. (Act X), 106. With regard to these points, the following has been said by Steer and Levinge, JJ. ". We think that though by the law of landlord and tenant, as applied in England, a person who takes and cultivates the lands of another, there being no express permission to cultivate on the side of the landlord, nor any express condition to pay rent on the part of the cultivator, would not be allowed to be regarded as a tenant, but treated as a mere trespasser, the peculiar circumstances of this country preclude the applicability of the technical doctrine of the English law of landlord and tenant to such a case. Here it is a very usual thing for a man to squat on a piece of land, or to take into cultivation an unoccupied or waste piece of land. Tenancy in a great many districts in Bengal commences in this way, and where it does so commence, it is presumed that the cultivator cultivates by permission of the landlord, and is under obligation to his landlord to pay him a fair rent, when the latter may choose to demand it. Thus, the established usage of the country regards these parties as landlord and tenant, and unless the landlord thus chooses to treat him, the cultivator is not regarded, as he would be by the law as administered in England, as a trespasser, but as a tenant; and he would be so,

56 THE LAW OF LANDLORD AND TENANT.

SECTION 18. although he may never have acknowledged the landlord's right, or entered into any express contract with him for the payment of rent. If he chooses to cultivate the zemindar's lands, and the zemindar lets him, there is an implied contract between them, creating a relationship of landlord and tenant"—*Nityanund Ghose* v. *Kissen Kishore*, W. R., 1864 (Act X), 82; 2 Board's Rep., 102. The mere fact of the jote having been held at an unvaried rent for twenty years, and on measurement having been found to be 125 bigahs instead of 102½ bigahs in respect of which the rent had been paid, does not preclude the tenant from the liability to pay for the excess—*Bibee Reazoonissa* v. *Shaikh Dad Ali*, 8 W. R., 326. The excess lands should be assessed at a fair and equitable rate, or where the defendant has held under a lease on the same terms as the other lands originally given under it—*Golam Ali* v. *Baboo Gopal Lal Thakoor*, 9 W. R., 65. This decision has been affirmed by the Privy Council, 19 W. R., 141, but nothing was said in the decision of the Privy Council as to this point. The existence of the alleged excess and the rate at which such excess land ought to be assessed must be proved—*Nubo Kishore Mundul* v. *Fakeer Puramanick*, 17 W. R., 558. It seems that a suit to assess rent upon land paying no rent at all is not a suit for enhancement of rent—*Baroda Kant Roy* v. *Radha Charan Roy*, 13 W. R., 163.

Where plaintiff fails to prove his case, suit must be dismissed.   A landlord, who has failed to show what the prevailing rate is, cannot ask the Court to give him a decree according to the rate which the defendant's witnesses admit the land will bear. There is no authority under Act X of 1859 to enhance the rent of a ryot to the rates which the land will bear; and, if plaintiff cannot prove the existence of his grounds of enhancement, the suit must be dismissed—*Jaun Ali* v. *Jan Ali*, 9 W. R., 149; *Juggessur Patty* v. *Ishan Chunder Ghose*, 20 W. R., 186; *Doma Roy* v. *Melon*, 20 W. R., 416. And where the suit is for enhancement, and the defendants set up a kubooleut, the Court cannot give a decree at the rate specified in the kubooleut, a suit to enhance being very different from a suit to recover arrears of rent at a rate originally fixed. A Privy Council case—*Soorasoonderee Debia* v. *Golam Ali*, 19 W.R., 141. See also *Jugessur Patty* v. *Ishan Chunder Ghose*, 20 W. R., 186. Nor can a decree be given at the ordinary rate—*Huronauth Roy* v. *Gobin Chunder Dutt*, 6 W. R. (Act X), 2. In the same way a Court cannot decree what it may consider to be fair and equitable rates, when the plaintiff merely asks for a decree at the prevailing rates. The Court must find specifically whether the rate claimed by the plaintiff is actually paid by the neighbouring ryots of the same class for similar, or what rate is so paid and decide accordingly—*Pelaram Kotal* v. *Nundcoomar Chuttoram*, 6 W. R. (Act X), 45. So where the plaintiff sues under this section, he is bound to prove the alleged rate he claims, and, on his failing to do so, the Court is not obliged to order an ameen to measure the lands to fix the rates—*Khola Mundel* v. *Piroo Sircar*, 6 W. R. (Act X), 18. But if a plaintiff sues on two separate grounds, and fails to prove one, he can have a decree in respect of the other—*Ram Kant Chuckerbutty* v. *Rajah Mohesh Chunder Singh*, 7 W. R., 172. See also *Bonmallee Churn Mytee* v. *Shooroop Hootait*, 14 W. R., 61.

A dur-izaradar can enhance.   A dur-izaradar can enhance the rents of an estate of which he holds a sub-lease—*Gunga Ram Bearer* v. *Ujoodhyaram Mytee*, 2 W. R. (Act X), 158.

THE LAW OF LANDLORD AND TENANT. 57

XIX. Every ryot having a right of occupancy shall be entitled to claim an abatement of the rent previously paid by him, if the area of the land has been diminished by diluvion or otherwise, or if the value of the produce or the productive powers of the land have been decreased by any cause beyond the power of the ryot, or if the quantity of land held by the ryot has been proved by measurement to be less than the quantity for which rent has been previously paid by him.

SECTION 19.

When ryot may claim abatement of rent.

Act X, 1859, section 18.

"Sections 18 and 19," it has been observed, "were passed for the benefit of the ryot, and not for the protection of the zemindar. Section 18 says that no ryot having a right of occupancy shall be liable to an enhancement of rent, except upon some one of the grounds therein specified; but section 19 is differently worded. It enacts that any ryot having a right of occupancy shall be entitled to claim an abatement of rent in any of the three cases mentioned therein, but it does not say that he shall not be entitled to an abatement upon any other grounds. Section 18 was to protect him from enhancement; and section 19 was intended to give him a right to abatement in certain cases, but not to protect the zemindar from liability to make abatement in any other case." Thus, where the jumma of a resumed *lakhiraj* estate had been reduced by Government on the condition that the rents of the ryots should be reduced in the same proportion, it was held that the ryots were entitled to the benefit of the stipulation made by Government on their behalf at the time when the jumma was reduced. It was, however, added that the right of abatement in this case only applied to the case of rents, of which the amounts had been fixed before the jumma was reduced by Government: and not to rents fixed by pottahs or kabuliats subsequently entered into—*Sukhawatoolah* v. *Puthoo Goldar*, 1 Ind. Jur., O. S., 7.

The ryot is not restricted to the grounds of abatement mentioned in this section.

The grounds of abatement, which are expressly recognized by this section, are:—

1*st.*—Diminution of area by diluvion or otherwise.

2*nd.*—A decrease in the value of the produce, or the productive powers of the land arising from causes beyond the ryot's control.

3*rd.*—When the quantity of land held by the ryot has been ascertained to be less than the quantity for which rent has been previously paid.

With regard to the first ground of abatement, a ryot whose land has diluviated has three courses open to him. He may either sue under this section for abatement of rent; or he may wait until sued by his landlord, and plead that he is entitled to a certain reduction on account of the diluviated land—*Afsurooddeen* v. *Mussamut Shorooshee Bula Dabee*, Marsh., 558; or he may complain of an excessive demand of rent, and sue for a refund of the sum which has been exacted from him. When a ryot had been compelled to pay an excess rent for 1265 of Rs. 99, for 1266 of Rs. 199, for 1267 of Rs. 195, for 1268 of

When area is diminished by diluvion, ryot can either sue for abatement;

or may sue for a refund of the excess taken from him;

9

58 THE LAW OF LANDLORD AND TENANT.

SECTION 19.

Rs. 1,126, in all Rs. 1,617, and sued the zemindar to recover the excess, it was held that the suit was not barred by limitation under section 30, Act X, 1859. "No doubt," observed the Court, "when a diluvion took place, the plaintiff had a right of suit to obtain an abatement of his jumma, if the zemindar had refused to grant such abatement. But he was not bound to sue for that purpose. He was not actually injured until compelled to pay the rent named in the pottah without the allowance of the abatement he claimed. Upon that payment having been extorted from him, he had a new right of action; and, as the suit would appear to have been brought within one year from that date, we think it was in time"—*Barry* v. *Abdool Ali*, W. R. (1864), 64; 2 Board's Rep., 85; *Raja Nilmani Singh* v. *Annadaprosad Mookerjee*, 1 B. L. R., F. B., 97; 10 W. R., F. B., 41.

or may set up the fact of a diminution in answer to a claim for arrears of rent.

Where, however, a ryot instead of suing for abatement waits until an action for arrears of rent has been brought against him by his landlord, and then claims a deduction on the ground of diluvion, the whole onus lies upon him of proving the extent of the deduction to which he is entitled, and of showing precisely what lands have disappeared. The zemindar, in proving that full rent has always been paid, has proved a sufficient *prima facie* case, which it is for the tenant to rebut—*Savi* v. *Obhoy Nath Bose*, 2 W. R. (Act X), 28. An occupancy-ryot is, however, entitled to abatement when the area of his holding has been reduced not only by diluvion, but by other causes also. Thus, when a portion of a ryot's land had been taken up by Government for a road, it was held that he was entitled to a deduction of rent from the zemindar for the land taken from him—*Din Doyal Lal* v. *Mussamut Thukroo Konwar*, 6 W. R. (Act X), 24; see also *Maharaja Dheraj Mahtab Chand Bahadoor* v. *Chittro Coomare Bebee*, 16 W. R., 201.

Other causes which entitle a ryot to an abatement. Land taken up by Government for a road.

Dispossession through defect of lessor's title.

In another case, where a tenant, after obtaining a lease for a certain quantity of land, was evicted from a portion of it, owing to the defective title of his lessor, it was held that he was entitled to an abatement of rent. "When a landlord," observed the Court, "leases any portion of land without any further stipulation with regard to the title, he does thereby impliedly undertake that he has sufficient title to support the lease, and he guarantees the tenant quiet possession and enjoyment. This is the result of the law of England, and we believe that it has always been held to be the same here"—*Brojonath Paul Chowdry* v. *Heera Lall Paul*, 1 B. L. R., A. C., 87; 10 W. R., 120. When once it is determined that a tenant is entitled to an abatement of rent, in consequence of the subject of the demise having been diminished, the only thing that requires to be settled is, what was the portion of the original rent which was referable to the portion of the tenure which has disappeared. If there is nothing in the pottah to show that the rent was apportioned in parcels to the different parts of the whole land, the only way to arrive at a conclusion as to how much of the whole rent is fairly attributable to this particular portion, is to deal with it as a matter of proportion,—that is, such a sum ought to be deducted from the whole rent as would bear to that whole rent the same proportion, as the annual value of the portion of the land that has disappeared bears to the annual value of the land originally leased.—*Id.,* 121.

Principle upon which the abatement is to be made.

This section only applies to occupancy-ryots, but all ryots and under-tenants, whether they have a right of occupancy or not, can claim an abatement of rent, if they can show that they are entitled to it on principles of natural justice and equity. Section 23, Act X, 1859, clause 3, conferred upon Collectors power to take cognizance of "all claims to abatement," whether preferred by occupancy-ryots, farmers, or under-tenants; and a Full Bench of the High Court has held that a suit for remission of rent, brought by a *putneedar* on the ground that certain portions of land included in his *putnee* had been resumed as *chakeran* by Government, would lie against the zemindar under Act X, 1859. "It is clear," observed the Court, "that a *putneedar* can be sued by the zemindar for rent under the 4th clause (1) of section 23, and it would be most inconvenient and unreasonable, and indeed would be at variance with the plain meaning of the words 'all claims to abatement of rent' in the 3rd clause, to hold that he is compelled to go to another Court to claim an abatement of his rent"— *Horo Kishen Banerjee* v. *Joy Kissen Mookerjee*, 1 W. R., 299. In the same way a howladar can sue for abatement—*Komlakant Doss* v. *Pogose*, 2 W. R. (Act X), 65. In another case a talookdar claimed an abatement of rent on the ground that a portion of his talook had been washed away by a river; and the question arose whether he was entitled to claim a diminution of rent on this account. The Court, however, held that he was so entitled, *unless there was an express stipulation that he should pay, whether the land was washed away or not*. "If a man," observed the Chief Justice, " stipulates to pay rent, it is clear he engages to pay it as a compensation for the use of the land rented; and independently of section 18 (2), we are of opinion that, according to the ordinary rules of law, if a talookdar agrees to pay a certain amount of rent, the tenant is exempt from the payment of the whole rent if the whole of the land be washed away, or of a portion of the rent if a portion only be washed away. According to English law, a tenant is entitled to abatement in proportion to the quantity of land washed away, and he is entitled to that abatement in a suit brought by the landlord for arrears of rent"—*Afsurooddeen* v. *Mussamut Shorooshee Bula Dabee*, Marsh., 558. This question was further discussed in a subsequent case, in which the tenant claimed an abatement, upon the ground that part of his land had been washed away, and that a part of it had been covered with sand. " We think," observed the Chief Justice, " upon principles of natural justice and equity, that, if a landlord lets his land at a certain rent, to be paid during the period of occupation, and the land is, by the act of God, put in such a state that the tenant cannot enjoy, the tenant is entitled to an abatement. The first question then is, whether there was any stipulation in the kabuliat, which precluded the tenant from claiming an abatement, if, by the act of God, any portion of his land was washed away? If it is found that, according to an express stipulation in the kabuliat, the tenant is not entitled to any abatement by reason of any part of the land being washed away by the act of God,

Sidenotes: SECTION 19. Any ryot or under-tenant can sue for abatement, though not under this section; If any part of the land leased has been resumed by Government through defect of the lessor's title; or if damage has been caused to the land demised by the act of God.

---

(1) Clause 4, section 23, Act X, 1859, was as follows:—" All suits for arrears of rent due on account of land, whether *kherajees* or *lakhiraj*, or on account of any rights of pasturage, forest rights, fisheries, or the like." This section is omitted from the present Act; but under section 33, all suits which were cognizable by a Collector under Act X, are now cognizable by the Civil Court under this Act.
(2) Section 19 of this Act.

SECTION 20. then the tenant is not entitled to abatement during the term of that lease. But it is said the lease is at an end; but we think then, when a tenant holds on after the expiration of the lease, he does so on the terms of the lease, at the same rent, and on the same stipulations as are mentioned in the lease, until the parties come to a fresh settlement. With regard to the land alleged to have been covered with sand, the Judge of the first Court will have to enquire if that portion was covered with sand, and thereby deteriorated or rendered wholly useless; because if the land has been deteriorated or rendered wholly useless, by the act of God, the tenant will be entitled to an abatement, provided there was no stipulation to the contrary in the kabuliat"—*Sheik Enayut Ulla* v. *Sheikh Elaheebuksh*, W. R., 1864 (Act X), 42 ; 2 Board's Rep., 62. At the same time, no ryot can claim abatement unless the depreciation in the value of the land has resulted from causes beyond his control—*Munsoor Ali* v. *Harvey*, 11 W. R., 291.

Fraud.

Fraud on the part of a lessor does not constitute a valid ground for abatement. Thus, where a zemindar gave out an estate in *putnee*, but concealed the existence of an intermediate under-tenure, the Court held that the *putneedar* was not entitled to an abatement of rent. In other words, that though the plaintiff might sue to be relieved of his contract, he could not sue for abatement under this section—*Shokoor Ali* v. *Umola Ahalya*, 8 W. R., 504.

Zemindars cannot sue Government for abatement.

It is, perhaps, almost needless to observe, that zemindars are not entitled to claim an abatement of rent from Government on account of diluvion, or any other cause, as the power of altering the public assessment is not vested by the Regulations in the Civil Courts of Judicature, but is reserved exclusively to the Executive Government—*Bhowanee Prosad Chuckerbutty* v. *Mussumat Coroona Mye*, 2 Sel. Rep., 242, and Sudder Dewanny Rep. for 1852, page 1094.

Act X, 1859, section 19.

Relinquishment of land by ryot after notice given.

XX. Any ryot, who desires to relinquish the land held or cultivated by him, shall be at liberty to do so, provided he gives notice of his intention, in writing, to the person entitled to the rent of the land or his authorized agent, in districts or parts of districts where the Fuslee year prevails, in or before the month of Jeyt, and in districts or parts of districts where the Bengallee year prevails, in or before the month of Pous, of the year preceding that in which the relinquishment is to have effect. If he fail to give such notice, and the land is not let to any other person, he shall continue liable for the rent of the land. If the person entitled to the rent of the land, or his agent, refuse to receive any such notice, and to sign a receipt for the same, the ryot may make an application on plain paper to the Collector in whose jurisdiction the lands are situate, who shall thereupon cause the notice to be served on such person or his agent in the manner provided in Section 14.

THE LAW OF LANDLORD AND TENANT. 61

This section does not apply to cases where the ryot has entered into SECTION 20. a lease for a specific term; where, for instance, a ryot had taken a lease, Section does not it was decided he could not relinquish his holding during the currency apply to ryots of the lease—*Kashee Singh* v. *Onraet*, 5 W. R. (Act X), 80; *Tilak* with lease. *Patak* v. *Mahabir Panday*, 7 B. L. R., App., 11; 15 W. R., 454; *Baboo Dwarka Doss* v. *Gopal Doss*, 1 Agra Rev. Ap., 22.

The notice to the landlord must, of course, be followed by relinquish- Notice, unless ment of the land. It is the relinquishment of the land, and not the relinquish-notice, which relieves the ryot from liability—*Nobin Chunder Rai* v. ment, is invalid. *Luckee Prea Dabee*, 1 W. R., 20; 2 Board's Rep., 200. The notice is not in what cases required by law to be in writing; but a verbal notice of relinquishment sufficient. is sufficient, provided that the landlord shows by his acts, by leasing out, for instance, the land to another tenant, that he has accepted the relinquishment—*Mahomed Gazee* v. *Shunker Lall*, 11 W. R., 53. Where a cultivating ryot, without giving notice, went away from the land he had occupied, and neither cultivated nor paid rent for it, it was held that the landlord was justified in assuming that he had relinquished it; and that the tenant had no right to ask to be reinstated in possession Absconding on the ground that he had not formally relinquished it—*Muneeruddeen* v. of ryot tan-tamount to *Mahomed Ali*, 6 W. R., 67. In the same way, where one of two relinquishment. joint tenants abandoned the holding, and left his co-sharer to cultivate the land and pay the rent, it was held that he had relinquished the land, and was not entitled to ask to be readmitted into possession— *Nuddea Chand Poddar* v. *Modhoo Soodhun Day Poddar*, 7 W. R., 153; *Haro Das* v. *Gobind Bhuttacharjee*, 3 B. L. R., App., 23; 12 W. R., 304. But the non-cultivation of a small portion of an ancestral jote by the admitted holders for one year, owing to their minority, does not amount to relinquishment—*Radha Madhub Pal* v. *Kalee Churn Pal*, 18 W. R., 41. The mere fact, however, of a tenant relinquishing his land, will not excuse him from the payment of rent, if he is otherwise liable to pay— *Cazee Syud Mahomed Agmul* v. *Chundee Lall Pandey*, 7 W. R., 250. And when a tenant who holds land for a term underlets it, he cannot determine the interest of his tenant by surrendering the term to the landlord—*Heeramonee* v. *Gunganarain Roy*, 10 W. R., 384. A tenancy from year to year does not *ipso facto* terminate at the end of the year—*Malodee Nashyo* v. *Bullubee Kant Dhur*, 13 W. R., 190.

This section does not imperatively require an application for service Service of notice of notice of relinquishment of land by a ryot to be made to the by Collector. Collector. The non-service of notice by the Collector cannot affect the rights of the tenant, if he can prove that, previous to his application to the Collector, he had given actual notice directly to the landlord himself, or to his authorized agent. The time referred to in the section has reference to the service of the original notice which the tenant is required to give without the intervention of the Collector—*Erskine* v. *Ram Coomar Roy*, 8 W. R., 221.

This section does not contemplate the relinquishment of part of a The relinquish-holding. A relinquishment to be valid must be of the entire holding— a holding not *Saroda Soondaree Dabya* v. *Hazee Mahomed Mundul*, 5 W. R. (Act permitted. X), 78.

In the case of a cultivating ryot, the notice of relinquishment Stamp on notice. can be written on plain paper, Act XVIII, 1869, section 15, clause 11;

SECTION 21. but in other cases a stamp of the following value is necessary under Schedule 1, No. 20 :—

(a.) When the amount of stamp-duty chargeable on the lease does not exceed Rs. 16. } The stamp-duty with which the lease is chargeable.

(b.) In any other case ... Rs. 16.

Act X, 1859, section 20.

What to be deemed an arrear of rent under this Act.

XXI. Any instalment of rent which is not paid on or before the day when the same is payable according to the pottah or engagement, or if there be no written specification of the time of payment, at or before the time when such instalment is payable according to established usage, shall be held to be an arrear of rent under this Act, and, unless otherwise provided by written agreement, shall be liable to interest at twelve per centum per annum.

Discretionary power vested in Courts to award interest on arrears of rent.

Instalments of rent not paid on the day they fall due are *liable* to interest at 12 per cent. per annum. The law, it will be observed, does not say that the unpaid instalments shall *bear* interest, but that they shall be *liable* to interest. By using the word "liable" the Legislature evidently intended to leave the Court a discretionary power of awarding interest or not. The obligation is not absolute—*Beckwith* v. *Kisto Jeebun Buxshee*, Marsh., 278 ; *Kasheenath Roy Chowdry* v. *Mynuddeen Chowdry*, 1 W. R., 154 ; *Rajah Sattyanand Ghosal* v. *Zahir Sikdar*, 6 B. L. R., App., 119; *Maharajah Dheraj Mahtab Chund* v. *Srimati Debkummare Debi*, 7 B. L. R., App., 26; *Radhika Prosunno Chunder* v. *Urjoon Majhee*, 20 W. R., 128. The Court also has a discretionary power to award interest from such date as it thinks proper—*Moharanee Inderjeet Kooer* v. *Khwajah Abul Hossein Khan*, 2 Board's Rep., 210. But, under ordinary circumstances, a landlord is entitled to interest unless the tenant can show that he has either paid, or tendered payment of his rent. As a debtor has to seek out his creditor and pay what is due, so a tenant must not wait till the rent is demanded of him, but must go to his landlord, and pay it on the day that it falls due—*Ranee Shurut Soondaree Dabya* v. *The Collector of Mymensingh*, 5 W. R. (Act X), 69. If a landlord does not claim interest as it falls due, but accepts sums due on account of principal on successive dates, and for a series of years, without making any demand for interest and without applying any of the sums paid to the discharge of the interest, the Court will be justified in holding that all claim to interest has been waived—*Dindoyal Pramanik* v. *Prankissen Paul Chowdhry*, Marsh., 394. But interest can under no circumstances be awarded where the plaintiff has obtained damages under section 44 ; for such damages are given in lieu of interest, and can only be decreed in addition to *rent* and *costs*—*Nobo Kanto Dey* v. *Rajah Barodakanth Roy*, 1 W. R., 100.

The tenant is bound to tender payment.

Waiver of interest.

Interest not awardable in addition to damages.

Meaning of "established usage."

"The established usage" means the established usage in the pergunnah, not the established usage between the parties—*Chytunno Chunder Roy* v. *Kedernath Roy*, 14 W. R., 99.

XXII. When an arrear of rent remains due from any ryot at the end of the Bengalee year, or at the end of the month of Jeyt of the Fuslee or Willayuttee year, as the case may be, such ryot shall be liable to be ejected from the land in respect of which the arrear is due : provided that no ryot having a right of occupancy, or holding under a pottah the term of which has not expired, shall be ejected otherwise than in execution of a decree or order under the provisions of this Act.

Sections 22 & 23.
Liability of ryot to be ejected for arrear due.
Act X, 1859, section 21.

A ryot cannot be ejected, under this section, for an instalment of rent which falls due in the middle of the year. The right to eject for non-payment accrues only when an arrear remains due at the end of the Bengalee year, or at the end of the month of Jeyt of the Fuslee or Willayuttee year, as the case may be—*Savi* v. *Chand Sirkar*, Marsh., 348; *Sreeram Biswas* v. *Juggernath Dass Mohunt*, 1 Ind. Jur., 187; 5 W. R. (Act X), 45. And under no circumstances can a landlord, who has received the rent of a subsequent year, eject a ryot on the ground that the rent of a previous year is due. A landlord having distrained for, and received the rent for 1268, then brought an action to recover the rent due for 1267, and to eject the tenant from the land ; but the Court held that the receipt of rent for 1268 barred the landlord's right to eject. "The receipt of rent for 1268," observed the Chief Justice, "had the same effect as if the plaintiff had at the commencement of 1268 created a new tenancy. If he had done so, it is clear that the defendant could not be ejected for non-payment of rent for 1267. So, if the plaintiff had obtained judgment in this suit to oust the defendant for the non-payment of rent for 1267, and had afterwards, instead of executing the judgment, allowed the defendant to continue in possession, and pay rent for 1268, it would have been a bar to his afterwards executing the judgment"—*Sheik Peer Bux* v. *Mouzah Ally*, Marsh., 25.

A ryot not liable to ejectment for arrears due in the middle of the year.

The receipt of rent of a subsequent year bars ejectment for arrears of previous year.

The liability of a holder of a *mokurruree istemraree ijarah* is to be determined by the conditions of his lease, and not by this section— *Mohunt Buloram Doss* v. *Jogendro Nath Mullick*, 19 W. R., 349.

Holder of mokurruree ijarah not under this section.

If a landlord eject a ryot of his own authority and without the intervention of a Court of law, he comes within section 15 of Act XIV of 1859, and the ryot can sue him under that section—*Jonardun Acharjee* v. *Haradhun Acharjee*, 9 W. R., 513.

Remedy in case of unlawful ejectment.

XXIII. When an arrear of rent shall be adjudged to be due from any farmer or other lease-holder not having a permanent or transferable interest in the land, the lease of such lease-holder shall be liable to be cancelled, and the lease-holder to be ejected : provided that no such lease shall be cancelled, nor the lease-holder ejected, otherwise

Act X, 1859, section 22.
Liability of farmer to have his lease cancelled for arrear adjudged due.

Proviso.

64   THE LAW OF LANDLORD AND TENANT.

SECTION 23.
than in execution of a decree or order under the provisions of this Act.

Application of section.
This section applies to farmers and other lease-holders who have not permanent or transferable interests in the land, and renders them liable to cancelment of their leases, or to ejectment for arrears of rent only. The right, therefore, need not be provided for in the lease—*Kadir Gazee* v. *Mahadebee Dossia*, 6 W. R. (Act X), 48. The section gives the landlord no right to eject for breach of any other conditions of the lease. The lease, therefore, must expressly stipulate that a breach in its conditions will be followed by ejectment; otherwise the landlord will have no right of re-entry, but must content himself with an action for damages. Thus, where a zemindar brought an action to eject an indigo planter for the breach of a stipulation in his lease, whereby the planter undertook to give up such part of the land as should be unfit for indigo, and not to sublet the same, it was held that the action would not lie. "We think," observed Peacock, C.J., "that the suit is one which would lie under Act X, 1859, if there had been a breach of a condition by which the ryot was liable to ejectment. Clause 5, section 25, Act X, 1859, provides for such a case. But in this case, although there was a stipulation, that the defendant should give up such part of the land as was unfit for the cultivation of indigo, and should not sublet the same, there was no stipulation that the tenant should be liable to ejectment for a breach of that stipulation. The defendant, therefore, was not liable to ejectment for a breach of that contract; even if it had been proved that a breach had been committed, he would have been liable only to a suit for damages"—*Goorooprosad Sirkar* v. *Philippe*, Marsh., 366; *Augur Singh* v. *Mohinee Dutt Singh*, 2 W. R. (Act X), 101.

No suit after arrears received.
The landlord cannot, after having obtained a decree and realized the arrears due, sue for ejectment—*Woomesh Chunder Chatterjee* v. *Shaikh Kumurooddeen Lushkur*, 7 W. R., 20.

Equitable relief in cases of forfeiture.
Section 52 provides that ejectment for non-payment of rent shall not be permitted if the total amount due is paid within fifteen days after the passing of the decree. That section, however, only applies to cases in which a lease becomes liable to be cancelled for non-payment of rent: it does not apply to cases in which landlords are entitled to re-enter for the breach of other conditions. In such cases it has been held that the Court must decide according to the contract between the parties, and must adjudge ejectment if the penalties of forfeiture have been incurred—*Ram Coomar Bhuttarcharjea* v. *Ram Coomar Sein*, 7 W. R., 132.

Courts will not adjudge forfeiture, if substantial relief can otherwise be granted.
The Courts, however, will not adjudge the penalty of forfeiture, if substantial justice can otherwise be done. "Cases of forfeiture," observed Mr. Justice Trevor, "are not favored when no injury has resulted; and in cases in which the injury can be estimated and compensated in money, our Courts have followed the doctrine of English Courts of Equity,—a doctrine which, in the matter of forfeiture for the non-payment of rent, has been recognized by the local Legislature, and have given relief; when, looking to the original intent of the parties in the case, it could give all that a party could in reason desire or expect. In the case before the Court, the intent of the lessor in demanding, and the lessee in giving, security, was simply to secure the punctual payment of the rent secured. This can be obtained by a decree short of an

absolute one for forfeiture, namely, by a decree for forfeiture, unless, **SECTION 24.** within fifteen days from the date of this decree, security equal to that withdrawn be replaced. By a decree of this nature the plaintiff will obtain all that he can in reason expect, and the relief, which has been sanctioned by the Legislature in analogous cases, will be extended to a class of cases falling within the same principle and requiring therefore the same mode of treatment"—*Alum Chunder Shah* v. *Moran & Co.*, 2 Board's Rep., 52.

Where a lease for a definite term contains a stipulation that the lease shall be forfeited on the breach of certain conditions, and the tenant holds over after the lease has expired, he is still bound by the conditions of his lease, and will be liable to ejectment if those conditions are broken—*Hari Prosonno Rai* v. *Bhugwan Chunder Panda*, 1 Board's Rep., 21. It may be suggested, however, that the mere fact of a tenant holding over after the expiry will not necessarily render him bound by the conditions of the lease, but much will depend upon the position of the parties, and their intention as gathered from the facts of the case. But, of course, a landlord may show by his actions that he has waived the conditions of the lease, and in such cases the right of forfeiture cannot be revived. The holder of a *putnee* tenure granted a *durputnee* of the same, and took a kabuliat from the tenant, in which it was stipulated that the landlord should have the right of re-entry, in case any arrears of rent remained unpaid within a month after the close of the year. The *durputneedar* defaulted, and the *putneedar*, instead of suing for possession on account of the breach of the condition, sued the *durputneedar* for arrears and in execution of his decree put up the tenure for sale. It was sold and purchased for Rs. 8,000. The purchaser was not called upon to execute any engagement; the rent was received from him in the usual way, and he was recognized as the holder of the *durputnee*. After a time the purchaser defaulted, and the *putneedar* then sued him for arrears of rent, and claimed to put in force against him the forfeiture clause of the old kabuliat, and to take khas possession of the *durputnee*. But the Court held that the right of forfeiture had been waived. "It is clear," observed the Court, "that the plaintiff might have acted upon the kabuliat against the old tenant who gave it; but having then waived his right of re-entry, he cannot in law" (that is, after selling the tenure in the ordinary manner prescribed by the law), "consider that engagement as a subsisting one between himself and the new purchaser"—*Deen Dyal Paramanick* v. *Juggeshur Roy*, Marsh., 252.

A tenant holding over is bound by the conditions of forfeiture contained in the lease.

Unless they have been waived by the landlord.

Where the parties stipulated that, on non-payment of any one of the instalments of rent, a sezawal should be appointed to collect the rents, and one was subsequently appointed, it was held that the appointment of such sezawal did not determine the lease, and that the defendant was liable for the deficiency in rent after the sezawul's collections were credited—*Fakiruddin Mahomed Ahason* v. *Phillipps*, 3 B. L. R., App., 53; 11 W. R., 464.

Appointment of sezawul does not determine lease.

XXIV. All suits which under the provisions of this Act may be brought by or against zemindars or other persons in the receipt of the rent of land, may be brought by or against surburakars or tehseeldars of

Act X, 1859, section 29.

Suits by or against surburakars or tehseeldars of estates held khas.

SECTION 25. estates held under khas management, whether such estates are the property of Government or of individuals.

Act VI (B. C.), 1862, section 9.

Proprietor's right to survey and measure his estates.

XXV. Every proprietor of an estate or tenure, or other person in receipt of the rents of an estate or tenure, has the right of making a general survey and measurement of the lands comprised in such estate or tenure, or any part thereof, unless restrained from doing so by express engagement with the occupants of the lands.

Can a proprietor not in receipt of the rents measure?

It is an open question whether a proprietor not in receipt of the rents of the estate is entitled to measure. It was held in one case, by Norman and Seton-Karr, JJ., that "the expression *in receipt of the rents*," overrides both the prior members of the sentence, and extends not only "to other persons, but also to the proprietor of the estate or tenure"—*Wise v. Ram Chunder Bysack*, 7 W. R., 415. The authority, however, of this decision was questioned in a subsequent case, Mitter, J., observing that "a man, who is the admitted proprietor of a mehal, is not bound to show that he is in actual receipt of the rents at the time when he applies to measure the land. The words 'in receipt of the rents' have no reference to the first part of the section, *i.e.*, to the words 'proprietors of tenures and estates;' but to the words 'other persons,' *i.e.*, other than those who are admittedly the proprietors of the tenure within which the lands are situated"—*Ranee Krishto Monee Debia v. Ram Nidhee Sircar*, 9 W. R., 331. By a proprietor, however, is meant a proprietor in possession. A proprietor who is not in possession of the property is not entitled to measure the land—*Pureejan Khetoon v. Bykunt Chunder Chuckerubtty*, 7 W. R., 96. "The words *any proprietor*," observed Peacock, C.J., "*or other person in receipt of the rents*, show that the proprietor who claims to measure must be a proprietor in possession, and not a proprietor out of possession, although he may be able to prove his title;" and should, therefore, a person's right to measure be disputed by an intervenor, the only question for the Court to try is, which of the two is in possession—*Kalee Doss Nundee v. Ramguttee Dutt Sein*, 6 W. R. (Act X), 10. The section is intended to provide for cases, where a proprietor or other person in possession of an estate, is opposed in making measurement by the occupants of the land, and not for cases where the title of the person claiming the right to measure is a matter in contest—*Durga Charan Mazumdar v. Mahomed Abbas Bhuya*, 6 B. L. R., 361; 14 W. R., 399. It is not, however, necessary that the proprietor should prove that he has actually received the rents of the estate; a proprietor who can show that he is in undoubted possession of the property is entitled to measure, whether he has previously received the rents of the estate or not—*Raj Chunder Rai v. Kishen Chunder*, 4 W. R. (Act X.), 16. The Court will refuse its assistance to a zemindar seeking its aid when such aid is solicited simply with a view to harass and oppress the tenant—*Dwarkanath Chuckerbutty v. Bhowanee Kishore Chuckerbutty*, 8 W. R., 11. With these restrictions every proprietor has the indisputable right of measuring his estate, unless restrained from doing so by express engagements with the occupants of the land—*Kebul Kishen*

A proprietor not in possession cannot measure.

Dass v. *Jaminee*, 5 W. R. (Act X), 47 ; *Ooma Churn Biswas* v. *Shibnath* SECTION 26. *Bagchee*, 8 W. R., 15.

The right to measure exists, whatever may be the nature of the subordinate tenures within the estate, and whether the rents of such tenures are fixed or not. This question was much discussed in the case of *Run Bahadoor Sing* v. *Muloorun Tewaree*, when Peacock, C.J., observed as follows:—"The plaintiff in this case is a proprietor of an estate, because he pays rent to Government. The defendant is not a proprietor within that definition. He is entitled to hold the land at a fixed rent. That does not prevent the plaintiff from having a right to measure it.......If he has the right given to him by law, he has a right to enforce that right, without being bound to state his reasons for enforcing it. If the defendant holds at a fixed rent, the plaintiff has a right to measure the land; if the rent is liable to be enhanced, the plaintiff has still a right to measure"—8 W. R., 149; *Tweedie* v. *Ram Narain Dass*, 9 W. R., 151.

The right to measure not affected by the land having been let out on fixed leases.

It is perhaps hardly necessary to observe that this section gives a zemindar no power to measure *lakhiraj* land. The zemindar's right of measurement merely extends to the rent-paying land comprised within the estate—*Prosunno Moyee Debia* v. *Chundernath Chowdry*, 10 W. R., 361; *Gholam Khejur* v. *Erskine*, 11 W. R., 445; *Ranglal Sahu* v. *Siali Dhar*, 3 B. L. R., App., 27; 11 W. R., 293. The rights which are possessed under this section by a proprietor of an estate, can be exercised by any lessee or under-tenant who is in receipt of the rents of the estate—*Watson and Co.* v. *Bhoonya Koonwur Narain Singh*, W. R., 1864 (Act X), 105 ; 2 Board's Rep., 151.

But zemindar cannot measure lakhiraj land.

XXVI. All dependent talookdars and other persons possessing a permanent transferable interest in land, intermediate between the zemindar and the cultivator, are required to register, in the sheristah of the zemindar or superior tenant, to whom the rents of their talooks or tenures are payable, all transfers of such talooks or tenures, or portions of them, by sale, gift, or otherwise, as well as all successions thereto, and divisions among heirs in cases of inheritance. And every zemindar or superior tenant is required to admit to registry and otherwise give effect to all such transfers when made in good faith, and all such successions and divisions: Provided that no zemindar or superior tenant shall be required to admit to registry or give effect to any division or distribution of the rent payable on account of any such tenure, nor shall any such division or distribution of rent be valid and binding without the consent in writing of the zemindar or superior tenant.

Act X, 1859, section 27.

Registry of transfers of talookdars, &c.

There are three classes of ryots recognized by the law:—*First.*—The cultivating or occupying ryot, whom the zemindar can eject under section 22, if default is made in the payment of the rent. *Secondly.*—

A transferable ryottee tenure, though virtually intermediate, need not be registered.

SECTION 26. Temporary lease-holders, whose leases are liable to be cancelled under section 23 for the same cause. *Thirdly.*—The holders of permanent and transferable tenures intermediate between the zemindar and the cultivator, whose tenures can be sold for arrears of rent, but not cancelled. It is this latter class of tenures which have to be registered under this section. It is necessary, therefore, to keep these distinctions in view, because doubts often arise as to whether a tenure is liable to registration or not: and this is a question which involves very important considerations. This may be illustrated by quoting the following case:—A zemindar sued a tenant for arrears of rent, and in execution of the decree sold the tenure. A third party then came forward, and sued for the cancelment of the sale, on the ground that he, and not the person against whom the decree had been given, was in lawful possession of the land. The zemindar took a preliminary objection, under section 106, Act X, 1859 (1), that the plaintiff had no ground of action, as the transfer of the under-tenure to him from the former under-tenant had not been registered. The Court, however, overruled the plea, on the ground that the tenure was a *mokurruree jote*, or ryotee tenure, and one therefore which it was not necessary to register. It was admitted that the land was not in the plaintiff's own occupation, but had been sublet to under-tenants; but the Court held that this did not make the plaintiff an intermediate holder, as subletting did not alter the nature of a tenure which was ryottee in its inception, and they therefore cancelled the sale, and restored the plaintiff to possession—*Karoo Lall Thakoor* v. *Luchmeeput Doogar*, 7 W. R., 15; to the same effect is *Wooma Churn Sett* v. *Haree Pershad Misser*, 1 B. L. R., S. N., 7; 10 W. R., 101. For a tenant is not at liberty to create an intermediate estate between himself and the landlord—*Hureehur Mookerjee* v. *Jodoonath Ghose*, 7 W. R., 114 (2).

No express penalty provided for non-registration.

Registration is as much for the benefit of the tenant as of the landlord, and it is perhaps on this account that no express penalty is attached to non-registration. "The only object," observed Markby, J., "of the provision appears to have been that the zemindar might have information as to who was his tenant. It is true, that no express penalty for omission to register is provided; but I cannot assume that because the Legislature has not expressly provided a penalty, therefore, this severe one of forfeiture was intended"—*Nobin Kishen Mookerjee* v. *Shib Pershad Pattuck*, 8 W. R., 96.

Zemindar need not recognize transfer.

Where a transfer has been made, the zemindar need not necessarily recognize it. "The current of decisions on this point," says Bayley, J., "has uniformly been that a zemindar is not bound to recognize any transfer in regard to which application has not been made to have such transfer registered in the zemindaree sheristah, unless it can be proved that the zemindar has not only known of the transfer, but has also *accepted* the transferree as his tenant; and the receipt of rent by the zemindar after such transfer has been held as one of the best proofs of the fact that of a zemindar having so accepted the transferree—*Sarkies* v.

---

(1) Section 63 of this Act.

(2) With reference to this, Mr. Bell says that, "in the Backergunge Districts, it was a matter of every-day occurrence for ryots at variance with their landlords to transfer their holdings in what was called "Zimba" to a neighbouring zemindar, thus interposing the neighbouring zemindar between themselves and their own landlord."

Kali Coomar Roy, W. R., 1864 (Act X), 98. He need not even SECTION 26. recognize a transfer where the lessee's interest is transferable, if in so doing he defeats his own right of re-entry—*Nund Kishore Singh* v. *Ranee Ismed Kooer*, 20 W. R., 189. He is not in fact bound to recognize any transfer made without his knowledge and consent, and which is unregistered, and it is sufficient for him to bring his suit against the party from whom he receives rent or whose name is recorded in his sheristah—*Huree Churn Bose* v. *Meharoonissa Bibee*, 7 W. R., 318; *Sadhun Churn Bose* v. *Gooroo Churn Bose*, 15 W. R., 99; *Kasheenath Punee* v. *Luchmonee Pershad*, 19 W. R., 99.

Any improper transfer, however, does not deprive the old surburakar Effect of improper transfer. of his rights, or entitle the zemindar to get khas possession—*Kasheenath Punee* v. *Lukhmonee Pershad Patnaik*, 19 W. R., 99. But the transferree has no legal status as against the zemindar until the transfer has been registered; and, if ejected from his holding, "he cannot sue the zemindar, for possession, until he has himself been recognized as tenant, or has been registered as such in the zemindar's sherishtah"— *Mookta Keshee Dossia* v. *Pearee Chowdhrain*, 7 W. R., 158. It must be borne in mind also that the transfer of his tenure by a *putneedar* is not binding on the zemindar unless made strictly in accordance with the provisions of Regulation VIII of 1819—*Watson* v. *Collector of Rajshaye*, 13 Moo. I. A., 160; 3 B. L. R., P. C., 48; 12 W. R., P. C., 43.

A zemindar is not bound to give effect to any subdivision of a No division of tenure previously registered as undivided—*Watson and Co.* v. *Ram* tenure without consent of zemindar. *Soonder Panday*, 3 W. R. (Act X), 165; *Upendra Mohan Tagore* v. *Thanda Dasi*, 3 B. L. R., A. C., 349; 12 W. R., 263. If, however, the zemindar practically recognizes the division, it is not necessary that there should be any consent in writing on his part—*Nubo Kishen Mookerjee* v. *Sreeram Roy*, 15 W. R., 255. The section refers to divisions and distributions made after Act X of 1859 came into operation—*Allender* v. *Dwarkanath Roy*, 15 W. R., 321.

Where, however, a landlord has recognized a transfer by receiving Recognition by rent from the transferree, he cannot, although the transfer has not been landlord supplies the place of registered in his sheristah, go back and sue the old tenant; but must registration. proceed against the transferree whom he has recognized as his tenant— *Nobo Coomar Ghose* v. *Kishen Chunder Bonnerjee*, 2 Board's Rep., 165. As such receipt of rent amounts to a recognition of the transfer— *Mrityun Jaya Sirkar* v. *Gopal Chandra Sirkar*, 2 B. L. R., A. C., 131; 10 W. R., 466; *Bharut Roy* v. *Gunga Narain Mohapattur*, 14 W. R., 211; *Dhunput Singh Roy Bahadur* v. *Vellayet Ali*, 15 W. R., 211; *Allender* v. *Dwarkanath Roy*, 15 W. R., 320; *Meah Jan Munshi* v. *Kurrunamayi Debi*, 8 B. L. R., 1. In the same way, where a zemindar has brought a tenure to sale for arrears of rent, he cannot proceed against the old tenant for arrears which have become due since the sale, he must proceed against the purchaser, although the sale may not have been registered in his sheristah—*Gopeekisto Gosamee* v. *Ram Comul Misry*, Marsh., 212.

As to whether, in the case of a *benamee* transaction, the landlord is When lease has been taken entitled to proceed against the *benameedar*, or against the person benamee, the landlord beneficially entitled, there seems some conflict of opinion, the majority lord may sue real of the Judges apparently holding that the landlord may proceed against tenant. the persons really in possession — *Bepin Behary Choudhry* v. *Ram*

70   THE LAW OF LANDLORD AND TENANT.

SECTION 27. *Chandra Roy*, 5 B. L. R., 235; 14 W. R., 12. The cases on this point, however, were decided under Act X of 1859, and turn more or less on the question of the jurisdiction of the Revenue Courts. It may be said that the law is thus stated by Peacock, C.J., in *Rajkishore Mozoomdar* v. *Heeralall Bukshee*, Marsh., 188. " In determining this case, it was necessary to try whether Heeralall was the real proprietor, and whether Roopchand was merely his agent. The Judge had power to determine that question, and has found that the lease was *benamee*, and that Heeralall was the actual farmer and the person beneficially interested in it. That being so, we are of opinion that Heeralall, as the real proprietor, was liable for the arrears of rent. It is a general rule of English law, that where an agent enters into a contract in his own name as principal, without disclosing the fact that he is merely acting as agent, the principal, when discovered, is liable to be sued upon the contract. But the principal is not liable upon the contract of his agent, if the other party to the contract, with full knowledge of the facts, and having the power and means of deciding to whom he will give credit, elects to give credit to the agent in his individual character." A similar view was taken in the Full Bench case of *Prosonno Coomar Paul Choudhry* v. *Koylash Chunder Paul Choudhry*, 2 Ind. Jur., 327; 8 W. R., 428.

Rights of unregistered transferree.
Although the sale of an under-tenure has not been recognized by the landlord as registered, it must not be assumed that the purchaser has no right as connected with the property, for a *bonâ fide* purchaser at an execution-sale may even, though his name be not registered in the zemindar's sheristah, sue for a declaration of title and possession—*Hurrish Chunder Mookerjee* v. *Annund Chunder Chatterjee*, 9 W. R., 279. The facts of this last case do not seem very clear. Again a transferree of an under-tenure is a person sufficiently interested in the protection of the tenure to stop its sale, even though the transfer has not been registered—*Khetter Paul Singh* v. *Luckhee Narian Mitter*, 15 W. R., 125; *Anand Lall Mookerjee* v. *Kalika Persaud Nissa*, 20 W. R., 59.

Suit lies to compel registration.
When a zemindar refuses to register a transfer, the tenant's remedy is by action in the Civil Court, and the decree of the Court will supersede the necessity of registration; but under no circumstances need a landlord register the subdivision of a holding—*Watson and Co.* v. *Ram Soonder Panday*, 3 W. R. (Act X), 165. And the limitation will run from the time of such refusal and not from the time of the purchase —*Radhika Pershad Sadhoo* v. *Gooroo Prosunno Roy*, 20 W. R., 125. Of course, a holding can be subdivided with the zemindar's consent; and it has been held that a farmer, who is confessedly authorized to receive the surrender of a holding, can likewise sanction the subdivision of a holding, and that this sanction, in the absence of fraud and collusion, will be binding upon the zemindar—*Huree Mohun Mookerjee* v. *Gora Chand Mitter*, 2 W. R. (Act X), 25. But before a suit can be brought to compel registration, the transferree must make a formal application to the landlord to register—*Bhooputee Roy* v. *Umbika Churn Banerjee*, 17 W. R., 169.

Act X of 1859, section 30.
Limitation of certain suits.

XXVII.   All suits instituted for the recovery of damages on account of the illegal exaction of rent or of any unauthorized cess or impost, or on account of the

refusal of receipts for rent paid, or on account of the SECTION 28.
extortion of rent by confinement or other duress, or on
account of the excessive demand of rent, and all suits for
abatement of rent, and all suits to eject any ryot or to
cancel any lease on account of the non-payment of arrears
of rent, or of the breach of the conditions of any contract
by which a ryot may be liable to be ejected, or a lease
may be liable to be cancelled, and all suits to recover the
occupancy of any land, farm, or tenure from which a ryot,
farmer, or tenant has been illegally ejected by the person
entitled to receive rent for the same, and all suits arising
out of the exercise of the power of distraint for arrears
of rent conferred on zemindars and others, by this or
any other Act or out of any acts done under color of
the exercise of the said power, shall be commenced
within the period of one year from the date of the
accruing of the cause of action, and not afterwards.

The limitation laid down by this and the four following sections is Saving of limitation not affected by Act IX of 1871 (The Indian Limitation Act), as this Act. section 6 of that Act expressly saves the limitation prescribed by any Act not thereby specially repealed.

The "one year" referred to in this section must be calculated accord- "One year" to be ing to the British calendar—*Khasro Mandar* v. *Premlal*, 9 B. L. R., tish calendar. App., 41 ; 18 W. R., 403.

It seems that a suit against an ijaradar, entitled to the rents, can be Illegal ejectment. brought under this section by a ryot who has been illegally ejected—*Mussamut Gobind Monee* v. *Rajendro Kishore Chowdhry*, 15 W. R., 18; and so can a suit against a zemindar so long as he has ejected illegally, even though his right to eject may be good and he might have succeeded had he proceeded legally—*Gunga Gobind Roy* v. *Kala Chund Surma*, 20 W. R., 455. And a superior holder who dispossesses a ryot is liable not merely for the profit which he makes by letting out the land, but to make good the loss which the ryot sustains by being dispossessed—*Huruck Lall Shaha* v. *Sreenibash Kurmokar*, 15 W. R., 428.

When matters in dispute have been referred to arbitration, and one party refuses to submit to the award, a new cause of action different from any of those mentioned in this section arises—*Raj Narain Roy* v. *Muddoo Soodun Mookerjee*, 20 W. R., 19.

In 1857 the plaintiff gave a lease of a garden to defendant who agreed to plant within five years from the date thereof 2,000 betel-nut trees. The defendant failed to do so. In 1867 the plaintiff brought a suit for ejectment, on account of the breach of the contract entered into by the defendant. Held that, under this section, the suit was barred—*Kali Kamal Mazumdar* v. *Shib Suhai Sukul*, 3 B. L. R., App., 47 ; 11 W. R., 452.

XXVIII. Suits for the delivery of pottahs or kabuliats, Act X, 1859, section 31.
Limitation of suits for and for the determination of the rates grant of pottahs, &c. of rent at which such pottahs or

72   THE LAW OF LANDLORD AND TENANT.

SECTION 29. kabuliats are to be delivered, may be instituted at any time during the tenancy.

A suit for a kabuliat may be brought without previous notice of enhancement at any time during tenancy—*Brae* v. *Kumal Shaha*, 4 W. R. (Act X), 5. The words "during the tenancy" implying that the position of tenant has already been determined—*Muhesh Dutt Pandey* v. *Seetul Sonar*, 1 All., 506.

Act X of 1859, section 32.

XXIX. Suits for the recovery of arrears of rent shall be instituted within three years, from the last day of the Bengal year, or from the last day of the month of Jeyt of the Fuslee or Willayuttee year, in which the arrear claimed shall have become due : Provided that if the suit be for the recovery of rent at a higher rate than was payable in the previous year, such rent having been enhanced after issue of notice under Section 13 of Act X of 1859, or under Section 14 of this Act; and the enhancement not having been confirmed by any competent Court, the suit shall be instituted within three months from the end of the Bengal year, or of the month of Jeyt of the Fuslee or Willayuttee year, on account of which such enhanced rent is claimed.

Limitation of suits for arrears of rent.

Section not affected by Limitation Act.

It has already been stated that the provisions as regards limitation laid down in this section are not affected by the Indian Limitation Act of 1871. It was also held formerly that the provisions of the old Limitation Act (Act XIV of 1859) did not apply to cases under the corresponding section of Act X of 1859—*Poulson* v. *Modoosoodun Paul Choudry*, 2 W. R. (Act X), 21. And it was consequently further decided that no deduction of time will be allowed even to a person who has *bonâ fide* prosecuted his suit in a wrong Court—*Modhoosoodun Moozumdar* v. *Brojonath Koond Choudhry*, 5 W. R. (Act X), 44. Nor on account of the minority or other legal disability of the plaintiff. "It can hardly be supposed," observed Peacock, C.J., "that the Legislature, in passing Act XIV, 1859, would have introduced into it provisions as to disability affecting the limitation clauses of Act X, 1859, which had not been introduced into that Act when it was passed. It could scarcely have been the intention of the Legislature, that, if a person was an infant at the time his rent became due to him, he should be allowed three years after the attainment of his majority, for the purpose of suing his ryots for rent due, inasmuch as such a provision would in some cases give him a right to sue for his rents eighteen or twenty years after they became due"—*Dinonath Panday* v. *Roghoonath Panday*, 5 W. R. (Act X), 41. It seems, however, that under certain circumstances a deduction of time may be allowed in accordance with a decision of the Privy Council. Ranee Shorno Moye brought to sale, under Regulation VIII of 1819, a *putnee* for arrears of rent due in 1857. The *putnee* was sold : the arrears were paid out of the purchase-money, and the purchaser was put into possession. A suit was then

No deduction of time allowed for minority, &c.

Where tenure is sold for arrears of rent and the sale is reversed, the arrears are held to accrue from reversal of sale.

brought to set aside the sale of this *putnee* talook on the ground of irregularity. The lower Court decreed the suit, and cancelled the sale on the 26th December 1860, and this decision was upheld by the High Court on appeal on the 30th June 1863. The effect of this judgment was that the Ranee had to pay back the purchase-money to the purchaser, and the *putneedar* recovered possession of his talook with mesne profits. The Ranee then brought a suit for the arrears of 1857, which she had realized from the purchase-money, but which on the cancellation of the sale she had been compelled to refund. Her suit was, however, dismissed on the ground that it was barred by section 32 of Act X, 1859 (section 29 of the Act), as the suit should have been brought within three years from the time the arrears first became due. The result of this decision was that the Ranee was deprived of her rent for 1857, and the *putneedar* got back his *putnee*, and at the same time relieved himself from the obligation of paying the rent due for that year. Their Lordships, however, thought that, "upon the fair construction of section 32, the time had really not run; that upon the setting aside of the sale, and the restoration of the parties to possession, they took back the estate, subject to the obligation to pay the rent; and that the particular arrears of rent claimed in this action must be taken to have become due in the year in which that restoration to possession took place; and that the appellant was therefore not barred from her remedy"—*Ranee Shornomoyee* v. *Shooshee Mokhee Burmonia*, 12 Moo. I. A., 242; 3 B. L. R., P. C., 11; 11 W. R., P. C., 5. The result of this decision seems to be that, so long as a plaintiff is *bonâ fide* engaged in prosecuting or resisting suits as to rights without which he would be unable to sue, his right cannot be considered to have come into existence, until such litigation has ceased, the decision having frequently been followed by the High Court of Calcutta—*Eshan Chunder Roy* v. *Khajah Asanoollah*, 8 B. L. R., 537 (Note); 16 W. R., 79; *Dindoyal Paramanik* v. *Radha Kishori Debi*, 8 B. L. R., 536; 17 W. R., 415; *Mohesh Chunder Chakladar* v. *Gunga Monee Dossee*, 18 W. R., 59; *Huronauth Roy Choudhry* v. *Golucknauth Choudhry*, 19 W. R., 18.

SECTION 29.

An arrear of rent is not due within the meaning of this section until the rent itself has been determined—*Komul Lochun Roy* v. *Moran and Co.*, 2 W. R. (Act X), 83. So, where an enhanced rent is fixed or determined for the first time after the expiration of the year in respect of which the rent is claimed, such rent becomes due *as from a passed date*, so as to enable the landlord to sue within three years from the end of the year in which the arrears would, if the rent had been previously fixed, have become due—*Joy Monee Dossee* v. *Huronath Roy*, 2 W. R. (Act X), 51. Before the repeal of Act X of 1859, it was possible for a landlord, who had obtained a decree for enhancement, to sue under section 30 of that Act for arrears of rent within one year from the date when the rent was finally settled by the decree on the suit for enhancement—*Joy Monee Dossee* v. *Hurronath Roy*, 2 W. R. (Act X), 51; *Madhub Chunder Ghose* v. *Radhika Chowdhrain*, 6 W. R. (Act X), 42.

Rent must be certain before suit for arrears will lie.

A declaratory decree does not, however, constitute a cause of action; and limitation runs from the date the rent fell due, and not from the date on which the declaratory decree was given. Thus, where a plaintiff in 1857 brought an action for the declaration of his right to enhance, and in 1864 obtained a decree, declaring that he was entitled to

Declaratory decree not a cause of action.

74   THE LAW OF LANDLORD AND TENANT.

SECTION 29. a certain enhanced rent, it was held that he could not then sue to recover the arrears at the enhanced rate which had accrued during the pendency of the suit. "The non-payment of the rent at the enhanced rates," observed Peacock, C.J., in delivering the judgment of the Full Bench, "and not the declaration of a Civil Court that the plaintiff had a right to enhance was the cause of action. The action for that cause might have been brought if the decree had never existed. A suit for arrears of rent at an enhanced rate may be brought after notice without first obtaining a decree in a declaratory suit that the plaintiff has a right to enhance............Parties are often put to much unnecessary expense and delay by these declaratory suits. There was no necessity in this case to bring a suit for a declaration of the right to enhance; at least, the arrears might have been sued for without such suit or a decree pronounced upon it"—*Doyamoyee Chowdrainee* v. *Bholanauth Ghose*, 6 W. R. (Act X), 77.

Dismissal of initiative suit by ryot voids proviso.
Where a ryot brings a suit to contest a notice of enhancement on the ground that he is a *mokurrureedar* holding under a pottah, such suit is a sufficient confirmation of the enhancement to take a subsequent suit for arrears of rent at the enhanced rate out of the operation of the proviso in this section—*Puddo Lochun Bhadooree* v. *Chunder Nauth Roy*, 5 W. R. (Act X), 51; 1 Ind. Jur., 170. But another case seems contrary to this, where it was held that a landlord's suit for rent at an enhanced rate according to notice was barred notwithstanding that a previous suit by a ryot contesting a notice of enhancement on the ground that he had paid rent at a uniform rate had been dismissed—*Huree Kishore Ghose* v. *Koomodinee Kant Banerjee*, 10 W. R., 41.

Miscellaneous.
A suit for arrears of rent, following a decree for a kabuliat, cannot date back further than the date of the decree for such kabuliat—*Jan Ali* v. *Gooroo Dass Roy*, 8 W. R., 338.

In a suit for arrears of rent a claim for abatement may be made by way of set-off in respect of land taken up by Government—*Deen Doyal Lall* v. *Mussamut Thakroo Koonwar*, 6 W. R. (Act X), 24.

Where plaintiff sued for arrears of rent and made his co-sharers *proformâ* defendants, it was held that such fact did not alter the real nature of this suit which was under the provision of this section—*Gunga Gobind Sen* v. *Gobind Chunder Doss*, 11 B. L. R., App., 31; 19 W. R., 347.

Under this section the rent of any portion of one year is recoverable at any time up to the last day of the third year after its close—*Bykunt Ram Roy* v. *Mussamut Shoorfoonissa Begum*, 15 W. R., 523. The object of the section being to fix the maximum period of time within which suits for arrears at enhanced rates ought to be brought, and not to create a bar to the institution of such suits before the expiration of the year on account of which the arrears are claimed—*Tarumonee Debia* v. *Joykisto Mookerjee*, 20 W. R., 329.

A suit of rent derivable by a lessor from tolls collected by the lessee from person resorting to an hût is not cognizable under this Act—*Savi* v. *Issurchunder Mundel*, 20 W. R., 146.

Omission to pay rent for 12 years does not constitute an adverse possession.
A landlord's right of action against his tenant for rent is one, it must be remembered, of yearly occurrence; and the tenant cannot consequently plead adverse possession against his landlord, simply because he may have omitted to pay his rent. "So long," observed Mr. Justice Markby, "as the relation of landlord and tenant exists, the mere omission by the tenant to pay his rent does not constitute an

THE LAW OF LANDLORD AND TENANT. 75

adverse possession, and the statute of limitation has no application— SECTION 30.
Troylucko Tarenee Dossia v. *Mohima Chunder Muttuck,* 7 W. R., 400. If,
however, a tenant openly sets up an adverse title, and holds adversely,
limitation runs—*Huronath Roy* v. *Jogender Chunder Roy,* 6 W. R., 218.

XXX. Suits for the recovery of money in the hands Act X, 1859, section 33.
Limitation of suits against agents for money, papers, or accounts. of an agent, or for the delivery of accounts or papers by an agent, may be brought at any time during the agency or within one year after the determination of the agency of such agent: Provided that if the person having the right to sue shall, by means of fraud, have been kept from the knowledge of the receipt of any such money by the agent, or if any fraudulent account shall have been rendered by the agent, the suit may be brought within one year from the time when the fraud shall have been first known to such person: but no such suit shall in any case be brought at any time exceeding three years from the termination of the agency.

This section is a transcript of section 33, Act X, 1859; but section 24 Meaning of "agent." of that enactment explained who these agents were. Section 24 was as follows :—"Suits by zemindars and others in receipt of the rent of land against any agents employed by them in the management of land or collection of rents, or the sureties of such agents, for money received or accounts kept by such agents in the course of such employment, or for papers in their possession, shall be cognizable by the Collectors, and shall be instituted and tried under the provisions of this Act, and shall not be cognizable in any other Court except in the way of appeal as provided in this Act." Section 33 of Act X, 1859, merely prescribed the limitation for suits instituted under section 24: and there could therefore be no doubt that the agents referred to "were agents employed by landholders in the management of land or collection of rents;" but section 24 which defined the meaning of the word agent, has been omitted from the present Act. There can be no doubt that naibs or gomastas specially authorized by writing are agents under this section. The word agent is by section 182 of the Indian Contract Act (Act IX of 1872) defined to be "a person employed to do any act for another, or to represent another in dealings with third persons." By section 186, the authority of agent may be expressed or implied. By section 187, an authority is said to be implied "when it is to be inferred from the circumstances of the case; and things spoken or written, or the ordinary course of dealings, may be accounted circumstances of the case." And by section 188, an agent having authority to carry on a business "has authority to do every lawful thing necessary for the purpose or usually done in the course of conducting such business." The law of agency is dealt with in Chapter 10 of the Contract Act.

Section 30.
The powers of agents.

With regard to an agent's power, it is, of course, obvious that, so far as the agent's authority extends, the landlord or principal is bound by all acts done in pursuance of that authority. So far there can be no doubt or difficulty whatever. The cases in which doubts and difficulties arise are those in which the agent has gone beyond his authority, and done some act which his instructions did not authorize; and then the question arises whether the principal shall or shall not be bound by it. As a general rule, an agent, employed in the management of land or the collection of rents, is armed with all the authority of the landlord in the discharge of the ordinary duties of his office. He can sign notices of enhancement, such notices being within the scope of the ordinary duties of a naib — *Digumber Mitter* v. *Gobindo Chunder Haldar*, Marsh., 354.

Cannot grant leases unless specially authorized.

There is, however, one well recognized restriction upon his authority: he cannot grant leases unless specially authorized by his landlord to do so. This restriction is imposed not only by the custom of the country, but by law. Regulation VIII, 1793, section 59, is as follows:—"No farmer, without special permission from the proprietor of the lands, shall grant a pottah extending beyond the period of his own lease; nor shall any agent grant a pottah without authority from the proprietor"—See *Golucknonee Debea* v. *Assimoodeen*, 1 W. R., 56; *Ooma Tara Debea* v. *Peena Bibee*, 2 W. R., 155; *Kali Coomar Das* v. *Sheikh Anees*, 3 W. R. (Act X), 1; *Unoda Pershad Banerjee* v. *Chunder Shekur Deb*, 7 W. R., 394; *Kenny* v. *Mookta Soonderee Debea*, 7 W. R., 419.

Limitation in suits against agents.

Suits brought under this section may be brought at any time during the agency, or within one year after the determination of agency, and the question when the agency is determined will probably now have to be decided according to sections 201—210 of the Indian Contract Act (IX of 1872).

Fraud.

In cases of fraud the cause of action arises from the date on which the plaintiff, using due diligence, became aware of the fraud. If the plaintiff omits, through mere negligence, to inform himself from accounts in his possession, that is his own *laches*. But if the accounts are falsified, or not rendered, that is a fraud on the agent's part. And even if the accounts are rendered, the plaintiff is entitled to such a time as

Principal must use due diligence in discovering the fraud.

would, with ordinary diligence, enable him to discover the fraud, and the cause of action would arise from such discovery—*Ramkant Chowdry* v. *Brojomohun Mozumdar*, 6 W. R. (Act X), 20; *Radha Kishore Roy* v. *Ameer Chunder Mookhoty*, 20 W. R., 386. But the landlord must use due diligence, for, as observed by Markby, J., in another case, "the Legislature never intended by this section that a man who did not take the trouble to look after his own interests, and carelessly chose to let accounts lie for a long period of time uninvestigated, could at any time after many years suddenly take up the accounts, examine them, and say in answer to any question of limitation, that he had not discovered the fraud until he chose to make the investigation. It is clear that the Legislature only intended to give the benefit of the extended period to a man who showed reasonable diligence in the investigation of his accounts"—*Dhunput Sing Doogar* v. *Rahman Mandal*, 2 B. L. R., A. C., 269; 11 W. R., 163; see also *Biddell* v. *Chuttardharee Lall*, 12 W. R., 116. When an agent renders his accounts, the zemindar has the means of finding out the fraud, and, under such circumstances, the suit must be brought within one year from the time when the accounts were rendered—*Mackintosh* v. *Womesh Chunder Bose*, 3 W. R. (Act X), 121. The word "any such money" clearly shows that the proviso relates to suits for money, and under that proviso, where a fraudulent account has been given in by the agent concealing the fact of the receipt of certain moneys, the zemindar has one year from the discovery of the fraud to bring a suit for such money—*Jan Ali Chowdry* v. *Ishan Chunder Sein*, 16 W. R., 149.

SECTIONS 31 & 32.

XXXI. Whenever a deposit on account of rent shall have been made under the provisions of this Act, or of Act VI of 1862, passed by the Lieutenant-Governor of Bengal in Council, no suit shall be brought against the person making the deposit, or his representatives, on account of any rent which accrued due prior to the date of the deposit, unless such suit be instituted within six months from the date of the service of the notice in Section 5 of the said Act VI of 1862, or in Section 47 of this Act mentioned.

Act VI. (B. C.), 1862, section 6.

Suit for further balance to be instituted within six months of service of notice of deposit.

It will be observed that a suit for arrears of rent, which accrued due prior to the deposit, must be brought within six months from the date of the *service* of the notice; that is to say, from the date on which the landlord received intimation that the deposit had been made. It must be presumed until shown to the contrary that notice was issued and duly served—*Bejoy Gobind Singh* v. *Karoo Singh*, 18 W. R., 531. And the notice must be in the form set out in Schedule B of this Act, if it omits any of the words used in such schedule, such omission is fatal to the claim—*Kunchun Molla Dossea* v. *Rajendro Chunder Roy Choudhry*, 18 W. R., 126. The deposit which is contemplated by this section is a deposit after the rents have *become due;* a tenant, who deposited rent before it became due, would not be entitled to claim the benefit of the special limitation prescribed by this section—*Tara Monee Koonwaree* v. *Jeebun Mundur*, 6 W. R. (Act X), 99. Where a zemindar had sold a *putnee* for arrears of rent, due in 1224, Mughee, the *putneedar* sued for the reversal of the sale, and deposited the rent for 1225. The sale was reversed, and the zemindar then sued for the rent of 1224, and was met with the objection that the suit should have been brought within six months from the date of the deposit of the rent of 1225. But the High Court held that this section did not apply, and that the zemindar was entitled to recover, as he had brought his suit within the three years allowed by law—*Sheikh Mohamed Shuhurroollah* v. *Mussamut Roomya Bibee*, 7 W. R., 487.

Deposit to be made after the rent has become due.

Notice must be in form of Schedule B.

Effect of reversal of sale after deposit.

XXXII. Every Naib or Gomashtah thereto specially authorised by any writing under the hand of his employer, shall, for the purposes of all suits for any of the causes of action mentioned in Sections 27, 28, 29, or 30 of this Act, be deemed to be the

Naibs or Gomashtahs to be deemed, in certain cases, authorised agents under Act VIII of 1859.

SECTIONS 33 & 34. recognised agent of such employer within the meaning of Section 13 of the said Act VIII of 1859, though such employer may be within the jurisdiction of the Court in which such Naib or Gomashtah may appear or make any application.

General power of attorney. Under the present Stamp Law, Act XVIII of 1869, Schedule 2, Art. 32, a general power of attorney requires a stamp of Rs. 8.

Suit to be brought in the name of the principal. A gomashtah cannot sue in his own name; he must sue in the name and on behalf of his employer; for no man can be plaintiff except the person or persons who have the right to recover. The only effect of this section is to enable the person who is employed in the collection of rents to do that as agent, which would otherwise have to be done by the plaintiff in person—*Moodhoo Soodun Singh* v. *Moran & Co.,* 11 W. R., 43. A duly appointed gomashtah can sue, not only for rents which fell due after his incumbency, but for rents which fell due before his appointment. He stands, in fact, in precisely the same position with respect to arrears of rent which accrued during the time of his predecessors, as he does with respect to rents which accrued during his own time—*Ib.*, 44.

XXXIII. From and after the time when this Act *Cognizance of suits under this Act.* shall commence and take effect in any place, the jurisdiction, save as regards any suits or proceedings then pending, of the Collectorate Courts in such place, under Act X of 1859 of the Governor-General in Council, and Act VI of 1862 of the Council of the Lieutenant-Governor of Bengal, to entertain suits, shall cease, and all suits brought for any cause of action arising under either of those Acts or this Act shall, from such time and in such place, be cognizable by the Civil Courts according to their several jurisdictions.

By Act III of 1870, B. C., certain suits and proceedings then pending in the Revenue Courts were transferred to the Civil Courts.

XXXIV. Save as in this Act is otherwise provided, *Proceedings to be regulated under Code of Civil Procedure.* suits of every description brought for any cause of action arising under this Act, and all proceedings therein shall be regulated by the Code of Civil Procedure passed by the Governor-General in Council, being Act No. VIII of 1859, and by such further and other enactments of the Governor-General in Council in relation to Civil Procedure as now are, or from time to time may be in force; and all the provisions of the said Act and of such other enactments shall apply to such suits.

Section 119 of the Civil Procedure Code (Act VIII of 1859) is made applicable to rent suits under the Act by this section—*Mussamat Drabamayi Gupta* v. *Taracharan Sen,* 7 B. L. R., 207; 16 W. R., 17.

SECTIONS 35—37.

XXXV. The cause of action in suits brought for the delivery of any pottah or kabuliat, or for the cancelment of any lease for the determination of rates of rent, for illegal exactions of rent, cess, or impost, for refusal of receipts for rent paid, for extortion of rent, for excessive demand of rent, for abatement of rent, for arrears of rent, and for refusing to register transfers, successions, or divisions under Section 26, shall be deemed to have arisen within the jurisdiction of the Court, which would have had jurisdiction to entertain a suit for the recovery of the land, or other immoveable property in relation to which the cause of action arose, and shall be brought in such Court and in no other Court.

Jurisdiction in certain suits.

Section 119 of Civil Procedure Code made applicable to rent suits.

XXXVI. If the land which, by the provisions of the next preceding Section, determines the place in which the cause of action in the suits in the said Section mentioned shall be deemed to have arisen, be situate within the jurisdiction of different Courts, the provisions of Sections 11 and 12 of the said Act VIII of 1859 shall apply to such suits, as if the same had been suits for the recovery of such land.

Provision when cause of action arises in different jurisdictions.

The suits which are enumerated in section 35, so far as the jurisdiction of the Courts are concerned, will be treated as suits for lands or other immoveable property; but all other descriptions of suits under this Act, must, as provided by section 5, Act VIII, 1859, be brought in the Court within the jurisdiction of which the cause of action shall have arisen, or within the jurisdiction of which the defendant at the time of the commencement of the suit shall dwell, or personally work for gain. With respect to the general question of the jurisdiction of the Civil Courts, see Broughton's Civil Procedure Code, 4th Ed., p. 41.

XXXVII. If any person, intending to measure any land which he has a right to measure, is opposed in making such measurement by the occupant of the land; or if any under-tenant or ryot, having received notice of the intended measurement of land held or cultivated by him, which is liable to such measurement, refuses to attend and point out such land, the person claiming

Proceedings in case of opposition made to the measurement of land.

Act VI (B. C.), 1862, section 9.

80   THE LAW OF LANDLORD AND TENANT.

SECTION 38. the right to measure such land may apply to establish his right to measure such land, in the Court which would have jurisdiction in case such suit had been brought for the recovery of such land, and such Court shall hear and determine the right to make such measurement, and, if the case shall so require, shall make an order enjoining or excusing the attendance of any such under-tenant or ryot. If any under-tenant or ryot, after the issue of an order enjoining his attendance, neglects to attend and to point out the land, it shall not be competent to him to contest the correctness of the measurement made, or any of the proceedings held, in his absence.

Separate application for each ryot not necessary. This section must be read in connection with section 25, which declares that proprietors generally are entitled to make a measurement and general survey of their property, unless restrained from doing so by express agreement with the occupants of the land. A single suit simply to measure lands may be brought under this section against several defendants although their rights and tenures are different—*Shushee Bhoosun Banerjee* v. *Nubo Coomar Chatterjee*, 8 W. R., 94.

A shareholder of joint estate cannot sue alone. A shareholder in a joint undivided estate cannot bring a suit under this section for the measurement of his share—*Santiram Panja* v. *Bycunt Panja*, 10 B. L. R., 397; 19 W. R., 280; *Pearee Mohun Mookerjee* v. *Rajkristo Mookerjee*, 20 W. R., 385.

Jurisdiction. The jurisdiction in this section means local, as well as pecuniary jurisdiction—*Pearee Mohun Mookerjee* v. *Rajkristo Mookerjee*, 20 W. R., 385.

Miscellaneous. The Court must be careful to satisfy itself before granting its aid under this section that the zemindar's motive is *bonâ fide* and is not to oppress the ryots—*Dwarkanauth Chuckerbutty* v. *Bhowanee Kishore Chuckerbutty*, 8 W. R., 11.

A ryot who refuses to attend and point out his land, is declared to be incompetent of afterwards contesting the correctness of the measurement, or any of the proceedings held in his absence: but he would not be bound by such measurement, unless notice had been duly served upon him under this section—*Jadub Chunder Halder* v. *Etwaree Lushkur*, Marsh., 498; 1 Board's Rep., 143.

An appeal from an order of a lower Appellate Court on an application under this section may be admitted on a six anna stamp—*Puriag Bhuggut* v. *Donzelle*, 14 W. R., 21.

Act VI (B. C.) 1862, section 10.
Measurement of land when it cannot be ascertained, who are the persons liable to pay rent.

XXXVIII. If the proprietor of an estate or tenure, or other person entitled to receive the rents of an estate or tenure, is unable to measure the lands comprised in such estate or tenure, or any part thereof, by reason that he cannot ascertain who are the persons liable to pay rent in respect of the lands, or any part of the lands comprised therein, such proprietor or other person may apply to the Court which would have had jurisdiction in case a suit had been brought for the recovery of such lands, and such Court thereupon, and on the necessary costs being deposited therein by the applicant, shall order such lands to be measured, and shall cause a copy of such order to be transmitted to the Collector in whose jurisdiction the lands are situate, together with the sum so deposited for costs, and the Collector shall thereupon proceed to measure such lands, and shall ascertain and record the names of the persons in occupation of the same, or, on the special application of the proprietor or other person aforesaid, but not otherwise, shall proceed to ascertain, determine, and record the tenures and under-tenures, the rates of rent payable in respect of such lands and the persons by whom respectively the rents are payable. If after due enquiry the Collector shall be unable to cause such lands to be measured, or to ascertain or record the names of the persons in occupation of the same, or if he shall (in any case in which such special application shall have been made as aforesaid) be unable to ascertain who are the persons having tenures or under-tenures in such lands, or any part thereof, then and in any such case such Collector may declare the same to have lapsed to the party on whose application such enquiry may have been made. If any person, within fifteen days after such Collector shall have recorded the name of such person as being in occupation of such land, or any part thereof, or shall have declared a tenure to have lapsed, shall appear and show good and sufficient cause for his previous non-appearance, and satisfy such Collector that there has been a failure of justice, such Collector may, upon such terms or conditions as may seem fit, alter or rescind such order according to the justice of the case.

SECTION 38.

Every proprietor of an estate, whether his property has been let out to *putneedars*, or any other description of under-tenants, is entitled to make a general survey of his estate under section 37; but it would seem that those persons only are allowed to make a detailed survey under this section, who are in receipt of the rents from the occupiers of the soil. In the following case the Court observed "The plaintiff in this case is the *putneedar*. Between him and the ryot there is the *durputneedar* and the *Shikmee Talookdars*. Now the ryots are not liable to pay rent to the plaintiff. They pay to the *Shikmee Talookdar*, who pays to the

Who may apply for measurement.

SECTION 38. *durputneedar*, who again pays to the *putneedar*. Section 10 (of Act VI of 1862), in our opinion, contemplates the case of a proprietor of an estate, who, by reason of inability to ascertain who are the persons liable to pay rent to him, is unable to measure his estate. The plaintiff cannot be ignorant of the person who is liable to pay rent to him, as he has given a *durputnee*: and his attempt, under section 10, to get the Collector's assistance to a minute measurement of the land held by each ryot, is simply with a view to harass and oppress them. He may be entitled to make a general survey of the land under section 9 of the Act, but this he has not asked for "—*Dwarkanath Chuckerbutty* v. *Bhowanee Kishore Chuckerbutty*, 8 W. R., 11.

Grounds on which application may be granted. An applicant under this section should prove that he cannot ascertain who are the persons liable to pay rent. If no enquiry is made to ascertain that such a state of facts existed, and the Collector takes proceedings, such proceedings are invalid—*Mahomed Bahadur Mojoomdar* v. *Raja Rajkishen Singh*, 10 B. L. R., 401 (Note); 15 W. R., 522. Nor can proceedings be taken on the application of one co-sharer in a joint undivided estate—*Ibid*; *Moolook Chand Mundul* v. *Modhossoodun Bachusputty*, 10 B. L. R., 398 (Note); *Shoorendro Mohun Roy* v. *Bhuggobut Churn Gangopadhya*, 10 B. L. R., 403 (Note); 18 W. R.,

One application may include many ryots. 332; *Santeram Panga* v. *Bycunt Panga*, 10 B. L. R., 397; 19 W. R., 280. And any number of ryots can be proceeded against in one application—*Solano* v. *Soobum Roy*, 6 W. R. (Act X), 4.

Intervenor. Where an intervenor objects that the applicant in not in receipt of the rents, the Court must determine whether the applicant or the intervenor is in receipt of the rent, and decide accordingly—*Baboo Nundoo Lall* v. *Smith*, 7 W. R., 188. Where the progress of measurement is interfered with by a third party claiming the land, the proper course is for the Collector to hold his hand leaving it for the parties to seek their remedy in Court—*Wise* v. *Bansee Shaha*, 16 W. R., 51.

Power of the Collector. This section merely empowers revenue officers to decide what rate of rent the tenant of a particular parcel of land has been paying, and does not empower them to declare that rent at a certain rate shall be paid simply because rent at that rate has been paid by the tenants of neighbouring lands—*Anunt Manjhee* v. *Joy Chunder Chowdhry*, 12 W. R., 371. He is to record the state of things as actually existing, and not what he thinks ought to be the rates—*Bala Thakoor* v. *Meghburn Singh*, 14 W. R., 269. Nor can a Collector assess the rate of rent on land which has hitherto paid no rent—*Sree Misser* v. *Crowdy*, 15 W. R., 243. Nor can he determine summarily the character of the holdings under the estate—*Wise* v. *Lakhoo Khan*, 16 W. R., 50.

Proceedings must be in strict accordance with terms of section. The Court will not hold any person bound by the finding in this section, unless it is shown beyond a doubt that the proceedings of the revenue officers referred to have been conducted in strict accordance with the terms therein set forth—*Dinobundhoo Chowdhry* v. *Dinonath Mookerjee*, 19 W. R., 168.

Objection to be taken at the time of proceedings. And when the measurement has been completed without any objection having been made to it while on progress, the proceedings ought not to be set aside on objection made subsequently—*Goluck Kishore Acharjee* v. *Kesha Majhee*, 15 W. R., 23.

No proceedings valid under this section to enhance rents. This section is intended to assist the proprietor to measure the lands when he cannot ascertain who the ryots are, what lands are in their occupations, and what rent they have to pay, but not to enable him to enchance the rents, or resume rent-free lands by throwing the *onus* on the *lakhirajdar* to prove his rent-free holding—*Sharoda Persaud Gangooly* v. *Raj Mohun Roy*, 18 W. R., 165.

SECTIONS
39—41.

XXXIX. The Collector shall, as soon as conveniently may be after he shall have finally completed any such measurement and record, return a copy thereof to the Court by which such measurement had been ordered, and such Court shall receive and record the same ; and every decision of the Collector made in pursuance of the provisions of Section 38 shall be appealable, as if the same had been an order of the Court into which such copy had been returned, made upon the day on which such copy was so returned ; but, save as aforesaid, every decision of such Collector made in pursuance of the provisions of Section 38 shall be final.

Proceedings on completion of such measurement.

XL. The provisions of the said Act VIII of 1859, and the Acts amending the same, or of any other Act or Acts for the time being in force in Civil Courts in Bengal, relating to the evidence of witnesses, to procuring the attendance of witnesses and the production of documents, and to the examination, remuneration, and punishment of witnesses, shall apply to all proceedings before any Collector under Section 18; and for the purposes aforesaid, the Collector shall have all the powers and authorities in and by such Acts or any of them conferred upon the Court.

Collector's powers.

XLI. All measurements made under this Act shall be made according to the standard pole of measurement of the pergunnah in which the land is situated.

Act VI (B. C.), 1862, section 11.

Measurement to be made by the pergunnah pole.

Formerly there were conflicting decisions as to the power of the Collector to decide, in cases of dispute, what was the standard pole of the measurement of the pergunnah ; but it is now decided by a majority of the Full Bench (Couch, C.J., Bayley and L. S. Jackson, JJ., dissenting) that where there is a dispute solely on the ground that the pole, with which the measurement is attempted to be made, is not the standard pole of the measurement of the pergunnah, and the parties are at issue as to what is the length of the standard pole, the Collector has jurisdiction to enquire into and decide as to what is the true length of the standard pole—*Srimati Manmohini Chowdhrain* v. *Prem Chand Roy*, 6 B. L. R., 1; 14 W. R., F. B., 5. This decision was under section 11 of Act VI (B. C.) of 1862, but the wording of that and this section is exactly the same.

84   THE LAW OF LANDLORD AND TENANT.

SECTIONS 42—44.

Weight to be given to Canoongoes papers in fixing the standard.

In determining the question of the length of the standard pole, due credit must be attached to the Canoongoes papers, which have always been recognized to be of great weight in questions connected with pergunnah rates, standards of measurements and similar statistics; and it is no ground for rejecting these papers that the local *hât* does not correspond with the English cubit of 18 inches: for the *hât* varies in length in different pergunnahs—*Nund Duntpat* v. *Tara Chand Prithee-haree*, 2 W. R. (Act X), 13. It sometimes, indeed, happens that there are two different standards of measurement in the same pergunnah; and when this is the case, the standard which is current in a particular locality or *tuppah* must be followed—*Bhogobutty Churn Bhattacharjea* v. *Tameerooddeen Moonshi*, 1 W. R., 225, and *Sarbanund Pandey* v. *Ruchia Pandey*, 4 W. R. (Act X), 32.

Register of suits.

XLII. All suits brought under any of the provisions of this Act shall be entered in a special register of the Court kept for that purpose.

This section was enacted for purely statistical purposes, and not for the purpose of separating into parts the jurisdiction exercised by one Court—*Jallalooddeen* v. *Burn*, 18 W. R., 99.

Act VI (B. C.), 1862, section 12.

Form of plaint in suits for arrears of rent.

XLIII. In any suit hereafter to be brought for the recovery of an arrear of rent, the plaint shall specify the name of the village and estate, and of the pergunnah or other local division in which the land is situate, the yearly rent of the land, the amount (if any) received on account of the year for which the claim is made, the amount in arrear, and the time in respect of which it is alleged to be due. If the arrear is alleged to be due from any ryot, the plaint shall further specify the quantity of land; and where fields have been numbered in a Government Survey, the number (if it be possible to give it) of each field.

Act VI (B. C.),. 1862, section 2.

The Court may in certain cases award to the plaintiff additional damages not exceeding 25 per cent.

XLIV. In any suit hereafter to be brought for rent under the provisions of this Act, if it shall appear to the Court that the defendant has, without reasonable or probable cause, neglected or refused to pay the amount due by him, and that he has not, before the institution of the suit, tendered such amount to the plaintiff or his duly authorized agent, or in case of the refusal of the plaintiff or such agent, to receive the amount tendered, has not deposited such amount in the Court before the institution of the suit in manner hereinafter mentioned, it shall be lawful for the Court SECTION 45. to award to the plaintiff, in addition to the amount decreed for rent and costs, such damages, not exceeding twenty-five per centum on the amount of rent decreed, as the Court may think fit. These damages, if awarded as well as the amount of rent and costs decreed in the suit, shall carry interest at the rate of twelve per centum per annum from the date of decree until payment thereof.

This section formed no part of Act X, 1859, and was passed under special circumstances, to enable the Courts to deal with cases in which tenants combined to withhold the payment of their rents. The penalties it imposes are highly penal, and cannot be awarded unless it is shown that the tenant has, without reasonable or probable cause, neglected to pay the amount that is due. A man is not liable to damages, merely because he may from poverty, illness, or some unavoidable cause, have failed to pay his rent. Nor can damages be awarded unless they are specially claimed, and the absence of probable cause expressly alleged in the plaint—*Hora Mohun* v. *Omeshchandra Dutt*, 1 Board's Rep., 200. It is for the Court to determine what is a reasonable and probable cause; but it has been held that the mere pendency of an enhancement suit is not of itself a sufficient excuse for a tenant omitting to pay or tender the rent which is admittedly due at the old rate—*Nobokanto Dey* v. *Raja Borodakanth Roy Bahadoor*, 1 W. R., 100. It must be borne in mind that damages under this section are given in lieu of interest, and can only be awarded in addition to the *rent* and *costs of the decree*, see page 62.

Under what circumstances damages are to be awarded.

Are in lieu of interest.

XLV. In any suit hereafter to be brought for rent under the provisions of this Act, if it shall appear to the Court that the plaintiff has instituted the suit against the defendant without reasonable or probable cause, or that the defendant had, before the institution of the suit, duly deposited in the Court, in the manner hereinafter mentioned, the full amount which the Court shall find to have been due to the plaintiff at the date of such deposit, it shall be lawful for the Court to award to the defendant, by way of compensation, such sum, not exceeding twenty-five per centum on the whole amount claimed by the plaintiff, as the Court may think fit ; and such sum, with interest at the rate of twelve per centum per annum until payment thereof, shall be recoverable from the plaintiff in like manner as sums ordered to be paid by decrees of such Court.

Act VI (B. C.), 1862, section 3.

The Court may award compensation not exceeding 25 per cent. on the amount sued for, to a defendant improperly sued.

86   THE LAW OF LANDLORD AND TENANT.

Sections 46 & 47.

Act VI (B. C.), 1862, section 4.

Under-tenant or ryot may, after tender, &c., pay into Court, without any action being brought against him, what he admits to be due to his Zemindar, &c.

XLVI. If any under-tenant or ryot shall, at the Mâl Cutcherry for the receipt of rents or other place where the rents of the land or other immoveable property held or cultivated by him are usually payable, tender payment of what he shall consider to be the full amount of rent due from him at the date of the tender to the Zemindar or other person in receipt of the rent of such land ; and if the amount so tendered shall not be accepted, and a receipt in full shall not be forthwith granted, it shall be lawful for the under-tenant or ryot, without any suit having been instituted against him, to deposit such amount in the Court having jurisdiction to entertain a suit for such rent, to the credit of the Zemindar or other person aforesaid : and such deposit shall, so far as the under-tenant or ryot, and all persons claiming through or under him, are concerned, in all respects operate as, and have the full effect of, a payment then made by the under-tenant or ryot of the amount deposited to such Zemindar or other person.

Payment into Court to have effect of payment to Zemindar or other person entitled.

When defendant entitled to set-off.

In a suit for rent where defendant claimed credit for a sum which he had deposited under the provisions of section 4, Act VI (B.C.) of 1862, in the Deputy Collectorate of the subdivision within which the plaintiff's Mâl Cutcherry was situate giving notice to the plaintiff under section 5, it was held that the defendant was entitled to a set-off— *Grish Chunder Sein* v. *Eastern Bengal Jute Company*, 10 W. R., 492.

Tender must be made and refused before deposit.

A party is not, however, entitled to benefit from a deposit made under this section if it was paid in without a tender to and refusal by the opposite party—*Kristo Protibar* v. *Alladinee Dossee*, 15 W. R., 4.

Zemindar entitled to know interest of depositor.

Where a party wishes to make known to a zemindar that he has a right to a tenure, the rent of which the zemindar refuses to accept from him, it is not sufficient for him to put the money into Court in the name of the recorded tenant along with his own name without stating what his claim is, he should give distinct notice to the zemindar of the interest which he claims—*Mrityun Joya Sirkar* v. *Gopaul Chunder Sirkar*, 2 B. L. R., A. C., 131 ; 10 W. R., 466.

Act VI (B. C.), 1862, section 5.

Proceedings on making a payment into Court and drawing out the money.

XLVII. Such deposit shall be received in such Court on the application of the under-tenant or ryot, or his agent, made in writing, and on the under-tenant or ryot, or his agent, making a declaration in the form, or, as nearly as circumstances will admit, in the form set forth in the Schedule (A) hereto annexed,

THE LAW OF LANDLORD AND TENANT. 87

and the Court shall give a receipt for the same under its seal. If the declaration shall contain any averment which the person making the declaration shall know or believe to be false, or shall not know or believe to be true, such person shall be subject to punishment according to the law for the time being in force for the punishment of giving or fabricating false evidence. Upon receiving the money so deposited, the Court shall issue a notice to the person to whose credit it has been deposited, in the form set forth in the Schedule (B) hereto annexed; and such notice shall be served by the Court, without the payment of any fee, either upon the person to whom it is addressed, or upon his Naib, Gomashtah, or other agent; and in the absence of any such agent, it shall be served by sticking up a copy of the same in the said Court, and another copy upon the Mâl Cutcherry for the receipt of rents, or other place where the rents are usually paid for the land in respect of which the money has been deposited. If the person to whom such notice is issued, or his duly authorized agent, shall appear and apply that the money in deposit be paid to him, it shall be immediately made over to him.

Section 48.

Stamp on deposits.
These sections have made one most important change in the law. Under the old procedure, a ryot who wished to deposit his rent had to make application to the Court in writing, upon paper bearing a stamp of such value as would be necessary on the institution of a suit for arrears of rent; under the law as it at present stands, such applications will be treated as miscellaneous petitions, and be written on stamp paper of the value of 8 annas. The rulings on the subject of deposits are arranged under section 31.

The Court would apparently have no power in case the zemindar objected to the deposit to make any enquiry as to the quantity of land held by the ryot, and the circumstances under which he had been ejected from it—*Bacharam Paul* v. *Asgur Fukeer*, 10 W. R., 423.

XLVIII. The defendant in any suit instituted under any of the provisions of this Act, may, if he have duly tendered the same to the plaintiff before the institution of the suit, pay into Court such sum of money as such defendant may consider to be due to the plaintiff, without paying in any costs incurred by the plaintiff up to the time of such payment, and such sum shall be immediately paid out of Court to the plaintiff. If after such payment the plaintiff elects

Act VI (B. C.), 1862, section 7.

After action brought, defendant may pay into Court, without costs, money tendered before action brought.

SECTIONS 49—51.

Costs if plaintiff goes on and recovers no more. to proceed in the suit, and ultimately recovers no further sum than shall have been paid into Court, the plaintiff shall be charged with the whole costs of the suit incurred by the defendant; but if the plaintiff ultimately recovers a further sum than shall have been paid into Court, the defendant shall be charged with the whole costs of the suit.

XLIX. The defendant, in any suit instituted under *If no previous tender has been made, defendant may pay into Court what he admits to be due, with costs on that sum.* any of the provisions of this Act, may, without having made any tender before action brought, pay into Court such sum of money as he shall consider to be due to the plaintiff, together with the costs (to be fixed by the Court, if necessary, as of a suit originally instituted for the amount so paid into Court) incurred by the plaintiff up to the time of such payment, and such sum shall immediately be paid out of Court to the plaintiff. If after such payment the plaintiff elects to proceed in the suit and ultimately recovers no further *Costs if plaintiff goes on with the suit.* sum than shall have been paid into Court, he shall be charged with all costs incurred by the defendant subsequently to such payment; but if the plaintiff ultimately recovers a further sum than shall have been paid into Court, the defendant shall be charged with costs as upon a suit originally instituted, for the whole amount for which the plaintiff ultimately obtains a decree, but shall have credit thereout for the amount of costs paid into Court by him in the first instance.

L. No warrant of arrest before judgment shall be *No warrant of arrest before judgment.* issued in a suit for arrears of rent due in respect of a dependent talook or other transferable tenure which may be liable to sale in execution of any decree which may be passed in the case.

As to what are transferable tenures, see section 23, page 42.

LI. It shall be lawful for any person entitled to *Mesne profits may be claimed in suits for recovery of land.* recover the possession of land under any of the provisions of this Act, to include in his plaint a claim for the mesne profits of the land.

Principle on which mesne profits to be calculated. For the principle on which mesne profits should be calculated, see *Baboo Purmessuree Pershad Narain Singh* v. *Aghur Singh,* 7 W. R.,

THE LAW OF LANDLORD AND TENANT.   89

78, and *Ranee Asmad Kooer* v. *Maharanee Inderjeet Kooer*, 9 W. R., 455 SECTION 52.
(F. B.). When a cultivating ryot is ejected by his zemindar, the mere
rent of the land realized by the zemindar from another tenant, is not
necessarily the measure of damage sustained by the ryot and recoverable
by him as mesne profits—*Bhiro Chandra Mozoomdar* v. *Bamundas
Mookerjee*, 3 B. L. R., A. C., 88; 11 W. R., 461.

A regular suit for mesne profits will lie after a suit for possession, if Separate suit for
in the latter suit no question of mesne profits was raised or decided—   mesne profits.
Pratab Chandra Binwa v. *Rani Swarnamayi*, 3 B. L. R., App., 81;
12 W. R., 5; see also *Baboo Gauri Brijnathpersad* v. *Budhoo Singh*,
2 B. L. R., S. N., 16; 10 W. R., 486.

The cause of action in respect of mesne profits accrues on the date on When cause of
which, but for the fact of dispossession, the plaintiff would have been action accrue.
entitled to receive them—*Lakhi Kant Das Chowdhry* v. *Ram Dyal
Dass*, 5 B. L. R., App., 61; 14 W. R., 82. Mesne profits can be
decreed only for six years before the institution of suit. Interest may
be allowed year by year during period of dispossession—*Muneeram
Acharjee* v. *Sreemutty Turungo*, 7 W. R., 173. A plaintiff is bound by
his own assessment of mesne profits—*Karoo Lall Thakoor* v. *Forbes*,
7 W. R., 140.

Where a decree-holder obtains possession of an estate in execution, Wrongful pos-
he is not at liberty to sue the ryots for rents falling due before the date sessor liable to
of his taking possession. His proper course is to sue the late wrongful ditor for mesne
possessor for mesne profits including rents—*Umes Chandra Roy* v. profits.
Shastidhar Mookerjee, 3 B. L. R., App., 99; 12 W. R., 35. With
respect to the subject of mesne profits generally, see Broughton's Civil
Procedure Code, 4th Ed., pp. 58, 312, 317.

LII. Any person desiring to eject a ryot or to cancel Act X, 1859, section 78.
Suits for ejectment or a lease on account of non-payment
cancelment of lease. of arrears of rent, may sue for such
ejectment or cancelment and for recovery of the arrear
in the same action, or may adduce any unexecuted decree
for arrears of rent as evidence of the existence of such
arrear in a suit for such ejectment or cancelment. In
all cases of such suits for the ejectment of a ryot or the
cancelment of a lease, the decree shall specify the
amount of the arrear, and if such amount, together with
interest and costs of suit, be paid into Court within
fifteen days from the date of the decree, execution shall
be stayed.

The only suits for ejectment contemplated by this Act are those Equitable relief
consequent on the non-payment of arrears of rent, a suit therefore for afforded by this
ejectment from land assigned for building purposes brought upon a section extends
contract by which the defendant had bound himself on certain conditions to lease-holders.
to give up the land was held not to lie—*Ramnarain Mitter* v. *Nobin
Chunder Moordafarash*, 18 W. R., 208; see also *in the matter of
Brohommoyee Bewah*, 9 B. L. R. (Note), 109; 14 W. R., 10. This
section applies to all cases of suits for the ejectment of a ryot,
or for the cancelment of a lease for the non-payment of rent. It applies

13

SECTION 53.

not only to cases in which it is sought to eject a ryot, under section 22, for non-payment of rent, or for the cancelment of a lease for non-payment of rent under section 23, but also to cases in which it is sought to cancel a lease, or eject a ryot for non-payment of rent under an express stipulation contained in the agreement between the parties that, in the event of non-payment, the lease shall be forfeited. The words are general " in all cases of suits," and not in all cases of suits brought for the purpose of enforcing the provisions of section 23—*Jan Ali Chowdery* v. *Nittyanund Bose*, 10 W. R., F. B., 12; *Lullo Singh* v. *Thakoor Pershad*, 2 All., 249. The equitable relief, therefore, can be granted so as to keep the judgment-debtor in possession—*Baboo Gokhlanund* v. *Lalljee Sahoo*, 21 W. R., 11.

Time how computed.

If the decree is altered or amended on review or appeal, the fifteen days' grace dates from the final decree in the case—*Rada Mohun Mondul* v. *Buckshee Begum*, Marsh., 471. And the day on which the decree was passed should be excluded from the computation—*Shoopalul Singh* v. *Nabee Ashruf Khan*, 3 All., 342.

Discretionary with Court to extend time.

It would seem that the Court, though it cannot shorten the period of grace which this section allows, can, in the exercise of its discretion, stay execution for a longer period than fifteen days. This discretionary power is also vested in the Appellate Court—*Nobokisto Mookerjee* v. *Ramessur Goopto*, 18 W. R., 412 (Note); 2 Wyman (Act X), 75; *Rao Baneeram* v. *Ramnath Shaha*, 10 B. L. R., App., 2; 18 W. R., 412.

Section does not apply to middlemen.

Middlemen who have a permanent or transferable interest in land are not liable to be ejected under this section—*Nand Lall Ghose* v. *Sidi Nazir Ali Khan*, 1 Board's Rep., 1. So when in a suit under section 78, Act X of 1859, to eject the defendant from certain lands and to recover arrears of rent, the defendant was in the habit of receiving the rents of his tenants, and was bound only to pay a certain sum on account of Government revenue and village expenses, and was also entitled to sell or mortgage his rights, it was held that he was not a tenant but a subordinate proprietor, and that the suit therefore could not be brought under the above section—*Mussamut Balool Bebee* v. *Jugut Narain*, 4 All., 172; see also *Tirbhobun Singh* v. *Jhono Lall*, 18 W. R., 206.

It is absolutely necessary that the decree should specify the amount of arrears, and if it fails to do so it ought to be set aside—*Shah Ali Hossein* v. *Naudar Khan*, 2 All., 62.

LIII. Whenever in any suit brought by any Zemindar or other person in receipt of the rent of land, to eject any cultivator not having a right of occupancy, or to eject any farmer or other tenant holding only for a limited period after the determination of his lease or tenancy, or any agent after the determination of his agency, or to enforce any attachment or ejectment expressly authorized by any Regulation or Act, the Court shall pass a decree in favor of the plaintiff, no application in the form provided in Section 212 of the said Act VIII of 1859 shall be necessary, but the Court

Court to issue immediate execution in certain cases.

shall forthwith, upon the plaintiff depositing in Court **SECTION 54.** the necessary expenses, make an order for delivery of possession in execution of the decree: Provided, however, that in cases to which Section 52 of this Act is applicable, no such order shall be made until after the expiration of fifteen days from the date of the decree.

To justify a holding after expiry of a lease, a direct consent of the landlord is necessary. Where tenants have no right to hold over, their use and occupation of land is a trespass, they are liable not for the rents as tenants but for damages as trespassers—*Mackintosh* v. *Gopee Mohun Mozoomdar*, 4 W. R., 24. But another case seems contrary to this in which it was held that, where a tenant held over and was allowed to continue in possession by the landlord, an implied agreement existed between the landlord and the tenant, and under such circumstances the tenant was entitled to hold on until a legal notice to quit was served on him—*Jumant Ali Shah* v. *Chowdhry Chutturdhari Sahi*, 16 W. R., 185; see also *Tofaoll Khan* v. *Woopean Khan*, 9 W. R., 123. A tenant who held over for eight years without a pottah was held to be a yearly tenant, and not liable to ejectment without notice—*Sadhoo Jha* v. *Bhugwan Chunder Opadhya*, 1 Ind. Jur., 75; 5 W. R. (Act X), 17. *Effect of holding over after expiry of lease.*

If the landlord continues to receive rent for a fresh period, he must be considered to have acquiesced in the tenants continuing to hold on the terms of the original lease and cannot turn out the tenant or treat him as a trespasser, without giving him reasonable notice to quit. This is according to English law and the general principles of justice—*Per* Peacock, C.J., in *Ram Khelawan Singh* v. *Mussamut Soondra*, 7 W. R., 152. *Where landlord consents.*

A ryot, who holds over after the expiry of his lease in spite of his landlord, is liable to pay at rates current for the same kind of land in the village—*Tommy* v. *Soobba Kurim Lall*, 2 W. R. (Act X), 73. *Where landlord dissents.*

LIV. It shall not be lawful for the Court to entertain any application for stay of execution of any such order pending any appeal, and no person who shall have been evicted under any such order shall be restored to possession so long as the decree under which such order was issued shall remain unreversed. *In such cases execution not to be stayed pending appeal.*

Sections 53 and 54 were substituted for section 25, Act X, 1859, which authorized the Collector to grant summary assistance to any zemindar who wished to eject a ryot, not having a right of occupancy, or an under-tenant holding over after the determination of his lease. Under the present procedure, a zemindar, who wishes to invoke the assistance of the Court, must proceed by a regular suit for ejectment. If he obtains a decree, he will be entitled to ask for immediate execution, except in cases to which section 52 is applicable. Now section 52 must be read with sections 22 and 23. Section 22 provides that no "ryot having a right of occupancy or holding under a pottah, the term of which has not expired, shall be ejected otherwise than in execution *Ejectment of non-occupancy ryots and under-tenants holding over after the lease has expired.*

of a decree or order under the provisions of this Act." Similarly, section 23 exempts from summary ejectment "farmers or other leaseholders not having a permanent or transferable interest in the land, whose lease is liable to be cancelled for non-payment of arrears of rent." These two classes of cases, therefore, would be those to which section 52 is applicable, and in which immediate execution could not be given. In other cases, such, for instance, as cultivators not having a right of occupancy, or farmers or other tenants holding over after the termination of their lease or tenancy, immediate execution would issue on the passing of the decree.

Act. X 1859, section 80.

If person required by the decree refuse to grant pottah, Court may do so.

LV. When a decree is given for the delivery of a pottah, if the person required by the decree to grant such pottah refuse or delay to grant the same, the Court may grant a pottah in conformity with the terms of the decree under the signature and seal of such Court, and such pottah shall be of the same force and effect as if granted by the person aforesaid.

Act X, 1859, section 81.

Refusal to execute kabuliat as required by the decree.

LVI. When a decree is given for the delivery of a kabuliat, if the person required by the decree to execute such kabuliat shall refuse to execute the same, the decree shall be evidence of the amount of rent claimable from such person, and a copy of the decree under the signature and seal of the Court shall be of the same force and effect as a kabuliat executed by the said person.

Before a decree can be allowed as evidence under this section, the plaintiff must ask the defendant to execute the kabuliat, and he must refuse—*Shaikh Misser* v. *Kazee Syud Naser Ali*, 20 W. R., 33.

Act VI. (B. C.), 1862, section 17.

Process not to issue simultaneously against both person and property.

LVII. Process of execution in any suit instituted under this Act may be issued against either the person or the property of a judgment-debtor, but process shall not be issued simultaneously against both the person and property.

Act X, 1859, section 92.

No execution to be issued after three years from date of judgment.

LVIII. No process of execution of any description whatsoever shall be issued on a judgment in any suit for any of the causes of action mentioned in Sections 27, 28, 29, or 30 of this Act, after the lapse of three years from the date of such judgment, unless the judgment be for a sum exceeding five hundred rupees, in which case the period within which execution may be had shall be regulated by the general rules in force in SECTION 58. respect to the period allowed for the execution of decrees of the Court.

In calculating whether a judgment exceeds Rs. 500, all costs, Cost of execution whether incurred before or after the decree, must be taken into con- to be reckoned as sideration. Thus, where a judgment was under Rs. 500, but the value judgment. of the stamps incurred in taking out execution raised the amount to above Rs. 500, it was held that the judgment must be considered as one for a sum exceeding Rs. 500. "In deciding," observed the Court, "a general point of law of this description, we cannot do better than be guided by the general principles of law, which we find in Act VIII, 1859. Section 188 of that Act explains that under the denomination of costs, are included the whole of the expenses necessarily incurred by either party on account of the suit, and in enforcing the decree passed therein, such as the expense of stamps, &c. In any suit under Act VIII, 1859, it is clear from these sections that the value of stamps required and used in enforcing a decree would be held to be included in the judgment; and we would apply the same law to judgments in Act X suits"—*Campbell* v. *Abdul Huc*, 6 W. R. (Act X), 8.

Where the judgment is for a sum not exceeding Rs. 500, no execu- Application for tion can be issued after the lapse of three years from the date of the execution, if presented before decree. The meaning of this is, that no application can be received the lapse of three for the execution of such a decree after the lapse of three years; but carried out after an application, presented before the lapse of three years, can be carried the expiration of out after that period has expired. "We think," observed Peacock, C. J., in the case of *Hera Lall Seal* v. *Poran Matteah*, 6 W. R. (Act X), 84, "that, giving a reasonable construction to the section, the meaning is, that no execution shall issue upon a decree, unless a proper application for execution be made within three years from the date of the decree. If the meaning of the section is that the warrant of execution must be signed within three years, a party might be deprived of the fruits of his judgment in a case in which he has to execute it against the heirs or representatives of the judgment-debtor, though he may have acted with the greatest diligence.........The Deputy Collector has declined to issue the warrant, on the ground that he has no jurisdiction to issue a warrant after three years from the date of the judgment, notwithstanding that the application was made to the Collector, and the *tullubana* lodged, within the period of three years. We think he had jurisdiction, and he must be directed to hear and determine the case upon its merits." This decision has been confirmed by the more recent Full Bench case, where it was held that the word "issued" is to be interpreted to mean "sued out" or "applied for with success," that is, no application for process of execution shall be successful, unless the application for it is made, or it is sued out within three years—*Rhidoy Krishna Ghose* v. *Koylash Chandra Bose*, 4 B. L. R., F. B., 82; 13 W. R., F. B., 3. In the Full Bench case, the delay, if it can be called delay, was caused by the Court alone, but where the delay is on the part of the judgment-creditor he is barred—*Lalla Ram Sahoy* v. *Dodraj Mahto*, 20 W. R., 395.

The date of the judgment is the date of the final judgment in The three years must be reckoned the case. Where a case has been appealed, the three years must be from date of final judgment.

SECTION 59. reckoned from the date of the decree of the Appellate Court. In all such cases the period of limitation runs, not from the date of the original decree, but from the date at which the appeal was determined—*Gyan Chunder Roy* v. *Kalee Churn Roy Chowdhry*, 7 W. R., 48.

Act X of 1859, s. 105 (part).
Act VIII of 1865 (B. C.), s. 4 (part).

Procedure on sale of under-tenure.

LIX. Whenever a decree may be passed for an arrear of rent due in respect of an under-tenure which by the title deeds or the custom of the country is transferable by sale, and the judgment-creditor shall make application for the attachment and sale of such under-tenure, the Court shall, so soon as such under-tenure shall have been ordered to be sold, cause to be hung up in some conspicuous part of the building in which such Court sits, and of the buildings in which the Collector and Judge of the District, within which the land comprised in such under-tenure is situate, and to be affixed on some conspicuous place on such land, and on some conspicuous place in the town or village in or nearest to which such land is situate, a notice for the sale of such under-tenure on some fixed date not less than twenty days from the hanging up of such notice in such Court.

Transferable under-tenures hypothecated to landlord for rent.

All under-tenures which are transferable by sale, are hypothecated to the landlord for the rent; and the tenant cannot, by disposing of the tenure to a third party, deprive the landlord of his lien upon it. Thus, where the plaintiff had purchased, under a Civil Court decree, the rights and interests of a tenant in a certain under-tenure, and this under-tenure was afterwards brought to sale for arrears of rent by the zemindar, it was held that the purchaser under the Act X sale, and not the plaintiff, was entitled to possession—*Khoobaree Rai* v. *Roghoobur Rai*, 2 W. R., 131; *Gopaul Mundul* v. *Soobhudra Boistobee*, 5 W. R., 205; *Mussamut Safuroonissa* v. *Saree Dhoobee*, 8 W. R., 384; see also *Ramjeebun Choudhry* v. *Pearyloll Mundle*, 4 W. R. (Act X), 30; *Golam Chunder Dey* v. *Nuddiar Chand Adheekaree*, 16 W R., 1. But another decision seems contrary to these in which Phear, J., says:— "The power which a Revenue Court has in this behalf is given to it by section 105 of Act X of 1859" (sections 59 to 61 of this Act), "and we think that those provisions only enable the Revenue Court to seize and sell that which at the time is the property of the judgment-debtor. There is nothing in the whole Act as we read it to indicate that the Legislature contemplated for a moment that the property of any other person than the judgment-debtor should be sold for the debt of the latter, even though that property had previously been the property of the judgment-debtor."—*Pran Bandhu Sirkar* v. *Sarbasundari Debi*, 3 B. L. R., A. C. (Note), 52; 10 W. R., 434. And this decision is followed out in *Samiraddi Khalifa* v. *Huris Chandra*, 3 B. L. R., A. C., 49, where Loch, J., says:—"But it was further urged that, under the provision of section 112 of Act X of 1859 (section 68 of this Act), the tenure of the ryot was hypothecated for the rent. This is a mistake.

The produce of the land is held to be hypothecated, and a zemindar, instead of bringing a suit for arrear, may recover the same by distraint and sale of the produce." But it is now decided that the tenure is hypothecated—*Sham Chand Koondoo* v. *Brojonath Paul,* 21 W. R., 94. Where, however, the rights and interests of a tenant in an under-tenure are sold by the Civil Court, and the zemindar recognizes and adopts the purchaser as his tenant, giving him a new lease of the land, he cannot then proceed against the under-tenure for arrears which accrued before the purchaser came into possession. He must realize such arrears, as he would realize any other debt from the former tenant—*Umurt Lal Bose* v. *Soorubee Dosse,* 2 W. R. (Act X), 86.

<small>SECTION 59.</small>

A tenure purchased in execution of a decree for the current rent due therefrom cannot be again resold for the arrears of rent which had accrued on account of arrears of former years. Those arrears become the personal debt of the former proprietor, and must be recovered from him. The tenure itself is hypothecated for the rent of the current year, and can only be sold for arrears of the current year—*Mussamut Luteefun* v. *Shaikh Meah Jan,* 6 W. R., 112; see also *Sumbhoo Chunder Singh* v. *Ram Narain Doss,* 9 W. R., 217.

<small>Tenure cannot be resold a second time.</small>

Where a tenant commits default and purchases the tenure when sold in execution of a decree against himself, he cannot claim the benefit of the law relating to auction-purchasers under this Act and section 11 of Regulation VIII of 1819—*Meheroonissa Bibee* v. *Hur Churn Bose,* 10 W. R., 220. The proprietor of a talook which was about to be sold for arrears of rent, entered into an arrangement with the plaintiff whereby in consideration of a share in the purchase he agreed to use his influence to urge on the sale and to secure the purchase to the plaintiff. Under this arrangement, the plaintiff became the purchaser of the talook, and the former proprietor obtained a share of the purchase. A suit by the plaintiff to oust the under-tenants was dismissed, as the plaintiff took only as a purchaser in an ordinary execution-sale—*Srinath Ghose* v. *Haronauth Dutt Chowdhry,* 9 B. L. R., 220; 18 W. R., 240.

<small>Defaulting tenant cannot himself purchase.</small>

In executing a decree for arrears of rent, a Court, under this section, has power only to seize and sell that which at the time is the property of the judgment-debtor. When, therefore, a decree was obtained against persons who were originally proprietors of the land, but who, at the time of the decree and subsequent sale, had ceased to have any interest therein, the purchaser at the sale in execution of such decree took nothing—*Dowlut Ghazee Choudhry* v. *Moonshee Munoor,* 15 W. R., 341; *Meah Jan Munshi* v. *Kurrunamayi Debi,* 8 B. L. R., 1.

<small>Only the property of the judgment-debtor can be sold.</small>

Where a plaintiff had obtained an *ex parte* decree against a defendant, and in execution of that decree had sold the defendant's under-tenure, and this *ex parte* decree was afterwards set aside, it was held that the sale was valid, though the decree under which it had taken place was invalid, and the defendant was not allowed to recover the under-tenure: unless he could prove that the purchase was not a *bonâ fide* one: and that the purchaser was acting in collusion with the decree-holder— *Jan Ali* v. *Jan Ali Choudhry,* 1 B. L. R., 56; 10 W. R., 154. Peacock, C.J., in delivering judgment, referred to the case of *Chunder Kanto Surma* v. *Bissesur Surmah Chuckerbutty,* 7 W. R., 312, in which Norman, J., had made the following remarks:—" It is important to observe that, if a sale takes place in execution of a decree in force

<small>Is sale under an *ex parte* decree, which is afterwards set aside, valid?</small>

SECTIONS 60 & 61.

Effect of reversal of decree on sale.

and valid at the time of the sale, the property in the thing sold passes to the purchaser; and if the decree or judgment be afterwards reversed, the reversal does not affect the validity of the sale or the title of the purchaser."

No suit will lie to set aside the sale of an estate in execution of a decree for arrears of rent at enhanced rates according to a prior decree obtained *ex parte* for enhancement, subsequently reversed on special appeal. This case was decided under Act X of 1859, and Norman, J., says:—" We think it clear that the Lower Courts were right in dismissing the suit. The now plaintiff had his remedy, under section 58 of Act X of 1859, to apply to set aside the judgment within fifteen days after the process for enforcing the judgment was executed, if the story he now sets up is true. He might have paid the money into Court, or applied to stay the proceedings in the second suit pending the appeal in the first. He had no right to hold back and pay nothing, and, having done so, he must take the consequence. As it is, the decree became final, and the sale under it was perfectly regular. And although the defendant is not in the position of a purchaser without notice of the proceedings in the suit, we think he has a perfectly valid title to the property he has bought "—*Doorga Pershad Pal Choudhry* v. *Jogesh Prokash Gungopadhya*, 4 W. R. (Act X), 38. It may be remarked with respect to this case, that section 58 of Act X of 1859 has been omitted from this Act; but section 119 of Act VIII of 1859 made applicable to rent-suits by section 34 of this Act repeats in almost identical terms the direction given in section 58 of Act X of 1859, and by the Limitation Act (Act IX of 1871), Schedule 2, Division 3, Art. 157, an application by a defendant for an order to set aside a judgment *ex parte* must be made within thirty days of the passing of such judgment. In another case, however, a contrary view was held by the Court, where Morgan, J., says:—" On the reversal of the decree in execution of which the sale took place, the sale itself made while that decree was under review fell"—*Sheikh Bhoolloo* v. *Ram Narain Mookerjee*, W. R. (1864), 129.

Effect on sale when decree is barred by limitation.

When it appeared that a decree was barred by limitation, the sale in execution of such decree was declared invalid—*Golam Asgar* v. *Lakhimoni Debi*, 5 B. L. R., 68; 13 W. R., 273, so also when the original decree was passed without jurisdiction—*Jadunath Kundu Choudhry* v. *Braja Nath Kundu*, 6 B. L. R., App., 90.

Act VIII of 1865 (B. C.), section 5.

Contents of notice of sale of under-tenure.

LX. Every such notice shall specify in the words used in the plaint in the suit in which the decree was made, the name of the village, estate, and pergunnah, or other local division in which the land comprised in the said under-tenures is situated, the yearly rent payable under the said under-tenure, and the gross amount recoverable under the said decree.

Act X of 1859 section 105(part).

Under-tenures not to be sold while other execution in force.

LXI. No order for the sale of any such under-tenure shall be made in execution of a decree for recovery of arrears of rent payable in respect thereof, when a warrant of execution has been previously issued against **Section 61.** the person or moveable property of the judgment-debtor, so long as such warrant remains in force. If, after sale of any such under-tenure in execution of such decree, any portion of the amount decreed remains due, process may be applied for, and issued against, any other property, moveable or immoveable belonging to the debtor.

Section 57 enacts that process of execution may be issued against either the person or the property of a judgment-debtor, but not simultaneously against both person and property. Having laid down this general rule, section 65 enacts that in the execution of any decree for the payment of money under this Act, not being money due as arrears of rent of a saleable under-tenure, the judgment-creditor may apply for execution against any immoveable property belonging to his debtor, if satisfaction of the judgment cannot be obtained by execution against the person or moveable property of the debtor, within the district in which the suit was instituted. It is clear, therefore, that, as a general rule, process of execution for a money decree under this Act is not to be levied in the first instance by attachment of immoveable property. The Legislature seems to have been anxious to guard against the sale of immoveable property in execution of decrees in · rent-suits, until the moveable property should have been first exhausted. The only exception made is in the case of transferable under-tenures which can be sold in the first instance for their own arrears : but "no order for the sale of any such under-tenure can be made when a warrant of execution has been previously issued against the person or moveable property of the judgment-debtor so long as such warrant remains in force." " From which," observed Peacock, C.J., " I infer that the Legislature considered that no other execution could be issued before the application to sell the under-tenure, except an execution against the person or moveable property of the debtor. I can scarcely conceive that the Legislature, if they had considered that an attachment of the general immoveable property of the debtor might be made in the first instance, would not have provided that the under-tenure should not be sold so long as a warrant should remain in force against the other immoveable property, as well as when a warrant should remain in force against the moveable property. I therefore think that, even for arrears of a saleable under-tenure, the other immoveable property of the debtor cannot be attached in the first instance"—*Desaratulla* v. *Nawab Nazim Nazar Ali Khan*, 1 B. L. R., A. C., 217 ; 10 W. R., 341.

Immoveable property other than the under-tenure in arrear not to be sold till the moveable property is exhausted.

Any Court which sold immoveable property without on the first instance proceeding against the moveable property or the under-tenure in arrear would act without jurisdiction. For the terms of section 105 of Act X of 1859 clearly lay down two rules: first, that, so long as any warrant of execution issued against the person or moveable property of the judgment-debtor remains in force, no application for the sale of the tenure can be received ; and, secondly, that, till the tenure in which the · arrears accrued be sold, other landed property cannot be brought to sale—*Jokee Lall* v. *Nursing Narain Singh*, 4 W. R. (Act X), 5.

Execution must issue against moveable property first.

SECTIONS 62 & 63.

Act VIII (B.C.), 1865, section 2.

How the sale may be stayed by person interested in under-tenure.

LXII. If the sum due under the decree, together with interest to date of payment, and all costs of process, be paid into Court at any time before the sale commences, whether by the defaulting holder of the under-tenure, or any one on his behalf, or any one interested in the protection of the under-tenure, such sale shall not take place; and the provisions of Section 13 of Regulation VIII of 1819, for the recovery of sums paid by person other than the defaulting holder of the under-tenure to stay the sale of the under-tenure, shall be applicable to all similar payments made under this Section.

Effect of deposit by under-tenant of rent due.

An under-tenant who has saved his superior tenure from sale by depositing the amount of rent due, not only has the security of the tenure which he preserves and of which he can obtain possession on application to the Collector, but he also has a right to recover the amount deposited by him as a loan in an ordinary suit—*Ambika Debi* v. *Pranhari Das*, 4 B. L. R., F. B., 77; 13 W. R., F. B., 1.

Act X, 1859, section 106.

If third party claim to be the lawful possessor of such under-tenure, Court to stay the sale and to enquire into and adjudicate upon the claim, upon decree being paid or secured.

LXIII. If after attachment and before sale of any such under-tenure as aforesaid in execution of a decree for arrears of rent due in respect of such under-tenure, any third party may prefer a claim alleging that such third party and not the person against whom the decree has been obtained is the proprietor of such under-tenure, and was in lawful possession of the same at the time when such decree was obtained, the Court shall not postpone such sale, unless and until such third party shall have deposited in Court the amount of the decree, or given sufficient security for the same. Provided, always, that no transfer of an under-tenure which, by the provisions of this Act or any other law for the time being in force, is required to be registered in the Sherishtah of the Zemindar or superior tenant, shall be recognized unless it has been so registered, or unless sufficient cause for non-registration be shown to the satisfaction of the Court.

Non-registered transfers not to be recognized.

An unregistered under-tenant cannot sue for reversal of a sale, except in cases of fraud.

In the absence of fraud, a third party, whose name is not registered in the zemindar's sherishtah, and who has not been recognized as the tenant, cannot sue for the reversal of the sale. When, therefore,

THE LAW OF LANDLORD AND TENANT. 99

an unregistered tenant wishes to protect his under-tenure from sale, his SECTION 64. only course is to deposit the amount of the decree under the last preceding section: if in spite of the deposit the under-tenure is then sold, a suit will lie in the Civil Court to reverse the sale—*Sheikh Afzul* v. *Lalla Gurnarain*, 6 W. R. (Act X), 59 (F. B.).

This section would seem to apply only to cases in which the existence of the under-tenure and the decree-holder's right as landlord are admitted, not when they are denied, and an adverse proprietary title is set up by the claimant as owner of the land—*Golam Chunder Dey* v. *Nuddiar Chand Adheekaree*, 16 W. R., 1. <small>This section applies only when relation of landlord and tenant exists.</small>

Where land has been attached in execution of a rent decree and it is released from attachment either under section 246 of Act VIII of 1859 or section 106 of Act X of 1859, the order for release of attachment is final and not subject to appeal, and can only be impugned by a regular suit—*Urjoon Sahoy* v. *Rajah Nilmoney Singh Deo*, 20 W. R., 90.

LXIV. If a decree is given in favor of a sharer in a joint undivided estate, dependent talook, or other similar tenure, for money due to him on account of his share of the rent of an under-tenure situate in such undivided estate, talook or tenure, no order for the sale of such under-tenure in execution of such decree shall be made unless and until all moveable property (if any) which such judgment-debtor may possess within the jurisdiction of the Court in which the suit was instituted, shall have been seized and sold in execution of such decree, and the sale of such property (if any) shall have proved insufficient to satisfy the judgment. In such case, such under-tenure, if of the nature described in Section 59, may be seized and sold in execution of such decree, according to the ordinary procedure of the Court, and not in the manner provided in the said Section, and every such sale shall have such and the same effect as the sale of any immoveable property sold in execution of a decree not being for arrears of rent payable in respect thereof. <small>Act X, 1859, section 108. Execution of decrees given in favor of sharers in undivided estates or tenures.</small>

A sharer in a joint undivided estate, dependent talook, or other similar tenure, cannot cause the tenure itself to be sold in execution of a decree for his share of the rent; he can only sell the rights and interests of his tenant in such under-tenure, so far as his own share is concerned. The tenure will be sold under the ordinary procedure of the Court for the sale of immoveable property. Where a decree-holder is only a sharer in a joint undivided estate, and the property sold is a share in a gantee tenure, the sale was declared to have taken place under this section, under which only the rights and interests of the defaulter can pass—*Meetoonjoy Choudhry* v. *Khetter Nauth Roy*, 5 W. R. (Act X), 71 ; *Nundo Lall Roy* v. *Gooroo Churn Bose*, 15 W. R., 6. <small>A co-sharer cannot cause sale of tenure for his share of rent.</small>

SECTIONS 65 & 66.
Act X of 1859, section 109.

LXV. In the execution of any decree for the payment of any money under this Act, not being money due as arrears of rent of a saleable under-tenure, if satisfaction of the judgment cannot be obtained by execution against the person or moveable property of the debtor within the district in which the suit was instituted, the judgment-creditor may apply for execution against any immoveable property belonging to such debtor.

Act VIII (B.C.), 1865, section 16.
Purchaser to acquire the under-tenure, with certain exceptions, free of incumbrances.

LXVI. The purchaser of an under-tenure under the provisions of Sections 59 and 60 of this Act, shall acquire it free of all incumbrances which may have accrued thereon by any act of any holder of the said under-tenure, his representatives or assignees, unless the right of making such incumbrances shall have been expressly vested in the holder by the written engagement under which the under-tenure was created, or by the subsequent written authority of the person who created it, his representatives or assignees, provided that nothing herein contained shall be held to entitle the purchaser to eject khoodkast ryots or resident and hereditary cultivators, nor to cancel *bonâ fide* engagements made with ryots or cultivators of the classes aforesaid by any holder of the under-tenure or his representatives, except it be proved in a regular suit to be brought by such purchaser for the adjustment of his rent, that a higher rent would have been demandable at the time such engagements were contracted by his predecessor. Nothing in this Section shall be held to apply to the purchase of a tenure by the previous holder thereof, through whose default the tenure was brought to sale.

Incumbrances not void—only voidable.

This section is a re-enactment of section 16 of Act VIII of 1865 (B. C.), and gives the landlord power to avoid all incumbrances created by the tenant, unless the making of such incumbrances has been expressly vested on the holder of the tenure. These incumbrances, however, are not void but only voidable. Markby, J., says :—" The decisions on the Regulations of 1793 of 1822, and Act VI of 1862 (B. C.), are all in *pari materiâ*, and I think it must now be taken as an established principle of law, that no sales for arrears of rent have *ipso facto* the effect of cancelling the tenures created by defaulting owners, but merely to give the purchaser the power to do so if he thinks proper "—*Madhusudan Kundu* v. *Ramdhan Ganguli*, 3 B. L. R., A. C., 431 ; 12 W. R., 383 ;

THE LAW OF LANDLORD AND TENANT. 101

Iswar Chandra Chuckerbutty v. *Bistu Chandra Chuckerbutty*, 3 B. L. R., App., 97; 12 W. R., 32.   SECTION 67.

An auction-purchaser cannot, without notice, cancel a pre-existing under-tenure—*Gobind Chunder Bose* v. *Alimooddeen*, 11 W. R., 160.   Notice condition precedent to cancellation of tenure.

Limitation to avoid incumbrances or under-tenures is twelve years from the time when the sale becomes final and conclusive. See Act IX of 1871, Sch. 2, Art. 120.

The right of occupancy of a ryot holding such right is preserved— *Nil Madhab Karmokar* v. *Shibu Pal*, 5 B. L. R., App., 18; 13 W. R., 410. Khoodkast ryots referred to in this section mean resident and hereditary cultivators—*Koontee Debee*. v. *Hirdoy Nath Duneepa*, 16 W. R., 206, and the mere fact of a ryot residing in a mouzah other than that in which his land is situate does not preclude him from being a resident cultivator within the meaning of this section—*Nubokishore Biswas* v. *Jadub Chunder Sircar*, 20 W. R. 426. The auction-purchaser of a *mokurruree* tenure cannot set aside rights of occupancy existing from a period prior to the creation of such tenure. Act VIII of 1865 refers only to incumbrances created subsequently—*Bholanath Ghosal* v. *Kedarnath Banerjee*, 19 W. R., 106.   What rights preserved.

This section does not apply to sales of portions of tenures—*Harasundari Dasi* v. *Kistu Mani Choudhrain*, 5 B. L. R., 37; 13 W. R., 257.

A purchaser at a sale in execution of a decree, under Act VIII of 1865 (B.C.), cannot be ousted from the property purchased by him without proof that the decree and sale were fraudulent, and that he (the purchaser) was a party to, or had notice of, the fraud—*Damudar Roy* v. *Nimanand Chuckerbutty*, 7 B. L. R., App., 1; 15 W. R., 365. And where a proprietor of a talook which was about to be sold for arrears of rent, entered into an arrangement with the plaintiff, whereby in consideration of a share of the purchase, he agreed to use his influence to urge on the sale and to secure the purchase to the plaintiff. Under this arrangement, the plaintiff became the purchaser of the talook, and the former proprietor obtained a share in the purchase. A suit by the plaintiff to oust the under-tenants was dismissed; the plaintiff took only as purchaser in an ordinary execution-sale and did not benefit by this section—*Srinath Ghose* v. *Haronath Dutt Choudhry*, 9 B. L. R., 220; 18 W. R., 240.   Fraud.   Collusive sale.

A house is not an incumbrance within the meaning of this section— *Shibdas Bandapadhya* v. *Bamandas Mookhapadhya*, 8 B. L. R., 237; 15 W. R., 360.   A house no incumbrance.

The cause of action of a purchaser of a tenure sold free of incumbrances under a sale for arrears of rent due in respect of it accrues when he purchases it but not before, and this is even the case when the person at whose instance the tenure is sold purchases it, and sues to recover possession from another who has trespassed previous to such sale, and has held possession for more than twelve years before suit—*Womesh Chunder Gooptoo* v. *Raj Narain Roy*, 10 W. R., 15.   When cause of action arises to auction-purchaser.

LXVII. The purchaser of an under-tenure sold under this Act shall apply to the Zemindar or other land-holder within fifteen days from the day of sale to have his name registered in the Zemindar or other   Act VIII (B. C.), 1865, section 17.   Zemindar how to proceed, if purchaser do not register.

land-holder's books as the purchaser, and shall execute a kabuliat on the same terms and conditions on which the under-tenure was held by the defaulter; and if such application be not made within fifteen days, it shall be lawful for the Zemindar or other land-holder to sue the said purchaser for the delivery of a kabuliat.

Sections 68 & 69.

Act X, 1859, section 112.
Produce of the land to be held hypothecated for the rent.

LXVIII. The produce of the land is held to be hypothecated for the rent payable in respect thereof; and when an arrear of rent, as defined in Section 21 of this Act, is due from any cultivator of land, the zemindar, lakhirajdar, farmer, dependent talookdar, under-farmer, or other person entitled to receive the rent of such land immediately from the actual cultivator thereof, instead of bringing suit for the arrear as hereinbefore provided, may recover the same by distraint and sale of the produce of the land on account of which the arrear is due, under the following rules:—provided always that, when a cultivator has given security for the payment of his rent, the produce of the land for the rent of which security has been given, shall not be liable to distraint. Provided also that no sharer in a joint estate, dependent talook, or other tenure in which a division of lands has not been made amongst the sharers, shall exercise the power of distraint otherwise than through a manager authorised to collect the rents of the whole estate, talook, or tenure, on behalf of all the sharers in the same.

Arrears of rent may be recovered by distraint under the following rules.

Cultivators who have given security to be exempt from distraint.

Proviso.

As to the question whether the produce of the land only and not the land itself is hypothecated for the rent, see the notes to section 59. This section will even apply to cases when the tenant has sublet the land, the crops of the sub-tenant being subject to distraint for rent due from the tenant—*Geetum Sing* v. *Buldeo Kahar*, 4 All., 76.

Act X, 1859, section 113.
No distraint in certain cases.

LXIX. Distraint shall not be made for any arrear which has been due for a longer period than one year, nor for the recovery of any sum in excess of the rent payable for the same land in the preceding year, unless a written engagement for the payment of such excess has been executed by the cultivator. *Sections 70 & 71.*

LXX. The power of distraint vested by Section 68 in Zemindars and other persons entitled to receive rent from cultivators of land, may be exercised by managers under the Court of Wards, Surburakars, and Tehseeldars of estates held under khas management, and other persons lawfully entrusted with the charge of landed property; and also by Naibs, Gomashtahs, and other agents employed by any such persons as aforesaid in the collection of rent, if expressly authorised by power of attorney in that behalf: Provided that if any illegal act is committed by any such Naib, Gomashtah, or other agent under color of the exercise of the said power, the person employing such agent shall be liable, as well as the agent, for any damages accruing by reason of such act. *Act X, 1859, section 114.*

Power of distraint to be exercised by managers under the Court of Wards, &c.

Proviso.

Gomashtahs employed in the collection of rent are not permitted to distrain, unless "expressly authorized by power of attorney in that behalf." To distrain for rent is not within the general scope of a gomashtah's authority, and the landlord would not, therefore, be liable for the acts of a gomashtah, who had not been expressly authorized by him to distrain. Where, however, a landlord did actually order the gomashtah to make the distress, he would be liable for the illegal distress, although it was not made under a written authority. So if the gomashtah paid to the landlord the proceeds of the distress, and the landlord received such proceeds, knowing that they had been obtained by distress, he would, by thus accepting and ratifying the act of the gomashtah, render himself as responsible for the act of the gomashtah, as if he had expressly authorized the illegal act—*Ramjoy Mundle* v. *Kallymohun Roy Chowdry*, Marsh., 282.

Gomashtahs cannot distrain unless specially authorized.

Ratification of illegal distress by landlord.

LXXI. Standing crops and other ungathered products of the earth, and crops or other products when reaped or gathered, and deposited in any threshing-floor or place for treading out grain, or the like, whether in the field or within a home-stead, may be distrained by persons invested with the powers of distraint under the provisions of this Act. But no such crops or products other than the produce of the land in respect of which an arrear of rent is due, or of land held under the same engagement, and no grain or other produce after it has been stored by the cultivator, and no other property whatsoever, shall be liable to distraint under this Act. *Act X, 1859, section 115.*

Standing crops, and crops gathered but not stored, liable to distraint.

104   THE LAW OF LANDLORD AND TENANT.

SECTIONS 72—74.
Act X, 1859, section 116.

With regard to what crops are subject to distress it is said as follows:—" We have considered the sections of Act X of 1859 by virtue of which the right of distress is now exercised in these provinces, and, having regard to the whole of those sections, we are of opinion that the term 'produce of land' is to be construed as equivalent to that which can be gathered and stored, crops of the nature of cereal, or grass or fruit-crops, and it does not apply to the trees from which the crops, if fruit-crops, are gathered. The law of distress in Act X of 1859 is substantially a re-enactment of the law of distress provided by Regulations XVII of 1793, and XXXV and XLV of 1795, and that again has evidently been adopted from the English Statute Law. Now by Statute Geo. 2, c. 19, s. 8, landlords are empowered to distrain corn, grass, or other product growing upon any part of the land demised, and it has been held that the term *product* in the section above quoted applies to such products only as are similar to those specified, to all of which the process of becoming ripe, and of being cut, gathered, made, and laid up when ripe, is incidental. Hence trees, shrubs, and plants growing in a nursery ground cannot be distrained for rent—Selwyn's N. P., p. 669. The provisions of Act X appear to us also to refer only to such produce of the land as becomes ripe and is cut, gathered, and stored "—*Sheo Pershad Tewary* v. *Mussamat Moleema Beebee*, 1 All., 7 c.

Act X, 1859, section 116.
Defaulter to be served with a written demand, &c., before or at the time of distraint.

LXXII. Before or at the time when distraint is made under this Act, the distrainer shall cause the defaulter to be served with a written demand for the amount of the arrear, together with an account exhibiting the grounds on which the demand is made. The demand and account shall, if practicable, be served personally on the defaulter, or, if he abscond or conceal himself, so that they cannot be so served, shall be affixed at his usual place of residence.

Act X, 1859, section 117.
Distress to be proportionate to the arrear if not paid or tendered.

LXXIII. Unless the amount of the demand is immediately paid or tendered, the distrainer may distrain property as aforesaid of value proportionate to the amount of the arrear with costs of the distress; and shall prepare a list or description of the said property, and deliver a copy of the same to the owner, or, if he be absent, affix it at his usual place of residence.

Act X, 1859, section 118.
Standing crops, &c., when attached, to be reaped and stored by the cultivator, or, if he neglect to do so, by the distrainer.

LXXIV. Standing crops and other ungathered products may, notwithstanding the distraint, be reaped and gathered by the cultivator, and may be stored in such granaries or other places as are commonly used by him for the purpose. If the cultivator neglect to do so, the distrainer shall cause the said crops or products to be reaped or gathered, and in such case shall store the same either in such granaries or other places as aforesaid, or in some other convenient place in the neighbourhood. In either case the distrained property shall be placed in the charge of some person appointed by the distrainer for the purpose. Crops or products, which from their nature do not admit of being stored, may be sold, before they are cut or gathered, under the rules hereinafter provided ; but in such case the distraint shall be made at least twenty days before the time when the crops or products, or any part of the same, would be fit for cutting or gathering.

LXXV. If a distrainer shall be opposed, or shall apprehend resistance, and shall desire to obtain the assistance of a public officer, he may apply to the Court, which under the provisions of this Act would have jurisdiction to entertain a suit for the rent for which such distrainer is about to distrain, and the Court may, if it thinks necessary, depute an officer to support the distrainer in making the distraint.

Distrainer may apply for aid to the Court upon occasion of resistance made or apprehended.

LXXVI. When any person, empowered to distrain property under Section 68 or Section 70, shall employ a servant or other person to make the distress, he shall give to such servant or person a written authority (which may be on plain paper) for the same, and the distress shall be made in the name and on the responsibility of the person giving such authority.

Persons empowered to distrain may give written authority to their servants to do so.

LXXVII. If at any time after property has been distrained, and prior to the day fixed for its being put up to sale as hereinafter provided, the owner of the property shall tender payment of the arrear demanded of him and of the expenses of the distress, the distrainer shall receive the same, and shall forthwith withdraw the distress.

Distress to be withdrawn if defaulter tender payment of arrear and expenses of attachment prior to the day of sale.

LXXVIII. Within five days from the time of the storing of any distrained crops or products, or if the crops or products do not from their nature admit of being stored, within five

Application for sale.

days from the time of making the distress, the distrainer shall apply for sale of the same to the Court, which would have jurisdiction to entertain a suit for the rent for which the distress was made.

Sections 79—81.

Act X, 1859, section 123.

LXXIX. The application shall be in writing, and shall contain an inventory or description of the property distrained, the name of the defaulter and his place of residence, the amount due, and the date of the distress, and the place in which the distrained property is deposited. Together with the application, the distrainer shall lodge in Court the amount necessary for the service of a notice upon the defaulter as hereinafter provided.

Form of application.

Cost of notice upon defaulter to be deposited by distrainer.

Act X, 1859, section 124.

LXXX. Immediately on receipt of any application under the provisions of the next preceding Section, the Court, to which such application shall have been made, shall appoint an officer to conduct the sale of such property, and shall cause to be served a notice [which shall be in the form contained in the Schedule (C) to this Act, or to the like effect] on the person whose property has been distrained, requiring him either to pay the amount demanded, or to institute a suit to contest the demand before such Court within the period of fifteen days from the receipt of the notice; and shall at the same time cause to be affixed upon some conspicuous place in the Court-house, a proclamation fixing a day for the sale of the distrained property, which shall not be less than twenty days from the date of the application; and shall deliver a copy of the proclamation to the peon charged with the service of the notice, to be put up by him in the place where the distrained property is deposited. The proclamation shall contain a description of the property, the demand for which it is to be sold, and the place where the sale is to be held.

Procedure by Civil Court on receipt of application.

The simple question to be determined in a suit under this section is whether or not the demand of the distrainer is a good and valid demand—*Doonee Mahtoe* v. *Sheo Narain Singh*, 21 W. R., 37.

Act X, 1859, section 125.

LXXXI. If a suit shall be instituted in pursuance of the aforesaid notice, the Court shall suspend proceedings in regard to the

Sale to be suspended when suit instituted.

sale of the distrained property, and shall certify to the officer appointed to conduct the sale of such suspension.

<small>SECTIONS 82—85.</small>

LXXXII. Any person, whose property has been distrained in the manner in this Act provided, may institute a suit to contest the demand of the distrainer immediately after the distraint of his property, and before the issue of notice of sale; when such suit is instituted, the Court shall suspend proceedings in respect of the sale of such property.

<small>Suit to contest distrainer's demand before issue of notice of sale.</small>

<small>Act X, 1859, section 126.</small>

Where, in a suit under this section to contest the demand, a question as to area was raised merely as a subordinate to the issue as to the amount of the rent due, without any dispute as to the relationship of landlord and tenant, it was held that the case did not come within section 102 of this Act—*Hurro Pershad Chuckerbutty* v. *Sreedam Chunder Chowdry*, 20 W. R., 15.

LXXXIII. The person whose property has been distrained may, at the time of instituting any such suit as aforesaid, or at any subsequent period, execute a bond with sufficient security, binding himself and his sureties to pay whatever sum may be adjudged to be due from him with interest and costs of suit: and when such bond is executed, the Court shall give to the owner of the property a certificate to that effect, or, if so requested, shall serve the distrainer with notice of the same, and upon such certificate being presented to the distrainer by the owner of the property, or served on him by order of the Court, the property shall be released from distraint.

<small>Distress to be withdrawn on receipt of Court's certificate that the owner has executed a bond to pay amount of decree with interest and costs.</small>

<small>Act X, 1859, section 127.</small>

LXXXIV. The estimated value of the claim made in any suit filed under the provisions of Sections 80, 82, and 96, or any of them, shall be deemed to be the amount of arrears of rent for which the distraint shall have been made.

<small>Value of claim in suits disputing distress.</small>

LXXXV. On the expiration of the period fixed in the proclamation of sale, if a suit to contest the demand of the distrainer be not in the meantime instituted in the Court and certified to the officer appointed to conduct the sale, such officer shall, unless the said demand,

<small>On expiration of period fixed in the proclamation of sale, if institution of suit to contest distrainer's demand have not been certified, sale may be proceeded with.</small>

<small>Act X, 1859, section 129.</small>

Sections 86—89.

with such costs of the distress as shall be allowed by him, be discharged in full, proceed to sell the property, or such part of it as may be necessary, in the manner hereinafter prescribed.

Act X, 1859, section 129.

Place and manner of sale of distrained property.

LXXXVI. The sale shall be held at the place where the distrained property is deposited, or at the nearest gunge, bazar, haut, or other place or public resort, if the officer appointed to conduct the sale should be of opinion that it is likely to sell there to better advantage. The property shall be sold by public auction in one or more lots, as such officer holding the sale may think advisable; and if the demand with the costs of distress and sale be satisfied by the sale of a portion of the property, the distress shall be immediately withdrawn with respect to the remainder.

Act X, 1859, section 130.

If fair price be not offered, sale may be postponed to another day, and shall be then completed, at whatever price may be offered.

LXXXVII. If on the property being put up for sale, a fair price, in the estimation of the officer holding the sale, be not offered for it, and the owner of the property or some person authorised to act on his behalf apply to have the sale postponed until the next day or the next market day, if a market be held at the place of sale, the sale shall be postponed until such day, and shall be then completed, at whatever price may be offered for the property.

Act X, 1859, section 131.

Payment of purchase-money.

LXXXVIII. The price of every lot shall be paid for in ready money at the time of sale, or as soon after as the officer holding the sale shall think necessary; and in default of such payment, the property shall be put up again and sold. When the purchase-money has been paid in full, the officer holding the sale shall give the purchaser a certificate describing the property purchased by him and the price paid.

Act X, 1859, section 132.

Proceeds of sale.

LXXXIX. From the proceeds of the sale of distrained property, the officer holding the sale shall make a deduction at the rate of one anna in the rupee on account of the costs of the sale, and shall transmit the amount to the Court, in order that it may be credited to Government. He shall then pay to the distrainer the expenses incurred by

THE LAW OF LANDLORD AND TENANT. 109

the distrainer on account of the distress and of the issue of the notice and proclamation of sale prescribed in Section 80, to such amount as, after examination of the statement of expenses furnished by the distrainer, he shall think proper to allow. The remainder shall be applied to the discharge of the arrear for which the distraint was made, with interest thereupon up to the day of sale; and if there be any overplus, it shall be delivered to the person whose property shall have been sold.

SECTIONS 90—92.

XC. Officers holding sales of property under this Act, and all persons employed by or subordinate to such officers, are prohibited from purchasing, either directly or indirectly, any property sold by such Officers.

Act X, 1859, section 133.

Officers holding sales prohibited from purchasing.

XCI. Officers holding sales of distrained property are required to bring to the notice of the Court any material irregularities committed by distrainers under color of this Act: and if in any case, on proceeding to hold a sale of property, such Officer shall find that the owner of the property has not received due notice of the distress and intended sale, he shall postpone the sale and report the case to the Court, and the Court shall direct the issue of another notice and proclamation of sale under Section 80, or pass such other order as may seem proper.

Act X, 1859, section 134.

All irregularities to be reported to the Court.

XCII. When any such Officer has proceeded to any place for the purpose of holding a sale, and no sale takes place either for the reason stated in the last preceding Section, or because the demand of the distrainer has been previously satisfied, no intimation of such satisfaction having been given by the distrainer to such Officer, the charge of one anna in the rupee on account of expenses shall be leviable, and shall be calculated on the estimated value of the distrained property. If the demand of the distrainer be not satisfied until the day fixed for the sale, the charge for expenses shall be paid by the owner of the property, and may be recovered by the sale of such portion thereof as may be necessary. In all other cases the Court shall make an order that such expenses shall be paid by the distrainer,

Act X, 1859, section 135.

Recovery of expenses if Officer proceed to place of sale and no sale take place.

Sections 93—95.

and shall in such order fix the amount to be paid by him; such amount not to exceed the sum of ten rupees; and the amount by such order directed to be paid may be recovered from such distrainer as if such order were a decree of such Court.

Act X, 1859, section 136.

Proceedings of Officers, &c., subject to revision and orders of Court.

XCIII. All proceedings, under this Act, of the Officers appointed to hold sales of distrained property, shall be subject to the revision and orders of the Court to which they respectively are attached, and the Court may require the submission of such reports and statements of business performed by such Officers as may be thought necessary.

Act X, 1859, section 137.

Second proclamation of sale.

XCIV. When a suit has been instituted to contest the demand of a distrainer, and the property has not been released on security, if the demand or any portion of it shall be adjudged to be due, the Court shall issue an order to the Officer appointed to conduct the sale of such property and furnish a copy of such order to the distrainer, authorising the sale of the property: and on the application of the distrainer, which shall be made within five days from the receipt by him of such copy of such order, such Officer shall publish a second proclamation in the manner prescribed in Section 80, fixing another day for the sale of the distrained property, which shall not be less than five nor more than ten days from the date of the proclamation; and unless the amount adjudged to be due with the costs of distress, including any costs of suit which may be ordered to be paid by the person instituting such suit, be paid intermediately, shall proceed to sell the property in manner hereinbefore provided.

Act X, 1859, section 138.

Procedure after institution of suit to contest distrainer's demand.

XCV. In all suits instituted to contest the demand of a distrainer, the distrainer shall be required to prove the arrear in the same manner as if he had himself instituted a suit for the amount. If the demand or any part thereof is found to be due, the Court shall make a decree for the amount in favor of the distrainer, together with such costs of suit as to such Court may seem proper, and the amount may be recovered by sale of the property as provided in the last preceding Section if the distress has not been withdrawn, and if any balance remain due after such sale, by execution of the decree against the person and any other property of the defaulter, or if the property has been released on security, by execution of the decree against the person and property of the defaulter and of his surety. If, on the other hand, the distraint is adjudged to be vexatious or groundless, the Court, besides directing the release of the distrained property, may award such damages in favor of the plaintiff as the circumstances of the case shall seem to require, and may decree the cost of the suit to be paid by the distrainer.

SECTION 96.

XCVI. If any person shall claim as his own, property which has been distrained for arrears of rent alleged to be due from any other person, such person may institute a suit against the distrainer, and such other person to try the right to the possession of the property in such Court, and in like manner and under the same conditions as to the time of instituting the suit and to the consequent postponement of sale, as a person whose property has been distrained for an arrear of rent alleged to be due from him may institute a suit to contest the demand. When any such suit is instituted, the property may be released upon security being given for the value of the same. If the claim is dismissed, the Court shall make an order for the sale of the property or the recovery of the value thereof, as the case may be, for the benefit of the distrainer, and for payment of such costs of suit to such distrainer, as to such Court shall seem fit. If the claim is upheld, the Court shall decree the release of the distrained property with costs, and such damages (if any) as the circumstances of the case may seem to require. Provided always that no claim to any produce of land liable to distraint under this Act, which at the time of the distress may have been found in the possession of a defaulting cultivator, whether such claim be in respect of a previous sale, mortgage, or otherwise, shall bar the prior claim of the person entitled to the rent of the land ; nor shall any attachment in exclusion of a

Act X, 1859, section 139.

Any person, whose property has been distrained for arrears of rent alleged to be due from another, may institute a suit against the distrainer.

THE LAW OF LANDLORD AND TENANT.

Sections 97—99.

Act X, 1859, section 141.
Persons prevented from suing in time to save their property from sale, may sue for damages.

judgment or decree of any Court prevail against such prior claim.

XCVII. If any person, whose property has been distrained for the recovery of a demand not justly due, or of a demand due or alleged to be due from some other person, is prevented by any sufficient cause from bringing a suit to contest the demand or to try the right to the property, as the case may be, within the period allowed by Sections 82 and 96, and his property is in consequence brought to sale, he may, nevertheless, institute a suit under this Act to recover damages for the illegal distress and sale of his property.

Before a tenant can obtain a decree for damages on the ground of illegal distraint, he must prove what loss he has actually sustained—*Oojan Dewan* v. *Prannath Mundul*, 8 W. R., 220.

Act X, 1859, section 142.
Also persons aggrieved by any illegal act of distrainer.

XCVIII. If any person empowered to distrain property, or employed for the purpose under a written authority by a person so empowered, shall distrain or sell, or cause to be sold, any property for the recovery of an arrear of rent alleged to be due otherwise than according to the provisions of this Act, or if any distrained property shall be lost, damaged, or destroyed by reason of the distrainer not having taken proper precautions for the due keeping and preservation thereof, or if the distraint shall not be immediately withdrawn when it is required to be withdrawn by any provision of this Act, the owner of the property may institute a suit under this Act to recover damages for any injury which he may have thereby sustained.

Act X, 1859, section 143.
Unlawful distraint.

XCIX. If any person not empowered to distrain property under Sections 68 and 70 of this Act, nor employed for the purpose under a written authority by a person so empowered, shall under color of this Act distrain, or sell, or cause to be sold any property, the owner of the property may institute a suit under this Act to recover damages from such person for any injury which he may have sustained from the distraint or sale. The said person shall, when the act complained of does not amount to criminal trespass, be liable to fine, which may extend

THE LAW OF LANDLORD AND TENANT. 113

to three hundred rupees or to imprisonment, simple or rigorous, which may extend to two months, or to both, in addition to any damages which may be awarded against him in such suit.

SECTION 100.

Section 98 contemplates the case of persons having authority to distrain, but who distrain otherwise than according to the provisions of the Act; but "this section," Peacock, C.J., says, "refers to the case of a person distraining under color of the Act when he is not empowered to distrain, and it is clear that, by the use of the words 'under color of the Act,' the Legislature did not mean under circumstances which were sufficient to induce the distrainer honestly to believe that he was justified in making the distress; if that had been their intention, they would not have enacted that the distrainer should be subject to the penalties for the offence of criminal trespass. Section 142 (section 99) gives an action against a person who shall distrain otherwise than under the provisions of the Act. That is an example of a suit arising out of the exercise of the powers of distraint; whilst section 143 (section 99) furnishes an example of a suit arising out of the exercise of the powers of an act done under color of the exercise of the said power"—*Joyloll Sheikh* v. *Brojonath Paul Chowdry*, 9 W. R., 163. And the section not only contemplates the case of a person who professes to follow the provisions of the law, though he has no power to distrain it, but also comprises the case of a person who, under color of the Act, does distrain, but does not do so according to the provisions of the Act—*Radha Mohan Naskar* v. *Jadu Nath Das*, 3 B. L. R., A. C., 261; 12 W. R., 68. So, if a person alleging himself to be a zemindar or other person entitled to receive rent immediately from the cultivator, should exercise the power of distraint and distrain and sell the property of the cultivator, and it should subsequently be found that he is not such zemindar or person entitled, he comes under the description of a person not empowered to distrain property, and the act which he does is done under color of the power of distraint, and the suit consequently comes within the terms of this section—*Ram Chandra Chowdhry* v. *Subal Patro*, 3 B. L. R., App., 74. And a plaintiff must establish distinctly that the defendant distrained when he was a mere trespasser, and when there was no reasonable foundation whatever for the allegation that he was entitled to the rent. The mere fact that the defendant had no legal right to make the distress will not be sufficient—*Raye Kumul Dassee* v. *Jhoroo Mollah*, 15 W. R., 543.

Penalty for illegal distraint.

Strict proof necessary.

C. Provided always that any suit which may be instituted under any of the last three Sections shall be commenced within three months from the date of the occurrence of the cause of action.

Act X, 1859, section 144.
Time for commencing suits for damages.

The three months are not necessarily to be reckoned from the date of the distraint. Thus, where property was attached on the 2nd April 1861, and was liberated from attachment on the 24th June, it was held that a suit for damages for the illegal distress and detention of the

Date from which the three months are to be reckoned.

16

114 THE LAW OF LANDLORD AND TENANT.

SECTIONS
101 & 102.
property was within time, if brought within three months from the 24th June—*Thukree Rai* v. *Heeramun Singh*, Marsh., 470; *Tarinee Churn Bose* v. *Shumboonath Panday*, 3 W. R. (Act X), 139.

Act X, 1859,
section 145.

Procedure on resistance to distraint, &c.

CI. If any person shall resist a distraint of property duly made under this Act, or shall forcibly or clandestinely remove any distrained property, the Court which would have jurisdiction in a suit for the rent for which such distraint was made, shall, upon complaint being made within fifteen days from the date of such resistance or removal, cause the person accused to be arrested; and if the offence be proved, and the offender be the owner of the property, shall order him to be imprisoned in the Civil Jail for six months, or until the whole arrear due to the distrainer, with all expenses and costs, shall be paid or levied by attachment and sale of the property of the offender under warrant of the Court. If the person convicted of the offence be any other than the owner of the property, he shall make good to the distrainer the value of the same, and shall further be liable to a fine not exceeding one hundred rupees, or, in default of payment thereof, to imprisonment for a period not exceeding two months.

A complaint under section 145 of Act X of 1859 was held not to be a suit—*In the matter of Amanatulla*, 6 B. L. R., 569; 15 W. R., 137. When an offence is alleged under this section, the Court is bound first to satisfy itself that the offence has been committed, and then the only order it can make against persons (not tenants) is that they shall pay the value of the crops distrained—*Prem Chand Laha* v. *Addoito Doss*, 20 W. R., 445.

No appeal from any decree of the District Judge for money below Rs. 100, unless it involve the right to enhance rent or a title to land.

CII. Nothing in this Act contained shall be deemed to confer any power of appeal in any suit tried and decided by a District Judge, originally or in appeal, if the amount sued for, or the value of the property claimed, does not exceed one hundred rupees, in which suit a question of right to enhance, or vary the rent of a ryot or tenant, or any question relating to a title to land or to some interest in land as between parties having conflicting claims thereto, has not been determined by the judgment.

Meaning of "District Judge."

The words "District Judge" in this section mean the Judge of the District; it will not, therefore, include a Subordinate Judge to whom a

THE LAW OF LANDLORD AND TENANT. 115

case has been transferred for disposal—*Iswar Chandra Sen* v. *Bepin Behari Roy*, 8 B. L. R., 188 (Note); 16 W. R., 132; *Doyal Chand Sahoy* v. *Nobin Chandra Adhikari*, 8 B. L. R., 180; 16 W. R., 235; *Moonshee Mahomed Munoor Mea* v. *Sreemutty Jybunee*, 10 B. L. R., App., 29; 19 W. R., 200 : nor does it include an Additional Judge— *Nobckisto Koondo* v. *Nazir Mahomed Sheikh*, 10 B. L. R., App., 30; 19 W. R., 201; so that in such cases a special appeal will lie.

Sections 103—105.

The word "suit" in this section includes all proceedings prior to decree as well as all proceedings subsequently to execution—*Kalee Doss Ghose* v. *Lall Mohun Ghose*, 19 W. R., 307.

Meaning of "suit."

Where the Judge avoids deciding the question of title there is no appeal—*Hurry Mohun Mozumdar* v. *Dwarkanath Sen*, 18 W. R., 42. There must be conflicting claims as to title before there can be a special appeal—*Sristeedhur Chuckerbutty* v. *Koonjo Behary Biswas*, 19 W. R., 261. And the conflicting claims must be between the plaintiff and defendant, and not between plaintiff and a third person, who was never made a party to the suit—*Shaikh Dilbur* v. *Issur Chunder Roy*, 20 W. R., 36. Where, in a suit under section 82, a question of area was raised merely as subordinate to the amount of rent due, it was held there was no appeal—*Huro Pershad Chuckerbutty* v. *Sreedam Chunder Chowdry*, 20 W. R., 15. Nor is there any appeal when the question is merely as to the amount of rent due—*Hurish Chunder Chuckerbutty* v. *Sreemutty Huree Bewah*, 20 W. R., 16. And where a shareholder cultivated land belonging to himself and other shareholders, a suit for money to be paid in respect of such land is substantially a suit for rent under this section, and therefore no special appeal lies—*Sreemutty Alladinee Dossee* v. *Sreenath Chunder Bose*, 20 W. R., 258.

Where no appeal lies.

CIII. No application for a review of any judgment or order passed in any suit brought under the provisions of this Act, shall be received by any Court after the expiration of thirty days from the date of such order or judgment, but nothing in this Section contained shall be deemed to apply to the High Court of Judicature at Fort William in Bengal.

Review of judgment.

This section applies merely to reviews of judgment and not to applications to set aside *ex parte* decisions—*Mussamut Drabamayi Guptia* v. *Taracharan Sen*, 7 B. L. R., 207; 16 W. R., 17.

CIV. Nothing in this Act contained shall be deemed to confer upon any Court, sitting as a Court of Small Causes, cognizance of any suit brought under the provisions of this Act, of which it would not have had cognizance if this Act had not been passed.

Small Cause Court not to have jurisdiction.

CV. If in any case the Court is satisfied that a party is unable to pay the cost of any necessary process in any suit under this

Power to issue process free of charge.

116	THE LAW OF LANDLORD AND TENANT.

SECTIONS 106—108.

Act, it may direct such process to be served free of charge.

Application of Act.

CVI. This Act shall take effect in those Districts in the Provinces subject to the Lieutenant-Governor of Bengal to which the said Lieutenant-Governor shall extend it by an order published in the *Calcutta Gazette*, and thereupon this Act shall commence and take effect in the Districts named in such order at the day and time which shall be in such order provided for the commencement thereof.

By Government Notification of the 24th February 1870, published in the *Calcutta Gazette* of the 2nd of March 1870, this Act commenced and took effect in the undermentioned Districts of the Lower Provinces of Bengal on the 13th April 1870, corresponding with the first of Bysakh 1277 of the Bengali year.

Bhaugulpore.
Bhaugulpore, Monghyr, Purneah.

Patna.
Patna, Gya, Chumparun, Sarun, Shahabad, Tirhoot.

Rajshahye.
Rajshahye, Bograh, Dinagepore, Maldah, Moorshedabad, Pubna, Rungpore.

Burdwan.
Burdwan, Bancoorah, Beerbhoom, Hooghly, Howrah, Midnapore.

Presidency.
Nuddea, Jessore, 24-Pergunnahs.

Dacca.
Dacca, Backergunge, Furreedpore, Mymensingh, Sylhet.

Chittagong.
Chittagong, Noakhally, Tipperah.

Certain enactments to cease to have operation in places in which this Act takes effect.

CVII. When and so soon as this Act shall commence and take effect in any District, the various provisions mentioned in Schedule (D) hereto annexed, shall cease to have operation or effect in such District, save so far as they repeal or modify any other Regulations or Acts, and save so far as regards suits or proceedings, which, before the time of the commencement of this Act, shall have been instituted before any Collector.

Pending suits to be carried on under former practice.

CVIII. Whenever any suit or other proceeding under the provisions of the Acts in the Schedule (D) mentioned, or of any of them, shall at the time when this Act comes into operation in any place have been instituted before any Collector or other officer, having under the provisions of the same Acts or of any of them, jurisdiction in such suit or proceeding, such suit or proceeding and all appeals therein shall be heard and determined, and execution of any decree or order therein shall be had, and the practice and procedure therein shall be such and the same, as if this Act had not been passed.

SECTIONS 109—111

CIX. Nothing in this Act contained shall be deemed to take away or abridge any power or authority conferred by an Act passed by the Lieutenant-Governor of Bengal in Council, entitled an Act to ascertain, regulate, and record certain tenures in Chota-Nagpore, on any person appointed to be a Special Commissioner thereunder, or on the Commissioner of the Division of Chota-Nagpore.

Act not to affect powers conferred by the Chota-Nagpore Tenures' Act.

CX. Nothing in this Act contained shall in any way affect any of the provisions of Act VII of 1868 of the Council of the Lieutenant-Governor of Bengal for the recovery of arrears of land revenue, and other demands recoverable as arrears of land revenue.

Act VII of 1868 saved.

CXI. This Act shall be called "The Landlord and Tenant Procedure Act, 1869."

Short title.

SCHEDULE A.

(*Referred to in Section XLVII.*)

I., A. B., of, &c., do solemnly declare that I did personally (or by my Agent, C.D.), on the   day of   tender payment to E. F. at his Mâl Cutcherry (or at   ) the place where the rent of the lands at   held or cultivated by me under or from the said E. F. are usually payable, of the sum of Rupees   as and for the whole amount due from me in respect of the rent of the said lands from the month of   to the month of   both inclusive. I further declare that the said E. F. refused to accept the said sum so tendered (or to give me a receipt in full forthwith for the same); and I do declare

SCHEDULE C. that, to the best of my belief, the sum of Rupees   so tendered, and which I now desire to pay into Court, is the full amount which I owe the said E. F. on account of the rent of the said lands from the month of   to the month of   both inclusive, and that I owe the said E. F. no further sum on account of the rent of the said lands.

SCHEDULE B.
(*Referred to in Section XLVII.*)
Court of
Dated the   day of   18
To E. F. of, &c.,

With reference to the within declaration, you are hereby informed that the sum of Rupees   therein mentioned is now in deposit in this Court, and that the above sum will be paid to you or to your duly authorized Agent on application ; and take notice that if you have any further claim or demand whatsoever to make against the said A. B. in respect of the rent of the said lands, you must institute a suit in Court for the establishment of such claim or demand within six calendar months from this date, otherwise your claim will be for ever barred.

[Copy of declaration in Schedule A. to be annexed.]

SCHEDULE C.
(*Referred to in Section LXXX.*)
FORM OF NOTICE TO OWNER OF DISTRAINED PROPERTY.

Court of
A. B., Distrainer.
(*Name, description, and address of the owner of the property.*)

Whereas the said A. B. has applied to have the distrained property specified below sold for the recovery of   alleged to be due to him as arrears of rent, you are hereby required either to pay the said sum to the said A. B., or to institute a suit in the Court of   to contest the demand within fifteen days from the receipt of this notice, failing which the property will be sold.

Dated this   day of   18   .

THE LAW OF LANDLORD AND TENANT. 119

SCHEDULE D.

(Referred to in Sections CVII and CVIII.)

Being Acts made inoperative in Districts in which this Act is in force.

Date and No. of Act.	Title of Act.	Extent of Repeal.
Act X of 1859 ...	An Act to amend the law relating to the recovery of rent in the Presidency of Fort William in Bengal.	The whole Act.
Act VI of 1862, passed by the Lieutenant-Governor of Bengal in Council.	An Act to amend Act X of 1859.	The whole Act.
Act IV of 1867, passed by the Lieutenant-Governor of Bengal in Council.	An Act to explain and amend Act VI of 1862, passed by the Lieut.-Governor of Bengal in Council, and to give validity to certain judgments.	The whole Act.

INDEX.

[*The Numerals refer to the Section of the Act, the Figures refer to the Page of the Book.*]

ABATEMENT
   of rent by order of court does prove alteration in the rate of rent so as to affect the presumption of s. 4, IV, 12, 13.
   what constitutes, in s. 51, Reg. VIII of 1793, XVI, 42.
   none on account of gradual decrease of rent, XVI, 42.
   of rent, limitation in suits for, XXVII, 71.
   grounds of, XIX, 57.
      diminution of area, XIX, 57.
      diluvion, XIX, 57.
      claims for, not confined to the three grounds mentioned in section, XIX, 59.
      reduction of personal or resumption of lakiraj estate, good ground for, XIX, 57.
      but no right when rents were fixed by pottahs or kabuliats, XIX, 57.
      must be owing to causes beyond tenant control, XIX, 57.
      land covered by sand, XIX, 59, 60.
      cause of action in suits for, dates from extortion of excess rent, XIX, 58.
      good plea on suit for arrears of rent, XIX, 58.
      onus however lies on tenant, XIX, 58.
      land taken up by Government for a road, XIX, 58.
      dispossession from defect in lessor's title, XIX, 58.
   on what principle to be made, XIX, 58.
   can be claimed in a suit for arrears, XIX, 58.
   all ryots or under-tenants can sue for, XIX, 59.
   howladar can sue for, XIX, 59.
   so can a talookdar, XIX, 59.
   zemindar cannot sue Government for, XIX, 60.

ACCOUNTS, see *Agent*.

ACCRETIONS TO UNDER-TENURES—
   general law of, in cl. 1, s. 4, Reg. XI of 1825, XVI, 45.
   tenant-at-will entitled to hold till evicted, XVI, 46.
   held under same legal condition as parent estate, XVI, 46.
   suit for a pottah for an accretion will only lie against the party to whom rent is payable, I, 2.
   belong to owner of under-tenure, XVI, 45.
   when liable to assessment, XVI, 46.

ACT—
   application of, I, 1.
   in what districts it has effect, CVI, 116.
   former enactments repealed by, CVII, 116.
   title of, CXI, 117.

ACT OF GOD—
   tenant not liable for rent if damage is done to land by, XIX, 59.

ADJACENT PLACES—
   meaning of term, XVIII, 52.

INDEX.

ADVERSE POSSESSION—
ryot setting up, against landlord cannot claim right of occupancy, VI, 17.
neglect of tenant to pay rent does not constitute an, XXIX, 74.

AGENT—
undisclosed principal of, can be sued by landlord for rent, XXVI, 70.
who is, XXX, 75.
naib and gomashta is, XXX, XXXII, 75—77.
powers of, XXX, 75.
cannot grant a lease unless specially authorized, XXX, 76.
limitation in suits against, XXX, 75, 76.
    in cases of fraud or fraudulent accounts, XXX, 75.
    due diligence to be used in discovering fraud, XXX, 76.
    when fraud alleged, one year from rendering accounts, XXX, 75.
can conduct suits if specially authorized, XXXII, 77.
    but suit must be brought in name of principal, XXXII, 78.
    and the special authority must be stamped, XXXII, 78.
cannot distrain unless specially authorized, LXX, 103.
can delegate to under-servant power of distraint, LXXVI, 105.

ALLUVION, see *Accretion*.

APPEAL
from order of measurement of Collector, XXXIX, 83.
does not lie from order of Judge in suits not exceeding Rs. 100, CII, 114.
nor as to amount of rent due, CII, 114.
unless question of title. &c., is involved, CII, 115.
when Judge avoids deciding title, there is no appeal, CII, 115.
must be conflicting claim before special appeal, CII, 115.
a minor collateral issue on the question of area will not give right of, CII, 115.

APPROPRIATION OF PAYMENTS
how and when to be made, XI, 32.

AREA
when diminished by diluvion, ryot can sue for abatement, XIX, 57.

ARREARS OF RENT—
purchaser under sale for, cannot evict occupancy-ryot, VI, 17.
definition of, XXI, 62.
courts can award interest on, XXI, 62.
    but not in addition to damages, XXI, 62.
due from ryot, ejectment for, XXII, 63.
due from leaseholders, ejectment for, XXIII, 63, 64.
when due from leaseholder, lease may be cancelled, XXIII, 63.
after realization of, landlord cannot sue for ejectment, XXIII, 64.
limitation in suits for, XXIX, 72.
deductions when allowed, XXIX, 72.
suit for, may be joined with suit for ejectment or cancelment, LII, 89.
unexecuted decree for, evidence in suit for ejectment, LII, 89.
suits for, at enhanced rates to be brought after notice within three months from end of year, XXIX, 73.
the rent must be determined before a suit at enhanced rates can be brought, XXIX, 73.
no suit for arrears, except within six months of deposit, XXXI, 77.
form of plaint in suits for arrears of rent, XLIII, 84.
in suit for, where no tender, damages may be awarded, XLIV, 84, 85.
reversal of sale of tenure for, gives a fresh cause of action, XXIX, 72.

ARREST BEFORE JUDGMENT
not permitted in suits for arrears due from intermediate tenures, L, 88.

INDEX. 123

ASSESSMENT
  of lakhirnj land,
    right to make, to be determined before a suit for kabuliat will
      lie, X, 26.
    by collector under Reg. VII of 1822.
      creates relation of landlord and tenant, XIV, 39.
      notice must be served after, where tenant not agreed
        to rates, XIV, 39.
  of accretions how to be made, XVI, 46.
ATTACHMENT
  of under-tenure, notice to be made, LIX, 94.
ATTENDANCE—
  power to compel, withdrawn from zemindar, XII, 32.
AUCTION-PURCHASER, see also *Sale*.
  under Act VIII of 1865, cannot eject occupancy-ryot, VI, 17.
  under Act XI of 1859,
    can cancel under-tenures, XVI, 48.
      but must exercise his right within a reasonable time,
        XVI, 49.
  of under-tenure sold for arrears
    acquires it free from encumbrances, LXVI, 100.
    certain encumbrances protected, LXVI, 100.
    cannot enhance rents of holding from permanent settlement, III, 8.
    cannot be ousted except on proof of fraud, LXVI, 101.
    cannot cancel under-tenure without giving notice, LXVI, 101.
    must exercise right within reasonable time, LXVI.
    cannot void rights of occupancy, LXVI, 101.
    fraud or collusion sale destroys right of, LXVI, 101.
    power of, in cancelling under-tenures, LXVI, 100, 101.
  to apply to zemindar for registration, LXVII, 101.
BASTOO LAND, see *Building Leases*.
BENAMEE—
  where lease is taken, landlord may sue the real lessee, XXVI, 69.
BHIKYA, XI, 31.
BOUNDARIES, see *Excess Land*.
BUILDING LEASE—
  land let on, not liable to enhancement, XVIII, 50.
  but homestead of ryot is not exempt from enhancement, XVIII, 50.
  fact of building being allowed to remain *primâ facie* proof that land
    was let for, XVII, 51.
BUKOOMAT, XI, 30.
BURDEN OF PROOF
  on the landlord in a suit for a kabuliat against the holder of a rent-
    free tenure, X, 26.
  on distrainer in suits to contest demand, XCV, 110.
CANCELMENT OF UNDER-TENURES—
  after sale of superior tenure to be made within a reasonable time,
    XVI, 49.
  of lease, see *Lease*.
CANOONGO PAPERS—
  value of, IV, 14.
  value of, as to standard pole, XLI, 84.
CAUSE OF ACTION—
  where sale of tenure for arrears is reversed, fresh cause of action arises
    from date of reversal, XXIX, 72.
  declaratory decree not a, XXIX, 73.

CESSES
> only recoverable when ryot has contracted to pay, XI, 30.
> contract to collect an illegal cess void, XI, 30.
> what are illegal, XI, 30.
> illegal, included in rent and paid for three years does not legalize, XI, 30.
> limitation in suits for unauthorized, XXVII, 70.

CIVIL COURTS—
> all suits under this Act to be brought in, XXXIII, 78.
>> where land is situated within the jurisdiction of two courts, XXXVI, 79.

CLASS—
> ryots of same, meaning of the term, XVIII, 51.

CODE OF CIVIL PROCEDURE—
> procedure under this Act regulated by, XXXIV, 78.
> section 119 of, made applicable to rent suits, XXXIV, 79.

COLLECTOR—
> interpretation of, I, 2.
> lands taken possession of by, as administrator cannot be sued for rent by superior landlord, I, 2.
> to serve notices
>> of relinquishment, XX, 60, 61.
> to make measurements, XXXVIII, 81.
>> when he has completed measurement, to return copy thereof to court, XXXIX, 83.
>> when orders of, appealable, XXXIX, 83.
>> powers of, as to summoning witnesses, XL, 83.
>> may decide what is standard pole, XLI, 83.
>> procedure to be observed by, in making measurement, XXXVIII, XL, 81, 83.

COLLUSIVE DECREE
> destroys right of auction-purchaser under section 66, LXVI, 101.
> can be set aside for fraud, LIX, 95.

COMPENSATION—
> suit for, in shape of rent is not a suit for rent, II, 4.
> for rent wrongfully extorted, XIII, 33.
> in what cases awardable to defendants after deposit, XLV, 85.

CONTRACT
> to pay illegal cess void, XI, 30.
> written as to cultivation not affected by Act, VII, 22.
> obligation to pay rent a contract single and entire, X, 28.
> to pay illegal cess invalid, XI, 30.

CO-PROPRIETOR—
> holding under one of several, gives right of occupancy, VI, 17.

CO-SHARER, see *Shareholder.*

COSTS—
> plaintiff subject to, if after tender he fails to obtain larger amount than payment into court, XLVIII, 87.
> on payment into court without previous tender, XLIX, 88.

CROPS—
> what may be distrained, LXXI, LXXIV, 103, 104.

CUSTOMARY—
> rates, meaning of, XVI, 45.
> rate, effect of using the words in lease, XVI, 44.

DAKHILAS, see *Receipts.*

DAMAGES, see *Exaction of Rent, Receipts, Distraint.*
    in what cases awardable in suits for arrears of rent, XLIV, 84, 85.
    cannot be awarded in addition to interest, XLIV, 85.
    but may be awarded in addition to rent, XLIV, 85.
    extent of, must be proved before decree for, XCVII, 112.

DECLARATORY DECREE
    obtainable under section 14, XIV, 39.
    not a cause of action, XXIX, 73.

DECREE, see *Execution of Decree.*
    when no date fixed on, for kabuliat, X, 29.
    for enhancement not to be retrospective, XIV, 37.
    for ejectment, should specify arrears due, LII, 90.
    when set aside whether sale of under-tenure invalid, LIX, 95, 96.

DEPENDENT TALOOKDAR—
    when holding at fixed rent from permanent settlement not liable to enhancement, XVI, 40.
    grounds of enhancement of rent of, XVI, 41.

DEPOSIT—
    where rent has been deposited, suit for previous arrears to be brought within six months, XXXI, 77.
    can only be made after tender of rent due, XXXI, XLVI, 77, 86.
    notice after, must be in accordance with Schedule B of the Act XXXI, 77.
    when, has been made, and plaintiff only entitled to that amount, defendant to have compensation, XLV, 85.
    to operate as payment, XLVI, 86.
    zemindar entitled to notice of interest of person who makes, XLVI, 86.
    when it renders defendant entitled to make it a set-off, XLVI, 86.
    after, notice to be issued by court, XLVII, 86, 87.
    by person claiming under-tenure when it is attached in execution of decree, LXIII, 98.
    procedure in making, XLVII, 86.
    stamp upon application for making, XLVII, 87.

DILUVION—
    a ground for abatement of rent, XIX, 57.
    and can be pleaded in answer to a suit for rent, XIX, 58.

DISABILITY, LEGAL
    no deduction allowed for, in rent suits, XXIX, 72.

DISPOSSESSION
    by landlord what amounts to, II, 4.
    from defect of lessor's title entitles tenant to proportionate abatement, XIX, 58.
    principle upon which the abatement is to be made, XIX, 58.

DISTRAINT—
    limitation in suits arising out of the exercise of, XXVII, 71.
    landlord of actual cultivator entitled to make, LXVIII, 102.
        unless cultivator has given security, LXVIII, 102.
    shareholders to distrain through common manager, LXVIII, 102.
    arrears at enhanced rates or of more than one year's standing not recoverable by, LXIX, 102.
    gomashtahs, unless specially authorized, cannot make, LXX, 103.
        responsibility of landlord for gomashtah's acts, LXX, 103.
        ratification of illegal distraint by landlord, LXX, 103.
    stored grain not liable to, LXXI, 104.
    notice to be served on defaulter, LXXII, 104.

DISTRAINT—(*Continued*).
  of standing crops, LXXIV, 104.
  distrainer if opposed to apply to court for assistance, LXXV, 105.
  agent can delegate his power of, LXXVI, 105.
  proceedings preliminary to sale, LXXVIII, LXXX, 105, 106.
  sale to be suspended, if suit to contest demand is instituted, LXXXI, LXXXIII, 106, 107.
  value of suit how to be estimated, LXXXIV, 107.
  procedure in conducting sale, LXXXVI, LXXXVIII, 108.
  application of proceeds of sale, LXXXIX, 108.
  irregularities to be reported to court, XC, XCI, 109.
  recovery of expenses of, where sale is stayed, XCII, 109.
  second proclamation of sale, XCIV, 110.
  in suit to contest demand, burden of proof lies upon distrainer, XCV, 110.
  damages for vexatious distraint, XCV, 110.
  suit by third party claiming the distrained property, XCVI, 111.
  suit for damages, for illegal distress and sale, XCVII, 112.
    for wrongful distraint, XCVIII, 112.
    for unauthorized distraint, XCIX, 112.
    for damages will lie whether distrainer acted *bonâ fide* or not, XCIX, 112.
    strict proof requisite to prove, XCIX, 113.
    for damages to be brought within three months, C, 113.
    date from which the three months is to be reckoned, C, 113.
  resistance of, penalty for, CI, 114.
  penalty for unauthorized distraint, XCIX, 112, 113.
  complaint under the section in suit, CI, 114.

DISTRICT JUDGE—
  " District Judge" in section 102 does not include Subordinate Judge, nor Additional Judge, CII, 115.

DIVISION
  of tenure, landlord need not give effect to or register, XXVI, 69.

EJECTMENT—
  ryot liable to, for arrears due at end of year, XXII, 63.
  remedy in case of unlawful, XXII, 63.
  leaseholder liable to, for arrears of rent. XXIII, 63.
    but only under order of court, XXIII, 63.
  leaseholder otherwise not liable to, except under conditions of lease, XXIII, 64.
  landlord cannot sue for, after he has realized arrears, XXIII, 64.
  limitation in suits for, XXVII, 71.
  suits for arrears of rent may be joined in suit for, LII, 89.
  unexecuted decree evidence of arrears in suit for, LII, 89.
  only those suits for ejectment for arrears are contemplated by the Act, LII, 89.
  receipt of rent after forfeiture bars the right of, XXIII, 64.
  barred, if amount is paid within 15 days from decree, LII, 89.
    even if lease provides for forfeiture on non-payment, LII, 90.
    the 15 days run from final decree, LII, 90.
    and a longer period may be granted, LII, 90.
  of non-occupancy-ryots and under-tenants holding over after expiration of lease, LIII, LIV, 90, 91.
    immediate execution in such cases to be issued, LIII, 90.

ENHANCEMENT, NOTICE OF
  in what month to be served, XIV, 33.
  in what cases necessary, XIV, 33, 34.
  in case of occupancy-ryots must show grounds as in section 18, XV, 34.

INDEX. 127

ENHANCEMENT, NOTICE OF—(*Continued*).
    requisites of, XIV, 35.
    what is good, XIV, 35.
    what is bad, XIV, 35.
    effects of, XIV, 37.
    judgment operates as, XIV, 37.
    failure to prove, XIV, 37.
    by whom to be issued, XIV, 37.
    on whom to be served, XIV, 38.
    naib may serve, XIV, 38.
    separate for each holding, XIV, 38.
        unless holding is consolidated, XIV, 38.
    objection as to, in special appeal, XIV, 39.
    ryots in government estates entitled to, XIV, 39.
    should not be prospective or retrospective, XIV, 37.

ENHANCEMENT OF RENT—
    rent paid in kind no bar to, II, 5.
    no ryot liable to, except after notice, XIV, 33.
    in what way ryot may contest, XV, 39.
    in suit to contest, court cannot fix rate of rent, XV, 40.
    grounds of, of dependant talookdar, XVI, 41.
    grounds of, of permanent transferable tenures, XVI, 45.
    dependant talookdars and others holding from permanent settlement, not liable to, XVI, 40.
    decree declaring right to, rebuts presumption that rent has been unchanged, XVII, 50.
    in suit for, where plaintiff fails, plaint must be dismissed, XVIII, 56.
    a decree cannot be given at admitted rates, XVIII, 56.
    by dur-izaradar, XVIII, 56.
    occupancy-ryot how liable to, XVIII, 50.
    grounds of, XVIII, 50.
        prevailing rate, XVIII, 51.
        rates paid by ryots of the same class, XVIII, 51.
        increase in value of produce, or productive powers of land, XVIII, 52.
        rule of proportion to be followed in adjusting rent to increase, XVIII, 52, 53.
    excess land, when liable to, XVIII, 55.

EQUITABLE RELIEF
    in cases of forfeiture, XXIII, 64.
    in suits for ejectment or cancelment, LII, 90.

ESTABLISHED USAGE—
    meaning of, XXI, 62.

ESTOPPEL—
    tenant estopped from denying landlord's title, II, 5.

EVICTION—
    does not destroy ryot's possession, IV, 13, 14.

EXACTION OF RENT—
    by landlord from ryot irrespective of ticca lease, XI, 31.
    suit by ryot for repayment of excess rent obtained by zemindar under legal process will not lie under section 11, XI, 31.
    penalty for illegal, XI, 31.
    what is illegal, XI, 31.
    by duress prohibited, XIII, 32.
    penalty in such cases, XIII, 33.
    limitation in suit for illegal, XXVII, 70.

EXCESSIVE DEMAND OF RENT—
    suit for, can be brought by ryot not having a right of occupancy, VIII, 24.
    but the rate of rent to be paid cannot be fixed in such suit, XV, 40.
    ryot whose land has diluviated can sue for, XIX, 57.
    when ryot may bring complaint of, XV, 39.
    limitation in suit for, XXVII, 71.

EXCESS LAND—
    co-sharer holding, can be sued for rent, IV, 14.
    when mentioned in notice must state actual quantity, XIV, 36.
    when suit for rent of, can be brought, XVIII, 55.
    when liable to assessment, XVI, 46.
    assessment of, XVIII, 55.
    holder of, not necessarily a trespasser, XVIII, 55.

EXECUTION OF DECREE
    in cases of ejectment, LII, LIII, LIV, 89, 90, 91.
    where amount of decree paid 15 days after, may be stayed, LII, 89.
    such 15 days may be extended in discretion of court, LII, 90.
    not to be stayed pending appeal, LIV, 91.
    for pottah, LV, 92.
    for kabuliat, LVI, 92.
    process not to issue simultaneously against person and property, LVII, 92.
    in suits under Rs. 500 not to issue after 3 years, LVIII, 92.
        the costs of execution to be reckoned in the Rs. 500, LVIII, 93.
        application for, made within 3 years, can be carried out after the 3 years, LVIII, 93.
        the 3 years dates from the final decree, LVIII, 93.
    for arrears against under-tenure, LXI, 96, 97.
    against immoveable property when permissible, LXV, 100.
    in favour of sharers in joint estates, LXIV, 99.

EX PARTE JUDGMENT—
    sale under, effect of, LIX, 94.

FARMER
    is a middleman, not a ryot, VI, 16.
    to issue notice of enhancement, XIV, 37.
    can sue for enhancement when zemindar issued notice before lease, XIV, 37.

FISHERY, see *Julkur*.
    lessee of, no right to the land covered by water, II, 4.
    no right of occupancy in, VI, 16.
    suit for kabuliat of, may lie, X, 29.
    right of occupancy cannot be acquired in, VI, 16.

FIXED RATES OF RENT—
    meaning of the term, III, 6.
    rent in kind may be, III, 6, 7.
    not affected by a trifling difference in jumma, III, 7.
    nor by an increase in rent through increase in lands, III, 8.
    nor by reduction in rent through reduction in lands, III, 7.
    nature of the holding need not be considered as to, III, 7.
    tenants at fixed rates in the same category as those who hold at rates assessable according to fixed rules, III, 7.
    nor by the payment in company's instead of sicca rupees, III, 7.
    when ryot suing for renewal of lease fails to prove it, VI, 20.
    who are entitled to hold at, III, 6.
    not affected by the consolidation of several jummas into one, III, 7.
    nor by subdivision of jumma, III, 7.
    land held at, from permanent settlement, III, 6.

FIXED RATES OF RENT—(*Continued*).
    presumption of 20 years' holding at, IV, 9.
    talookdars and other holders who have held at, from permanent settlement not liable to enhancement, XVI, 40.

FORFEITURE—
    waiver of, XXIII, 65.
        by receipt of rent, XXIII, 64.
    equitable relief in cases of, XXIII, 64.
    tenant holding over bound by conditions of, contained in the lease, XXIII, 65.
    right of, once waived cannot be revived, XXIII, 65.
    for non-payment of rent barred if decree is satisfied in 15 days, LII, 89.
        even if lease provides for forfeiture on non-payment, LII, 90.

FRAUD—
    on part of lessor is valid ground of abatement, XIX, 60.
    when auction-purchaser has knowledge of, voids rights, LXVI, 101.
    when agent is guilty of, limitation runs from discovery of, XXX, 75.
        due diligence to be used in discovering, XXX, 76.

GHATWALEE TENURES
    held on condition of service, XVI, 47.
    not liable to resumption if service is dispensed with, XVI, 47.
    holder of, not competent to grant lease in perpetuity, XVI, 48.
    rents of, not liable for debts of deceased owner, XVI, 48.

GOMASHTAH, see *Agent*.
    can serve notice of enhancement, XIV, 38.

GOVERNMENT ESTATE—
    ryots in, entitled to notice of enhancement, XIV, 39.

HEREDITARY—
    right of occupancy is, VI, 19.
    question as to this discussed, VI, 20, 22.
    putnee talook is *primâ facie*, XVI, 42.
    so is sarbarokaree, XVI, 42.
    right conveyed when the words *mokururee istemraree* are used, XVI, 43.
        but usage will supply the omission of the words, XVI, 43.

HOLDING OVER
    by tenant does not create right of occupancy, VI, 17.
    immediate execution may issue against tenant, LIII, 90, 91.
    notice must be given to tenant, LIII, 91.
    effect of, after expiry of lease, LIII, 91.
    tenant, bound by condition of lease, XXIII, 65.

HOUSE—
    occupancy-ryot can build a pukka house without landlord's consent, VI, 21.
    no encumbrance, LXVI, 101.

IMMOVEABLE PROPERTY—
    execution against, not to issue till moveable property is exhausted, LXV, 100.

IMPROVEMENTS—
    ryot not liable to enhanced rent upon, XVIII, 53, 54.

INSTALMENT
    of rent not paid is an arrear of rent, XXI, 62.

INTEREST
    awardable on arrears of rent, XXI, 62.
    but not in addition to damages, XXI, 62.
    waiver of, by landlord, XXI, 62.
    damages when awarded are in lieu of, XLIV, 85.
    may be given on compensation awarded, XLV, 85.
INTERMEDIATE TENURE—
    notice of enhancement must be served on holders of, XIV, 36.
    how holders of, to be enhanced, XIV, XVI, 36.
    not liable to enhancement, if held at fixed rents from permanent settlement, XVI, 40.
    effect of Government sale on, XVI, 48.
        are not void, but only voidable after such sale, XVI, 48.
        and within a reasonable time, XVI, 49.
    rent of, how to be enhanced, XVI, 41.
    grounds of enhancement of, XVI, 41.
        cannot be enhanced beyond customary rates, XVI, 42.
        rule for enhancement of, when customary rates do not exist, XVI, 42.
    accretions to, how to be assessed, XVI, 46.
    presumption in favour of, held at unchanged rent for 20 years, XVII, 49.
    proprietor of, required to register transfer in zemindar's sheristah, XXVI, 67.
        but recognition by landlord may supply the place of registration, XXVI, 69.
        section 52 does not apply to holders of, LII, 91.
    in suits for arrears of rent of, arrest before judgment not to issue, L, 88.
    procedure on sale of, LIX, 94.
    hypothecated to landlord for rent, LIX, 94, 95.
    sold for arrears, cannot be resold for previous arrears, LIX, 95.
    sale of, impeachable for fraud, LIX, 95.
    cannot be sold, while other execution against personal or moveable property is in force, LXI, 96, 97.
    person interested in, can stay the sale, LXII, 98.
    procedure where third party claims, LXIII, 98.
        but unregistered under-tenant cannot claim, LXIII, 98.
        unless he has been recognized by landlord as a tenant, LXIII, 98.
    voidable after sale of superior tenure for arrears, LXVI, 100.
        unless created by consent of superior holder, LXVI, 100.
JUDGMENT-DEBTOR—
    property of, only can be sold under the Act, LIX, 94.
    no sale of under-tenure for arrears while warrant out against person or moveable property of, LXI, 96, 97.
    only rights and interests of, are sold in a suit by sharer for arrears, LXIV, 99.
JULKUR—
    possession of, conveys no right of occupancy, VI, 16.
    lease of, does not include land covered by water, II, 4.
JUMMA-WASIL-BAKEE PAPERS—
    value of, as evidence, IV, 14.
JUNGLE-BOORIE
    leases, XVI, 47.
    right of ryot to hold under, XVI, 47.
    when rent of, considered as fixed, XVI, 47.
JURISDICTION, see *Civil Courts*.
    under this Act, CVI, 116.
    transferred in certain cases by Act III of 1870, XXXIII, 78.
        in certain cases, XXXV, 79.
        where arises in different places, XXXVI, 79.

INDEX. 131

KABULIAT—
every person who grants a pottah entitled to, X, 26.
binding on zemindar though pottah be not forthcoming, II, 4.
suit for, will not lie unless position of landlord and tenant, I, 1.
landlord cannot be released from conditions of, if no pottah, II, 4.
court can fix the term of, before decree, X, 29.
must be given if pottah is tendered, X, 26, 27.
trespasser cannot be sued for, X, 26.
nor holder of rent-free land, X, 26.
separate, cannot be sued for, for mâl waste lands included in lease and afterward brought under cultivation, X, 28.
in what cases to be registered, X, 29.
stamps required for, X, 29.
    in what cases exempt from stamp-duty, X, 29.
    by whom stamp-duty to be paid, X, 30.
decree for, how to be executed, LVI, 92.
see *Suit for a Kabuliat.*

KHAMAR, see *Neej-jote.*

KHAS MEHALS—
rent of ryots in Government, can only be enhanced after notice, XIV, 39.

KIND, see *Rents in kind.*

LAKHIRAJ, see *Rent-free.*

LANDHOLDER
cannot sue unless possession has been given, II, 3.
not responsible for tortious acts of third parties, II, 3.
cannot compel attendance of tenant, XII, 32.
damages against, for extorting payment by duress, XIII, 33.

LANDLORD AND TENANT—
relation of, must be established before a suit will lie, I, 1.
    if denied, court must determine whether it exists, I, 1.
    decree of Civil Court declaring zemindar's right to assess lands sufficient to establish relation of, I, 1.
    in what cases it has been held to exist, I, 1.
    in what cases it has been held not to exist, I, 2.
    may exist, where land is cultivated by tenant without permission, XVIII, 55.
right of tenant to possession, II, 3.
landlord's guarantee to tenant against eviction, II, 3.
granting lease to third party amounts to dispossession of tenant, II, 4.
any interference with tenant amounts to dispossession, II, 4.
where tenant dispossessed by no fault of landlord bound to pay rent, II, 4.
defaulting tenant cannot purchase at sale of his tenure, LIX, 95.
where lease merely gives right of julkur, tenant has no right to land covered by water, II, 4.
tenant setting up adverse title to landlord not entitled to presumption of section 4, IV, 10.
    nor entitled to right of occupancy, VI, 17.
higher rate of rent cannot be recovered than that mentioned in the notice, XIV, 39.
when lease existing, no notice of relinquishment need be given, XX, 61.
tenant estopped from denying landlord's title, II, 5.
shareholder may be a tenant, IV, 14.

LEASE
granted by person with limited interest binding upon lessor, but not upon reversioner, II, 4.
in what cases requires registration, II, 5.
stamp-duty required upon, II, 5.

LEASE—(*Continued*).
    lease to cultivators exempt from stamp-duty, II, 5.
    when second made to alter, the first must be stamped afresh, II, 6.
    interpretation of, in Stamp Act, II, 6.
    tenant holding over after, does not thereby create right of occupancy, VI, 17.
    as to right of occupancy where tenant has held under successive leases, VI, 18.
    rights of parties under, II, 4.
    of julkur does not include land covered by the water, II, VI, 4.
    holding over, after expiry does not create right of occupancy, VI, 17.
    failure to produce, does not void right of occupancy, VI, 18.
    right of re-entry under, VII, 23.
    how affects right of occupancy, VII, 23.
    continuous possession under several, gives right of occupancy unless express stipulation to the contrary, VII, 23.
    no notice of relinquishment need be given, XX, 61.
    liability of holder of *mokururee istemraree* to be determined by, XXII, 63.
    landlord cannot eject, except on breach of conditions of, XXIII, 64.
    but right of ejectment for arrears need not be provided in, XXIII, 64.
    cancelment of, for arrears, XXIII, 63.
    appointment of sezawul does not determine, XXIII, 65.
    where benamee, landlord may sue real tenant, XXVI.
    limitation in suit for cancelment of, XXVII, 71.
    effect of tenant holding over after expiration of, LIII, 91.
    suit for arrears of rent may be joined with suit for cancelment of, LII, 89.
    hereditary when the words "mokururee" or "generation after generation" are used, XVI, 43.
    but usage will supply the omission of the words, XVI, 43.
    "year by year" lease, XVI, 44.
    does lease with defined boundaries cover all land included within the boundaries, XVI, 46.
    specimen of jungle-boorie, XVI, 47.
    where full customary rate is fixed, that rate not to be exceeded, XVI, 47.

LESSEE
    entitled to quiet possession, II, 3.
    remedy if evicted, II, 3.
        by title paramount, II, 3.
        by mere stranger, II, 3.
    estopped from disputing lessor's title, II, 5.
    may sue for excess rent collected by zemindar, II, 3.
    must make lessor co-defendant in suit for possession, II, 3.

LESSOR
    guarantees quiet possession, II, 3.
    fraud on part of, does not constitute good ground for abatement, XIX, 60.

LIMITATION
    in suits by auction-purchaser to void tenures, LXVI, 101.
    general law of, does not apply to rent-suits, XXIX, 72.
    and no deduction of time allowed for minority, &c., XXIX, 72.
    suits to which limitation of one year applies, XXVII, 70.
    in suits for pottahs and kabuliats, XXVIII, 71.
        for arrears of rent, XXIX, 72.
        for arrears at enhanced rates, XXIX, 73.
    where sale of tenure for arrears is reversed, limitation runs from date of reversal, XXIX, 72.

LIMITATION—(*Continued*).
  in suits against agents, XXX, 75.
  in cases of fraud or fraudulent accounts, XXX, 75.
  in cases in which deposit is made, and further balance is claimed, XXXI, 77.
  in decrees for sums under Rs. 500, LVIII, 92.

MAL CUTCHERRY—
  notice may be fixed on, XIV, 33.

MANAGERS OF KHAS ESTATES
  can sue and be sued under this Act, XXIV, 66.
  can exercise the powers of distraint, LXX, 103.

MEASUREMENT—
  landlord has a right to make a, XXV, 66.
  but not, if he is not in possession, XXV, 66.
  right of, not affected by land being let out on fixed leases, XXV, 67.
  zemindar cannot measure lakhiraj land, XXV, 67.
  application to be made to Court by landlord if opposed in making, XXXVII, 80.
  value of stamp on which application is to be written, XXXVII, 80.
    separate application for each ryot not necessary, XXXVII, 80.
  to be made by Collector when landlord cannot ascertain who are the tenants, XXXVIII, 81.
  shareholder alone cannot obtain, XXXVII, 80.
  notice must be served before, XXXVII, 80.
  where ryot does not attend, he cannot afterwards contest, XXXVII, 80.
  landlord's intention must be *bonâ fide* as to, XXXVII, 80.
  where proprietor is unable to make, may apply to the Court, XXXVIII, 81.
    who may apply, XXXVIII, 81.
    grounds on which application may be granted, XXXVIII, 82.
    one application may include many ryots, XXXVIII, 82.
    intervenors, XXXVIII, 82.
  powers of Collector as to, XL, 82, 40.
  objection as to, to be taken during proceeding, XXXVIII, 82.
  when completed by Collector, copy to be returned to Court, XXXIX, 83.
  standard pole to be used in making, XLI, 83.
    responsibility of using the correct standard lies with Collector, XLI, 83.
  canoongoes papers of great weight in determining standard, XLI, 84.

MESNE PROFITS
  can be included in suit for possession, LI, 88.
  principle on which to be calculated, LI, 88.
  separate suits for, will lie, LI, 89.

MIDDLEMAN
  cannot acquire right of occupancy, VI, 15.
  difference with ryot, VI, 15.
  section 52 does not apply to, LII, 90.

MINORITY
  cannot be pleaded in bar of limitation in rent-suits, XXIX, 72.

MOKURUREE, see *Hereditary* and *Lease*.
  occupancy-ryot can grant mokururee lease, VI, 18.

MOUROOSEE
  holdings, XVI, 43.

NAIB, see *Agent*.

NAJAI, XI, 30.

NEEJ-JOTE LAND—
    under what circumstances right of occupancy can be obtained in, VI, 20.
    passes to purchaser on sale of zemindaree, VI, 20.

NOTICE
    of deposit, limitation after, XXXI, 77.
    of intended measurement to be given, XXXVII, 79.
    to be given to tenant holding over after lease, LIII, 91.
    of attachment and sale of under-tenure, how to be made, LIX, 94.
                              what to contain, LIX, 94.

OCCUPANCY, RIGHT OF—
    who are entitled to, VI, 16.
    who are not entitled to, VI, 17.
    loss or determination of, VI, 18.
    occupation of trespasser gives no, VI, 17.
    nor permissive occupation, VI, 17.
    nor possession in capacity of servant, VI, 17.
    nor can assignee of zemindar claim, VI, 17.
    sub-lessee cannot claim, VI, 17.
    can be pleaded after failure to prove pottah, VI, 19.
    how affected by a lease, VII, 23.
    cannot be voided by auction-purchaser, LXVI, 100.
    accrues after 12 years' holding, VI, 15.
    middlemen not entitled to, VI, 13.
        but only in land used for agricultural purposes, VI, 16.
    does not accrue in land used for building, VI, 16.
        nor for the erection of a school, VI, 16.
        nor in a julkur, VI, 16.
        nor in a tank, VI, 16.
    holding over after expiry of lease does not create, VI, 19.
    tenants-at-will acquire, VI, 19.
    accrues although rent is paid for part of the term to parties not entitled to receive it, VI, 17.
    accrues on land held for grazing purposes, VI, 16.
    holding under one of several co-proprietors gives, VI, 17.
    change in proprietary title does not affect, VI, 17.
    howladaree tenure gives, VI, 17.
    also a bhagdaree tenure, VI, 18.
    holding under several consecutive pottahs when there is no express stipulation to the contract gives, VI, VII, 18, 23.
    a yearly tenant holding for 12 years obtains, VI, 18.
    not forfeited on failure to produce written lease, VI, 18.
    an hereditary right, VI, 19.
    is transferable by sale when custom exists, VI, 19.
    such custom cannot be presumed, VI, 19.
    must be mentioned on doul, VI, 19.
        is transferable with consent of zemindar, VI, 19.
    under what circumstances can be acquired in *neej-jote* land, VI, 20.

OCCUPANCY-RYOT
    entitled to pottah at fair and equitable rent, V, 15.
    present rent presumed to be fair, V, 15.
    privilege of, not confined to those who till the soil, VI, 16.
    distinction between, and middlemen, VI, 15.
    inception of tenure to be considered in distinguishing between, and middlemen, VI, 16.
    cannot be evicted by purchaser for arrears of rent, VI, 17.
    can build pucca house on holding, VI, 21.
    when can transfer his tenure, VI, 19.
    can sub-let, VI, 18.
    does not thereby destroy his status of, VI, 18.

OCCUPANCY-RYOT—(*Continued*).
    can make mokurruree lease, VI, 18.
    need not register transfer of holding in zemindar's sheristah, XXVI, 68.
    rent of, can only be enhanced after notice, XIV, 33.
    grounds on which he can be enhanced, XVIII, 50.
    can resist notice of enhancement by complaint of excessive demand of rent, XV, 39.
    in suing for pottah, is barred by the allegations in plaint, IX, 25.
    can sue for abatement, XIX, 57.
    cannot be ejected otherwise than by Court, XXII, 63.
PAYMENT OF RENT
    to each shareholder his separate quota no evidence of consent to division of tenure, X, 28.
    appropriation of, when tenant evicts to specify, XI, 32.
    for current year not proof that rent of past year has been paid, XI, 32.
        but is *primâ facie* evidence of the fact, XI, 32.
    enforcement of, by zemindar withdrawn except under Act XII, 32.
    ryot must tender, XXI, 62.
PAYMENT INTO COURT
    in suits under the Act after tender, procedure, XLVIII, 87.
        before tender, XLIX, 88.
PAYMENTS, APPROPRIATION OF, see *Appropriation*.
PERMANENT SETTLEMENT—
    date of, III, 8.
    effect of holding from, at unchanged rent, III, 6.
        if rent has been changed, III, 8.
    holding from, secure against auction-purchaser, III, 8.
    but not if the rent has changed, III, 8.
    when land held from, nature of holding need not be considered, III, 7.
    presumption as to holding from, *see* Presumption.
    intermediate tenure held from, XVI, 40.
PERMANENT TRANSFERABLE TENURE
    when held at fixed rent from permanent settlement not liable to enhancement, XVI, 40.
    what is, XVI, 42.
    grounds of enhancement of, XVI, 45.
    persons holding, to register transfer in zemindar's sheristah, XXVI, 67.
        but recognition by landlord supplies the place of registration, XXVI, 69.
    attachment and sale of, notice how to be made, LIX, 94.
    sold for arrears cannot be resold for previous arrears, LIX, 95.
PLACES ADJACENT—
    meaning of, XVIII, 52.
PLAINT—
    form of, to be used in suits for arrears of rent, XLIII, 84.
    presented by agent to be drawn out in principal's name, 69.
    may include arrears of rent and ejectment, LII, 89.
PLEADINGS
    if inconsistent with claim of holding from permanent settlement voids presumption, IV, 10.
    plea of actual occupation not absolutely necessary, IV, 11.
    nor from the term of the decennial settlement, IV, 11.
    plea of holding from generation to generation construed as claiming from permanent settlement, IV, 11.
    similar rules apply to talookdars claiming under section 4, IV, 11.
    plaintiff, ryot, must stand or fall by, IX, 25.

PLEADINGS—(*Continued*).
        when suing for pottah at fixed rates, cannot ask for a pottah at fair rates, IX, 25.
        plaintiff, landlord, if not entitled to kabuliat at rent sued for, case to be dismissed, X, 27.

POTTAH, see *Lease*.
    ryot cannot sue for, unless in possession, II, 4.
    ryot entitled to quiet enjoyment on receiving. II, 3.
    absence of, does not release zemindar from condition of kabuliat, II, 4.
    ryot on failing to prove, can still prove right of occupancy, VI, 20.
    all ryots entitled to, II, 3.
    what particulars to contain, II, 3.
    at fixed rates to whom to be given, III, 6.
    occupancy-ryots entitled to, at fair rates, V, 18.
    as to right of occupancy when tenant has held under, VI, 18.
    non-occupancy-ryots entitled to, at such rates as may be agreed upon, VIII, 24.
    term of, to occupancy-ryot may be fixed by Court, IX, 25.
        but must not extend beyond 10 years, IX, 25.
        nor the landlord's tenancy, IX, 25.
    when ryot sues landlord for, he must be bound by the allegations in his plaint, IX, 25.
    ryot cannot sue for, unless relation of landlord and tenant exists, I, II, 1, 4.
    tender of, entitles grantor to kabuliat, X, 26.
    person holding under, cannot be ejected except by Court, XXII, 63.
    limitation in suit for delivery of, XXVIII, 71.
    cause of action in suits for delivery of, XXXV, 79.
    to be given by the Court, if landlord refuses to execute after decree, LV, 92.

PRESUMPTION OF HOLDING FROM PERMANENT SETTLEMENT
    not confined to holdings only, III, 7.
    hereditary transmission of property need not be proved to support, III, 8.
    proof of actual payment for every year not necessary to establish, IV, 12.
    nor receipts for 20 consecutive years, IV, 12.
    especially where landlord has refused to take rent, IV, 12.
    proof of uniformity in rates, not amount, necessary to raise, IV, 12.
    slight variation in rate will not destroy IV, 12.
    nor will proof of additional rent for additional land, IV, 13.
    nor exaction of a small illegal cess, IV, 13.
    joint-owner holding land under private arrangement cannot claim benefit of, IV, 14.
    when rent has not been changed for 20 years, IV, 9.
    probably not limited to suits under the Act, IV, 9.
    not precluded though there is an allegation of a pottah not proved, IV, 9.
    even though the pottah be a forgery, IV, 10.
    but it is precluded if pottah is subsequent to permanent settlement, IV, 10.
    ryot setting up adverse title, not entitled to benefit of, IV, 10.
    pleadings in order to raise, must be consistent with fact of holding from permanent settlement, IV, 10.
    plea that the tenure was the grandfather's and of long standing sufficient, IV, 11.
    where plea of holding for 40 or 50 years not sufficient to raise, IV, 11.
    where benefit of s. 4 claimed it is sufficient, IV, 11.
    proof necessary to establish, IV, 12.
        uniform rent for 20 years previous to suit must be proved, IV, 12.
        unexplained variation immaterial, IV, 12.
    consolidation or subdivision of tenure does not preclude, IV, 12, 13.

INDEX. 137

PRESUMPTION OF HOLDING FROM PERMANENT SETTLE-
MENT—(*Continued*).
a break in the holding rebuts, IV, 13.
but not if tenant has been unlawfully evicted, IV, 13.
nor by sale for arrears of revenue, IV, 14.
nor where holding was not mentioned in jumma-wasil-bakee papers,
VI, 14.
value of jumma-wasil-bakee and canoongoe papers as proof of, IV, 14.
under s. IV applies only to ryots, IV, 14.
as to talookdars and other tenures, XVII, 50.
decree declaring right to enhance rebuts, XVII, 50.
PREVAILING RATES—
what are, XVIII, 51.
PRODUCE—
increase in value of, a ground for enhancement, XVIII, 52.
but the increase must be a natural increase, XVIII, 53.
and must have been brought about otherwise than by agency of
ryot, XVIII, 53.
in adjusting the rent to the increase, the rule of proportion to be followed, XVIII, 53.
of land hypothecated for rent, LXVIII, 102.
PRODUCTIVE POWER OF LAND—
increase in, see *Produce*.
PROPORTION, RULE OF
when to be applied in adjustment of rents, XVIII, 52, 53.
PARVI-BHIKYA, XI, 30.
PUTNEE-TALOOK
is *primâ facie* transferable, XVI, 42.
PUTNEEDAR
is holder of a permanent transferable tenure, XVI, 42.
can sue for abatement, XIX, 59.
PUTWAREEAN, XI, 30.
QUIET ENJOYMENT—
implied contract for, II, 3
disturbance of, by title paramount, II, 3.
disturbance of, by mere stranger, II, 3.
RATIFICATION
of illegal acts of agent in cases of distraint, LXX, 103.
RECEIPTS—
evidence necessary to prove, IV, 13.
production of, advisable to prove fixed rates of rent, IV, 13.
damages for withholding, XI, 31.
what particulars to contain, XI, 32.
on proof of withholding of, Court must award some damages, XI, 31.
such damages can only be given for the withholding of receipts of money
payable as rent, XI, 32.
stamp on, XI, 32.
RECEIPT OF RENT
by landlord when amounts to recognition of transfer by ryot, VI, 20.
must specify year for which rent paid, XI, 32.
suits against persons in, may be brought against their managers,
XXIV, 65.
person in, may measure, XXV, 66.
when a waiver of forfeiture, XXIII, 65.
RE-ENTRY—
non-right of, except under conditions of lease, XXIII, 64.

19

REFUSAL
    of specification in receipt amounts to withholding of receipt, XI, 30.

REGISTRATION—
    what leases require, II, 5.
        such leases if unregistered not admissible in evidence, II, 5.
    of kabuliat, compulsory in what cases, X, 29.
    of under-tenures in zemindar's sherishtah, XXVI, 67.
        only transferable intermediate tenures need be registered, XXVI, 67.
        a ryottee tenure, though intermediate and transferable, need not be registered, XXVI, 67.
    penalty for non-registration, XXVI, 68.
    recognition by landlord supplies the place of, XXVI, 69.
    suit to compel, XXVI, 70.
    but zemindar need not register subdivision of a tenure, XXVI, 69.
    transferree must make application for, before suit to compel registration can be brought, XXVI, 70.
    rights of unregistered transferrees, XXVI, 70.
    in Court of suits brought under the Act, XLII, 84.
    but such is for statistical purposes only, XLII, 84.
    unregistered tenant cannot sue for reversal of sale, LXIII, 98.
    auction-purchaser to apply for, after sale, LXVII, 107.

RELINQUISHMENT
    of holding by ryot voids right of occupancy, VI, 18.
    notice of, in what month to be given, XX, 60.
        until given, ryot responsible for rent, XX, 60.
        to be served through Collector if landlord refuses to accept, XX, 60.
    any ryot can relinquish, XX, 61.
        but not where lease exists, XX, 61.
    part of holding not valid, XXI, 61.
    notice of, may be served by Collector, XX, 61.
    verbal notice of, in what cases sufficient, XX, 61.
    absconding of ryot tantamount to, XX, 61.
    stamp-duty upon notice of, XX, 61.

RENT—
    arrear of, see *Arrear*.
    fixed rate of, see *Fixed Rent*.
    annual amount of, must be inserted in pottah, II, 3.
    what suits for, cognizable under this Act, II, 4.
    co-sharer can be sued by the other co-sharers for, in particular cases, IV, 14.
    receipt of, by landlord does not amount to consent to transfer by ryot, VI, 20.
    the delivery of possession a condition precedent to action for, II, 3.
    payment of, condition precedent to claim of right of occupancy, VI, 16.
    even when made to parties not entitled to receive it, VI, 17.
    rate of, when the Court may determine, VI, 20.
    damages for sums exacted in excess of, XI, 30, 31.
    receipts for, what to contain, XI, 30, 32.
    what is an illegal exaction of, XI, 30.
    power to enforce payment of, other than under the Act, withdrawn from zemindar, XII, 32.
    damages for payment of, extorted wrongfully, XIII, 33.
    in suit for enhancement of, no more can be recovered than mentioned in notice, XIV, 39.
    Court cannot fix rates of, in suit to contest liability of enhancement, XV, 40.
    instalment of, unpaid is an arrear of rent, XXI, 62.

INDEX. 139

RENT IN KIND—
    value of, how to be estimated, II, 5.
    must be mentioned in the pottah, II, 3.
    may be changed into payment in money, II, 5.
    may be a fixed rate of rent, III, 6, 7.

RENT-FREE LAND—
    holder of, cannot be sued for a kabuliat, X, 26.
    until right to assessment has been established, X, 26.
    in suit for kabuliat for resumed lakhiraj, plaintiff must prove rate of rent asked for, X, 27.
    cannot be measured by zemindar, XXV, 67.

REVIEW OF JUDGMENT
    to be applied for within 30 days, CIII, 115.
    application to set aside *ex parte* decree not a, under the section, CIII, 115.

RYOT
    cannot sue for pottah when out of possession, I, 1.
    entitled to receive pottah, II, 3.
    when he has received lease entitled to possession, II, 3.
    landlord's implied guarantee to, against eviction, II, 3.
    landlord granting lease to third party amounts to dispossession of, II, 4.
    so does any interference with his possession, II, 4.
    not entitled to a pottah from a person to whom he does not pay rent, II, 4.
    right of, under a lease, II, 4.
    when he has fixed rate from permanent settlement, entitled to pottah at that rate, III, 6.
    and he cannot be enhanced by an auction-purchaser, III, 8.
    presumption as to his holding from permanent settlement, IV, 9.
    when he sets up adverse title to landlord not entitled to such presumption, IV, 10.
    the presumption of holding from permanent settlement applies only to, IV, 9.
    damages for excess rent exacted from, XI, 30, 31.
    entitled to separate notice for each separate holding, XIV, 38.
    but not when lands subdivided without consent of landlord, XIV, 39.
    failing to prove non-liability of enhancement, suit ought to be dismissed, XV, 40.
    rights of, who converts arable into orchard land, XVIII, 54.
    or who clears jungle land, XVIII, 54.
    desiring to relinquish land may give notice, XX, 60.
    on whom notice to be served, XX, 60.
    what amounts to relinquishment of land by, XX, 61.
    when can be ejected for arrears of rent, XXII, 63.
    opposing measurement, what to be done, XXXVII, 79, 80.
    if failing to attend after order cannot contest measurement, XXXVII, 80.

RYOT NOT HAVING A RIGHT OF OCCUPANCY .
    entitled to pottah at such rates as may be agreed upon, VIII, 24.
    but cannot sue landlord for pottah, VIII, 24.
    must either pay the rent demanded or quit, VIII, 24.
    but if permitted to stay, is only liable to pay a fair rent, VIII, 24.
    and this rent can only be enhanced after notice, VIII, 24.
    where landlord has distrained, can bring a suit for excessive demand of rent, VIII, 24.
    landlord cannot enhance rent of, unless he states ground, VIII, 24
    cannot take the initiative and contest enhancement, XV, 40.
    can claim abatement, XIX, 59.

140 INDEX.

RYOTEE KUDEEMEE TENURE
    not subject to enhancement under s. 51 of Reg. VIII of 1793, XVI, 41.

SALE
    for arrears of revenue.
        does not void presumption of holding tenure at fixed rates, IV, 14.
        effect of, on under-tenure, XVI, 48.
        what under-tenures are protected against, XVI, 48.
        object of the sale-laws explained, XVI, 48.
        effect of reversal of, after deposit, XXXI, 77.
        under-tenures after sale not void, but only voidable, XVI, 48.
    of under-tenures for arrears, LIX, LXVI, 94, 100.
    effect of sale under an *ex parte* decree which is afterwards set aside, LIX, 95, 96.
    notice of, what to contain, LX, 96.
    of under-tenure cannot be made while warrant out against the person or moveable property of the judgment-debtor, LXI, 96, 97.
    of immoveable property not to take place till moveable property and under-tenure in arrear are sold, LXI, LXV, 97—100.
    person interested in under-tenure can stay the sale, LXII, LXIII, 98.
    but unregistered under-tenant cannot sue for reversal of, except in case of fraud or deposit, LXIII, 98, 99.
    effect of, upon encumbrances, LXVI, 100.
        certain encumbrances protected, LXVI, 100.

SALE UNDER THE PUTNEE LAW—
    effect of, on under-tenures, XVI, 48.

SERVICE TENURES—
    zemindar cannot dispense with service and resume the land, XVI, 47.

SET-OFF—
    when defendant making deposit entitled to, XLVI, 86.

SEZAWUL—
    appointment of, does not determine lease, XXIII, 65.

SHAREHOLDER
    when holding land in excess of his share can be sued by co-sharers as a ryot, IV, 14.
    cannot sue joint-tenant for a kabuliat, X, 28.
    payment to, by tenant of his quota of rent, no evidence of division of tenure, X, 28.
        unless the rent has been separately paid by agreement, X, 29.
    cannot alone bring a suit for measurement, XXXVII, 80.
    decree in favour of, how to be executed, LXIV, 99.
    cannot distrain except through common manager, LXVIII, 102.

SHIKMEE
    lakhirajdar cannot be disturbed by auction-purchaser, XVI, 49.

SMALL CAUSE COURTS
    not empowered to try rent-suits, CIV, 115.

SPECIAL APPEAL—
    as to objection taken for the first time in, of landlord's inability to prove particular description of kabuliat sued for, X, 28.
    whether objection as to notice of enhancement can be taken in, XIV, 39.
    in what cases it will or will not lie, CII, 115.

SPECIAL CUSTOM—
    meaning of, XVI, 41.

INDEX 141

STAMP-DUTY
 on leases, II, 6, 7.
 to be paid by lessee, II, 8.
 cultivators' leases exempt from, II, 6.
 on kabuliats, X, 29.
  exemptions, X, 29.
 on receipts, XI, 32.
  exemption, XI, 32.
 on general power-of-attorney, XXXII, 78.
 on notices of relinquishment, XX, 61.
 on applications in cases of measurement, XXXVII, 80.
  deposit, XLVII.
 on written authority of agent to collect rents and to sue, 69.
 of servant to distrain, LXXVI, 105.

STANDARD POLE, see *Measurement.*

STIPULATION
 in contract contrary to right of occupancy, VII, 23.

SUBDIVISION OF A TENURE
 does not necessarily change the character of holding, IV, 13.
 zemindar may refuse to register, XXVI, 69.
 a farmer can sanction, XXVI, 70.

SUB-LEASE
 by occupancy-ryot, effect of, VI, 18.
 lessor determines rights of sub-lessee by surrendering to the landlord, XX, 61.

SUIT
 may be brought against manager of person in receipt of rent, XXV, 65.
 brought under this Act shall be entered in special register, XLII, 84.
  but such register is for statistical purposes only, XLII, 84.
 under the Act, payment into Court, XLVIII, 87.
 for arrears and for ejectment or cancelment may be joined together, LII, 89.
 the word, in s. CII, includes all proceedings before and after decree, CII, 114.

SUIT FOR A KABULIAT—
 only when relationship of landlord and tenant exists, X, 26.
 mere denial of relationship of landlord and tenant does not bar Court's jurisdiction in, X, 26.
 whether it would lie on mere allegation that the defendant is holding a specific quantity of land from under plaintiff, X, 26.
 person tendering pottah entitled to kabuliat, X, 26.
 does not lie against a trespasser, X, 26.
 nor against person who has not agreed to pay rent, X, 26.
 nor against holder of lakhiraj tenure, X, 26.
 is not the correct mode of establishing a title, X, 26.
 cannot be maintained unless pottah first tendered, X, 26.
 exception to this rule, X, 27
 if for an enhanced rent cannot be supported without notice, X, 26.
 cannot be maintained if landlord fails to prove the rate claimed, IX, 25; X, 27.
 need not necessarily be dismissed, if rate claimed is not proved, X, 27.
 does not lie for a portion of land in one holding, X, 28.
 does not lie by a shareholder against a joint-tenant, X, 28.
 except where special agreement is proved, X, 28.
 under such circumstances co-sharers need not be made parties, X, 29.
 will lie where plaintiff's share is not disputed, X, 29.
 does not lie against tenant having no right of occupancy, X, 29.
 does not lie for a right to fish, X, 29.

SUIT FOR A KABULIAT—(*Continued*).
> but does for the payment of the rents of a fishery, X, 29.
> decree in, should specify time from which kabuliat to take effect, X, 29.
> but where no term mentioned in the decree, kabuliat operates for a year, X, 29.
> limitation in, XXVIII, 71.
> may be instituted at any time during tenancy, XXVIII, 72.
> decree in, how may be executed, LVI, 92.

SUNNUD—
> talook held under, not subject to s. 51 of Reg. VIII of 1793, XVI, 41.

SURBURAKAR—
> tenure of, is permanent transferable, XVI, 42.
> not affected by unregistered transfer, XXVI, 69.

TALOOKDARS, see *Intermediate Tenure*.

TANK—
> no right of occupancy in, VI, 16.

TENANT-AT-WILL
> cannot take initiative, under s. 15, XV, 40.
> entitled to accretion of his holding, XVI, 46.

TENDER—
> ryot must tender payment to landlord, XXI, 62.
> where none, damages may be awarded, XLIV, 84.
> where not received, deposit may be made in Court, XLVI, 86.

TITLE—
> tenant setting up, adverse to landlord cannot claim right of occupancy, VI, 17.
> suit for kabuliat, not correct mode of establishing, X, 26.
> tenant estopped from denying landlord's, II, 5.
> change in proprietary title does not affect right of occupancy, VI, 17.

TOLLS
> sued for in shape of rent not a suit for rent, II, 4.

TRANSFER
> by occupancy-ryot, when valid, VI, 19.
> by ryot without right of occupancy does not give transferree right to add transferor's possession to his own, VI.
> by occupancy-ryot with consent of landlord gives transferree right of occupancy, VI, 17.
> of intermediate tenure required to be registered, XXVI, 67.

TRANSFERABLE TENURE, see *Intermediate Tenure*.
> in cases of occupancy-ryots, VI, 19.
> no warrant of arrest before judgment in suits as to, L, 88.
> instances of, XVI, 42.
> need not be mokururee, XVI, 43.

TREES
> are in holder of perpetual lease, II, 4.

TRESPASSER
> cannot be compelled to execute kabuliat, I, 1.
> trespasser cannot claim presumption, IV, 10.
> cannot acquire a right of occupancy, VI, 17.
> cannot be sued for kabuliat, X, 26.
> holder of excess land may be treated as, XVIII, 55.
> a ryot cultivating land without permission not necessarily a trespasser, XVIII, 55.

UNDER-TENURES, see *Intermediate Tenure*.

VOID AND VOIDABLE—
> distinction between, XVI, 48.

WAIVER, see *Interest, Forfeiture.*
WARRANT
    of arrest before judgment, none in suits as to intermediate tenures, L, 88.
YEAR BY YEAR—
    tenant of, holding for 12 years obtains right of occupancy, VI, 18.
    lease for, must be registered, II, 7.
    creates a yearly tenancy, XVI, 44.
ZEMINDAR—
    cases where action of, amounts to dispossession, II, 4.
    may sue to convert rent in kind to rent in money, II, 5.
    cannot claim abatement from Government, XIX, 60.
    power of, to compel attendance of tenant withdrawn, XII, 32.
    power of, to survey and measure lands, 6; XXV, 66.
    entitled to notice of interest of depositor, XLVI, 86.

www.ingramcontent.com/pod-product-compliance
Lightning Source LLC
Chambersburg PA
CBHW020306170426
43202CB00008B/515